By the same author

The Day Before America: Changing the Nature of a Continent

The Gulf Stream: Encounters with the Blue God

Oil and Water: The Struggle for Georges Bank

Uphill with Archie

A Son's Journey

William H. MacLeish

Simon & Schuster

New York London Toronto Sydney Singapore

SIMON & SCHUSTER
Rockefeller Center
1230 Avenue of the Americas
New York, NY 10020

SIMON & SCHUSTER and colophon are registered
trademarks of Simon & Schuster, Inc.

Designed by Jeanette Olender
Manufactured in the United States of America

1   3   5   7   9   10   8   6   4   2

Library of Congress Cataloging-in-Publication Data
MacLeish, William H., date.
Uphill with Archie : a son's journey / William H. MacLeish.
p.   cm.
1. MacLeish, Archibald, 1892–   2. MacLeish, Archibald, 1892—Family.
3. Poets, American—20th century—Biography.   4. Statesmen—United States—
Biography.   5. MacLeish, William H., date.   I. Title.
PS3525.A27 Z78 2000
811'.52—dc21
[B]   00-047076
ISBN 0-684-82495-7

ACKNOWLEDGMENTS

Uphill with Archie began with a nudge from Don Moser, editor of *Smithsonian* magazine, who was after something different from the environmental pieces I had been writing for him. He wanted a recollection of my late father, so recently late that it was hard for me to put him in perspective. I finally did, and Don published the result—"The Silver Whistler"—in October of 1983. Versions of stories in this book have appeared in such publications as *Civilization* (Nov.–Dec. 1995), *The New York Times Sunday Magazine* (11/8/92), and *Story Quarterly* (1984, #17), and on National Public Radio's *All Things Considered* (1/12/99). But it was "Whistler" that opened the door for me.

Others had already passed through that door. Roy Winnick spent years interviewing Archie and those who knew him and preparing a selection of Archie's letters (Houghton Mifflin, 1983). Scott Donaldson built on Roy's work and his own to plan and write Archie's biography *Archibald MacLeish: An American Life* (Houghton Mifflin, 1992). Scott opened his files to me, and in them I found a much needed counterweight to the confusions of memory.

A good many family members and friends helped with advice and criticism. My nephew A. Bruce MacLeish provided most of the photographs for the book. Charles Adams, my editor at Simon & Schuster, found me wandering afield in my first attempts and gently pointed out a better path. My neighbor Chris Jerome turned the completed text into better text. All these, and those not mentioned, I thank.

. . .

COVER: The painting of Uphill Farm was done in the late thirties by Alice Acheson, wife of Dean Acheson. Players in the croquet game are: Mimi, next to tree at left; Bill, next to tree at left-center; Archie, with blue-and-white jersey; Ada, with red coat; Dean, with yellow vest; Carolyn, in reddish dress. On the terrace are Alice, at left, and Ken.

This story is for

my daughters

Morellen and Meg.

It is dedicated to the memory

of my friend and agent

Jane Cushman.

Uphill with Archie

Only Your Life

ONE MORNING IN THE FALL OF 1981, MY FATHER AND I were sitting in the book room of the old house at Uphill Farm. November blew hard across the lawn and gardens. It blew on, northeast, across the Deerfield and Connecticut river valleys of western Massachusetts, toward the cone of Mount Monadnock on the horizon.

Ash logs burned in the high and shallow Rumford fireplace, and the smell of their burning mixed as it always did with the smells of well-used books in floor-to-ceiling cases running along the side walls. There were books everywhere in the house, but these were the favorites, bound and rebound in leathers and cloths, their pages gone the color of parchment.

My father wore a coat of Hebridean tweed that had once shown off the deep chest and small waist but now hung slack. When I had come into the room, he had been standing, looking out at my mother's garden. There wasn't much to see. The roses were mulched, the gravel paths patchy with last week's snow, the beds all put away for the winter. But the mere geometry was enough to call up, for him and for me, what had bloomed there—dahlias and lilies, peonies and hollyhock, phlox and a fiery red spike he once called "painted priest's prick."

My father swung around when he heard me, so that the light from the bay window was on his face. I was surprised yet again by how little his years had rearranged him: the high forehead was almost smooth; the wide-set brown eyes were calm, calmer than he ever was; the nose looked to be the same nose that was broken long ago in a water polo game. He opened his mouth to greet me, and the sight of the strong teeth and long upper lip reminded me of the horsey noises he used to make when he was in the orchard tasting his Northern Spies and Jonathans. He had shrunk a couple of inches to medium height, my height, but he was not stooped. He was seemly.

"You know," my father said, "I believe we now have the first truly silly president in the history of the republic." The front section of the *Times* lay on the floor, and I could see that he had been reading something about Ronald Reagan. I shared some of my father's feelings about the man, but I found it hard to rank him first among our chief executives in the dithering department. So I made some wisecrack, and we both laughed and sat down to take in the satisfactions of the fire.

The book room was the center of a place that still, in my fifty-fourth year, remained at the center of my life. That was where the family came to check on the day, to read the mail and the papers and, even after a television set had invaded it, to talk. We had drinks there, and after some feast in the dining room—most meals at Uphill Farm passed for feasts with me—we would regather there, some on the couch or in the deep chairs, others on the floor, and listen to music or slide into banter and laughter. I could see myself as a boy and then as a young man, sprawled on my back at right angles to my father with my head up on his ribs, listening to his voice roaming around under his shirt.

My father was "Dad" or "Pa" to me then, as my mother was "Mom." I had other names for him when he ticked me off—

"Arse Poetica" was one—but he didn't know about them. I never let them out of my mouth after I saw what happened to my older brother Ken when he thought he'd score points for himself by calling my father "Arch-yer-balls." An eternity (perhaps five seconds) passed in silence. I was scared breathless. Then my father gave a dry snicker I translated as "This one time only!" It wasn't until after my parents had died—he in April of 1982 at the age of ninety and she two years later at ninety-two—that I started calling them by their given names. It seemed strange at first, that familiarity, but then I began to see how it both freed me from filiality and evoked them in full, as people and not just parents.

My father was going over some papers in his chair by the window. Suddenly he looked up and handed one to me. It was the draft of a poem, a short one called "Whistler in the Dark." This is the final version:

> George Barker, British poet,
> writes a eulogy of Dylan Thomas,
> calls him whistler in the dark
> and great because the dark is getting darker.
>
> Is it? Was the dark not always darker?
> Have we not always had these silver whistlers?
> Listen! . . .
> >   That's Chaucer like a bobolink.
>
> I think it's not the darkness, Mr. Barker,
> makes for whistling well. I think

perhaps it's knowing how to whistle.
Listen! . . .

That's Dylan trilling like a lark.

At the top of the draft my father had written, "Bill, from his father." There had been a few other such transfers from him, so
swift in the giving that they outran acceptance. A dozen years
before, he had sent me another sheet of paper, a scrap really.
Over on the left, in a twitchy hand, were the words "Archie from
Father." On the right, my father had written "Bill from Dad."
And typed below, the ink going, was Emerson: "It is easy in the
world to live after the world's opinion; it is easy in solitude to
live after our own; but the great man is he who in the midst of
the crowd keeps with perfect sweetness the independence of
solitude."

I looked over my shoulder at the books behind me: Hemingway novels here, Dos Passos there, the works of other close
friends nearby. Then Trollope, Thackeray, Dickens. And, high
up, four volumes bound in dark blue with gold lettering: *Popular
Tales of the West Highlands,* stories collected in the Gaelic in the
middle of the nineteenth century and beautifully translated into
English. Archie read them to me over and over when I was
young, and the words and his way of saying them settled in my
mind. A voyage was not in the hills but over "seven bens and
seven glens and seven mountain moors." Clansmen rode out
not at dawn but "in the mouth of the morning."

My favorite was, and is, a story called "The Brown Bear of the
Green Glen." I saw myself as John, the youngest son of the King
of Erin. He, it was thought, "was not wise enough." But with the

help of the brown bear, he defeats his mean older brothers, saves his father's life, and wins as his wife the daughter of the King of the Green Isle. John is always running into giants who say things like, "Yes, yes, son of Erin's King, now I know thy matter better than thou dost thyself" and "Thy coming was in the prophecy."

I glanced down at the poem in my lap and then up at my father. He was reading and, at the same time, moving his cupped hand down his face, his thumb and forefinger caressing the sides of his nose. He had always done that, and yet it seemed special to me, as if I needed to pay attention to it, to him and to the time he had left.

Dylan Thomas had pleaded with his father to rage against his coming death, not to "go gentle." There would be no rage vented at Uphill Farm. It had been banished from the house, along with expressions of frustration, despair, boredom and all other "negative" vibrations. Even positive emotions were not allowed out unless fully under control, and only then when escorted by humor. Archie was as likely to let me see him wet his cheeks and rail at his mortality as he was to join the Reagan Revolution.

Besides, I didn't want to hear him rant. What I wanted was to tell the old man working in his corner how much I loved him. I decided to risk it and got up, crossed the room and stood by his chair. The words wouldn't come. What I said was, "Do you know how much I owe you?"

My father had the habit sometimes of moving his mouth as if he were tasting his words before he spoke them. He did that, looking up at me with a gentle smile.

"Only your life," he said.

I stood above him, flummoxed.

He saw me struggling and put his hand to my cheek. "And I could ask you that same unanswerable question," he said.

I retreated before he could ask it, for I knew I had no more of an answer to it than he had. I'd let my mouth run and had missed my mark. So I did what was expected of family members in such circumstances. I returned to my seat, assembled my frustrations in a manageable bolus, and swallowed them. In a minute or two, nothing was left of the situation but the beginnings of a sour stomach.

Only my life? I still haven't the faintest idea what Archie meant by that. When he wanted to be, he was equally the master of ambiguity as Ronald Reagan was of the wink. I now know that the unanswerable question had been something of a grail for him as a young poet. The particular questions that fascinated him then had to do with man's place in an uncaring universe—orders of magnitude more cosmic than a son's debt to his father.

My creation on a borrowed bed in Paris in the autumn of 1927 doesn't feel to me like a debt. That I and no other was the result owes more to chance than to Ada and Archie. The traits I believe Archie passed on to me—among them a fascination with language and its rhythms, the need for control, an unlimited capacity for worry, and a metabolism only slightly less supercharged than that of a pygmy shrew—did not come to me on loan. The safety and comforts and pleasures my parents subsequently provided for me, though I am indeed grateful for them, carried no terms of repayment that I see.

I think that what I did owe my father was not my life but a manifestation of his life: I owed him his fame. For half a century I borrowed it, using it as collateral to advance my own station. I came to think of it as a sun under which I could sit and get a nice tan. Unless I watch myself, I still do.

I read somewhere that fame is a collection of misunderstandings that gather around a person. I don't know when I first noticed the buildup around Archie. I was pretty small when I realized a lot of people knew about his poetry. As the years passed, I could see that he was becoming famous for being a poet who also had played college football and after that made names for himself as a lawyer, magazine journalist, high government official, playwright, lecturer, and teacher. It was the bunch of skills and not the one talent, I think, that elevated him.

He could hardly do anything without acing it. He was a winner at Yale, first in his class at Harvard Law School. He won three Pulitzers, two for his poetry and one for his verse play *J.B.* He received degrees and awards of every description, including the presidential Medal of Freedom and the National Medal of Literature (I gather he was the only American to win both). He knew unconscionable numbers of the powerful, the wealthy, the gifted, the celebrated. He wrote speeches for FDR and Adlai Stevenson; peppered his fellow citizens with encomiums to the republic and the blessings of democracy; and taught SRO classes at Harvard as the Boylston Professor of Rhetoric and Oratory. "Polymathic Papa," I used to sing. "Polymathic Papa, dontcha two-time me."

My mother, Ada, could have become famous. A few years before I was born, she had been a concert singer in Paris and had drawn fine reviews. In their early years together, she was a more accomplished artist than her husband, and I have built what-if stories around her staying with her art. They don't turn out well for Archie. There is no Uphill Farm in them, but there are necessities that force the children, especially me, to follow their own initiatives from an early age. And that I find intriguing.

Ada didn't give up singing for years but did abandon it as a career, much to the concern of her supporters, one of whom, also a singer, kept asking her, "Are you still with *that man?*" Ada said that her obligations to our family gave her no other choice. Whatever her reasons, she withdrew from what clearly was a central concern of her life and replaced it with a central concern for my father's life.

A year or so before I was born, my parents came back from a long stay in Paris and bought a big house on a ridge above the village of Conway, Massachusetts. They owned or rented several dozen houses thereafter, but the Conway place was their true home. Ada turned the foundations of an old barn just east of the house into her main garden. That was mostly for looking and sniffing. A bit farther east was her rock garden and, just over a little rise from that, her cutting garden. Every good day, she worked with tints and shapes and scents that changed with the season, and many of these she brought into the book room and the dining room, the parlor and the guest rooms. The tallest arrangements went down to the great music room, built for her when they bought the house.

A short woman, not much more than five feet two, Ada had fine, light-brown hair, always well permed, blue-gray eyes that could turn accipitral in an instant. She had beautiful legs and breasts that stayed firm; she boasted to me when she was into her seventies that she had finally decided to wear a brassiere. She struggled mightily with weight, but though she never looked heavy to me, she could never be slim—not with that strong barrel body. As an old woman, she once lay down on her back beside me on the book-room rug, suggested we raise our legs a few inches off the floor and kept hers there a half-minute longer than I could mine.

Ada had learned as a child how to run things: houses, kitchens, guests, men. She was as finished as her finishing school and her years in France could make her, but her wit regularly broke through the polish in flashes that were sometimes ribald, often brash, and usually sarcastic. When a banker friend drove up in a new and very expensive car equipped with everything then available, she looked it over carefully and then said, "It's wonderful, Bob, but where's the septic tank?"

I have not met a hostess like Ada. The seams of what she did, the effort required, rarely showed. All was done by her book. One afternoon, when she was entertaining out on the east terrace overlooking her garden, the maid of the time—there were many over the years—made an appearance. She wore a black uniform with a white lace apron and a tiny white hat, an outfit that must have galled her and made a joke of her in town. But she was game, and she knew the rules: Mrs. MacLeish had said that all guests should be announced on arrival. So she stopped in front of Ada, lifted her chin, and declared, "Madam, the pigs is here." And so they were, escapees from their pen up by the barn.

Friends were always coming up the hill for the weekend, friends who also knew fame or soon would. Even now, survivors of those gatherings, myself included, talk incredulously of the food and drink and conversation as if somehow we had been allowed to act in a hit play. Ada and Archie always dressed for dinner. Archie went for kilt and hose or white pants and a French sailor's jersey or, on special occasions, a Japanese ki mono. Ada appeared, and I mean appeared, in long and lovely floor-length gowns, necklaces and rings from a Fifth Avenue jeweler, and just enough of her favorite scents to dispel any doubts that she was the alpha of the evening.

Silence was not permitted at table. Archie and the men of the party rarely stopped talking, but whenever a hole did appear in the buzz and laughter, Ada would darn it with her wit. I know of only one instance when she didn't. She told me of an evening when the food was especially special (she often tasted every dish at table, before it was served to her guests, to make sure it met her standards) and the merriment in levitation. A woman who was doing for us at the time was passing the peas. As she rounded the southwest corner, she broke wind. I gather it sounded like the crack of a game rifle. Silence descended on the party like Triton's net. "Wal!" said the woman, "Hairken to me!" The diners did. Each sat, head bowed as if in prayer, mouth immobilized.

I know Ada had a good deal of fun doing what she did. But I'm pretty sure she was never able to forget for long what she could have been doing. Every other day or so, arranging flowers in her music room, she walked past two pianos facing each other curve in curve. She favored the Steinway. The Mason and Hamlin was for visiting musicians. Once in a while I played with her. But over the years the pianos gradually ceased being instruments and became furniture, well polished, well tuned—and silent. She still sang, with Ken and me and our guitars, but that couldn't have counted for much with her muse.

Ada had four children, but one, a boy, Brewster Hitchcock, died in 1921, in his seventh month of life, of what was then called "crib death." She almost never spoke of him. My brother

Kenneth was the eldest of the survivors, almost twelve years older than I. Then came my sister Mimi, six years older. I showed up in 1928. We were staggered too far apart to share childhoods. Mimi and I had a little of that, but Ken was out of college by the time I got to be ten. We were also strangers in temperament. Mimi was passionate and stubborn. Ken was at once sensitive and, in his younger years, cruel. I was the sunny one, or that is what everyone said.

Our family was not a good one for a girl to grow up in, at least not a girl who held to her own beliefs and ways of doing things. Mimi liked to eat her food slowly and did so, chewing away after the rest of us had polished our plates—usually within seconds of each other—and sat waiting on her. My mother often ordered her to stay at table until she had finished. She would do that, sometimes for an hour or more, and the look on her face was the look of Joan at the stake. Of the three of us, Mimi was the one who built her own life for herself. She kept in touch, on her terms.

Ken was Ada's favorite, but he had his problems with Archie, the kind of problems that left him wanting his father's approval to a degree that neither would nor could be met. Risk and danger were his way out. As a man, he dove to a record seven hundred feet in a Swiss lake, breathing an only partially tested mixture of gases. He dove on the *Andrea Doria,* the *Lusitania,* and other deep and dangerous wrecks. He raced cars and motorcycles, flew and parachuted. And when he felt the need, he let his mother know the risks involved in what he was about to do. He traveled the world and wrote about what he saw in language I envied.

I stayed and stayed at Uphill Farm, running for the stage door when it opened to me. Even as a young man, I took my departure from that hill town ridge as a mariner takes his from a headland, hoping to make my landfall there at the end of the voyage. Often enough I did. Often enough so that it is only a small stretch to say that the place held me as long as Archie and Ada lived there. That's where the fun was, where my father's sun was. It was, in the dear and departed sense of that word, gay.

If you didn't join in, if you felt out of sorts, you were expected to go to your room. My mother sent me there when I got grumpy, and she even sent herself there when she got "critical," her word for bouts with the blues. In a few hours, back she would be, her exuberance topped off and her repartee at the ready. The process worked so well in tamping down my darker impulses that it was not until well after my parents died that I took a real look at them.

I suppose what bothered me most as a boy was my penchant for conforming. "Live your life," Archie was fond of saying to me. "Don't let your life live you." Fine for him to say, with Ada running his base camp for him. Everyone at Uphill Farm was a lot bigger than I, a lot older than I, a lot more powerful in will, ego, and just plain experience. Adapt, piped a small voice behind my small ear. Adapt, or go to your room.

Adaptation wasn't at all difficult. I took to it as my father took to martinis. I studied my parents, learned from them how to perform in public. I adapted what I learned to my own realities—those of a small boy with blond curly hair and a charming smile—and went to work on myself. In time, I came to enjoy the company of adults far more than that of my peers. That was lucky in a way, since my parents were intent on culling all but the sons of the socially prominent from the list of those I could play with. In Conway in the thirties, that meant one boy who lived ten miles away.

It also meant that I started to think of childhood as contemptible. There is a West Highland tale about a giant who helps a prince, with the understanding that he will get the young man's first son as reward. The prince keeps giving him the sons of the hired help instead, and when the giant finds out, he seizes each imposter by the heels and dashes out his brains on a rock. I remember reading that story to myself for the first time, a boy with nothing to do on a rainy day but read, pissed off at the rain and my lot, thinking "Brats! Serves them right!" I still remember the noise the small heads made on the stone: "Sliochd."

As a conformer, I found it best to duck confrontation with my mother, probably because she had a drill sergeant's ability to turn my knee joints to jelly. I think she felt she had to be tough, since with me my father was such a pushover. I had to be friendly with her. I wanted to be friendly with him. That last doesn't jibe with all the stories in the national folklore about how sons should leave their fathers to find their manhood—or, alternatively, how the daddies should run the bubbas off. But closeness is what I wanted, and that is what I think he wanted, and that is what went on in one form or another for fifty years.

I am, like my father, loose of foot. My life has taken me down to Peru, out to sea, round and around this country. I live now only sixteen miles from Uphill Farm, across the Deerfield River. I am married to a poet who is as direct with me as I am evasive with her. I write books, each in some form about the environment. Two have been about the sea, one about how we have changed this land. I have loved writing them, traveling for them, making a film of one of them. Writing has moved from something I'd like to do if there weren't so many good writers already in my family, to something I do. It ranks with breathing—and worrying.

Every once in a while—a long while lately—someone asks me what it's like to be the son of a famous man. The question often awakens the memory of a little boy playing at being an adult, not wanting to know, but knowing, that he is the least of the company. I have never answered the question with any honesty. I laugh, usually, and shrug. Sometimes I say that it has been "interesting" or "fun." Once I told someone that I wouldn't recommend it, but that was more of a growl than a response.

Heywood Hale Broun, a fellow son of fame, had a friend who loved him enough to tell him a story about his predicament: "You," said the friend, "must fill big pairs of shoes; follow in footsteps; must not give way to anger, because you have been given so much more than others that you are not entitled to anger; must live up to your heritage, must be grateful for it." Broun could not find solace in unhappiness because that would be letting down his famous parents, writers Ruth Hale and Heywood Broun. If at times he felt like a failure, the friend concluded, it was because nobody can handle that assignment.

Being Archie's boy has something to do with that story. It has something to do, in my childhood, with a confusing combination of too much comfort and not enough challenge; something to do, in my manhood, with sticking too close for too long. It has most to do with spending bits and pieces of a half century with someone who knew how to whistle uncommonly well.

Jimmy, Meet Brownie!

SOMEWHERE ALONG THE WAY, WE LOST A GRAND-
mother. I don't know anything much about my mother's
mother, and neither does anyone else in the family. Ada rarely
mentioned her. She had plenty of stories about her father, but
only one I remember about the missing person. Ada was a child,
and she wanted very badly to have something happen, so badly
that she went into the room where her mother was in bed, something she wasn't supposed to do. She stood at the bed's foot and
started whining about what she wanted. Her mother shushed
her, but she couldn't stop. Suddenly there was this huge figure
looming over her, all wrapped in a sheet except for the staring
eyes. Ada bolted.

All I have learned is that Emily Boyle was born around 1860,
somewhere along the northern shore of the Gaspé Peninsula,
that great thumb that forms the southern edge of the St. Lawrence estuary. The Boyles may have had some money once, but
they seemed to be in reduced circumstances when Emily came
along. I think she spent some time with relatives in Montreal
and then, as a teacher, worked her way down to Albany and on
to Hartford, Connecticut. Somewhere I got the idea that she was
a lively soul, a cutup. I know from the two photographs I've
seen of her that she was very pretty. Her nickname was Dinah.

Dinah doesn't seem to have stayed lively long. In 1890 she
married William Arthur Hitchcock, a man in the process of
making himself. In 1892 Dinah had her one child, Ada, and

quite soon thereafter began to decline into general malaise and ineffectuality. Asthma and colitis accounted for some of her falling away. She died when I was two, and yet her enigmas keep her in my mind.

There have been Hitchcocks around the Connecticut River Valley since whites first arrived there. One marched off with his flintlock to fight the Indians and ended up dead; his widow received, among other communal considerations, a new gun. Another Hitchcock gained a certain renown for his ability, at the age of seventy, to leap without warning into the air and, with the toes of his left foot, snatch his hat from a nail driven into a cabin beam a foot above his head. And then there were the Hitchcock brothers, makers of furniture, including the cane-seated chair prized by antique dealers and auctiongoers. I have a pair, painted black and gold, in our house.

William Arthur was born in 1859 in Cornwall, Connecticut, in the hilly country of the Housatonic River watershed. He quit school to help keep his father, a tailor, from bankruptcy, then went into nuts and bolts, real estate, and banking. He and Dinah and the baby lived for a time on Lovely Street, just barely in the proper section of the workingman's town of Unionville, close to Hartford. Dinah had friends nearby in upscale Farmington, and before long they moved there.

William, a gregarious and opinionated man known in Farmington as Uncle Billy, found himself married to a woman less and less able to keep up with him. She had also given him a daughter instead of the son he wanted. So he named her "Jimmy" and in time came to rely on her as his hostess. On the sly, Billy took Jimmy to intertown baseball games. Sometimes, he parked his buggy next to that of Steve Lambert, a local saloon keeper. It was Steve who taught her what to look for in the game. Billy introduced Jimmy to golf and to bridge and to his friends and their wives. She loved him and she served him well.

Dinah, often bedridden, didn't seem to be much of a steadying force for her daughter. Ada ducked the proper when she could, with Steve Lambert and her father, and with the white birches across the street. She swung on them often, and one afternoon she got her bloomers entwined around a broken branch and sat there resolutely—and silently—until her father got home and rescued her. When her mother sent her up to Montreal to visit Boyle relatives, she bit some of the youngsters who had been invited over to play with her and sent the whole pack home. There was a new flush toilet in the house, only one. When Ada sensed that someone was feeling the call, she would get there first and sit snickering on the throne while, outside, knees were crossed and fists clenched. "The child," groaned one sufferer, "is notional."

She was also, like her father, musical. Her parents arranged for her to study the piano. Billy wasn't primarily concerned with her talent. He figured that if she were unable to attract or hold a man of means, at least she could provide for herself by giving piano lessons to local children. Ada had other ideas. As time went on, she took to using some of the clothing allowance from her father to pay for singing lessons.

I never heard that Ada's parents ever thought of sending her to college. Instead, they chose Westover, a finishing school in southwestern Connecticut. The school was run by Mary Hillard, a woman convinced that she had both the talent and the right to mess with the lives of any in her ken, old or young. She knew all about her sister's boy, Archie MacLeish, up at Hotchkiss, only forty miles away. She had just the girl for him, she thought, in her student Esther Cleveland, daughter of the White House Cleveland.

Mary Hillard invited her nephew to supper late in 1910 (I don't know whether Esther was there). Things were going well, except for the fact that one of the seniors invited to sit at the headmistress' table had not shown up. To fill the slot, another of Miss Hillard's invitees simply reached behind her, grabbed a passing skirt, and pulled. In the skirt was Ada Hitchcock, plump and pretty. And sitting directly across from her, she found when she recovered herself, was the guest of honor, a handsome, high-browed and obviously admiring young man with whom she was going to spend the next seventy-one years.

• • •

The MacLeishes and Hillards in my tree put a lot more of themselves on paper than did the Hitchcocks. Their letters were collected by descendants. Several privately published their memoirs for family distribution, and one—Archie's maternal grandfather—wrote a real book. I have copies of all these outpourings to correct or confound the family myths I took in by ear.

The myth I'm fondest of has Archie's father, Andrew Mac-Leish, fleeing Scotland for America because he couldn't take the pressure his mother put on him to "wag his pow i' the pulpit"— to enter the service of God. It isn't surprising that the urge to sermonize was strong in the family: MacLeish is a crunching of Gaelic words meaning "son of the servant of Jesus." MacLeishes are a sept or branch of a clan called MacPherson, or "son of the parson."

But Andrew did not carry that virus. What drove him over

the sea in 1856, as a lad of eighteen, was the urge to make something of himself and, in doing so, reunite himself with one Lilias Young, whose family had moved from Scotland to a wild place called Chicago. Andrew's family had been handweavers in a town near Glasgow. It was a remunerative trade in its time, but then came the steam looms and the factories, and the Mac-Leishes and their fellow artisans saw their traditions die in a matter of years. It was either enter the factories or leave or, if too old for either, endure. Andrew's grandfather Archibald endured. His father, also Archibald, went into the dry goods business in Glasgow. One of his uncles ended up heading a college of the University of Madras, and others escaped to England and Australia.

Andrew had learned the elements of retailing as an apprentice at drapers' establishments in Glasgow and London. With that meager accomplishment and the companionship of a friend similarly struck with wanderlust, he took passage aboard the iron steamship *City of New York* (which broke up and sank in an Atlantic storm a couple of years later), then transferred to the Erie Railway.

Chicago, Andrew writes in a bare-bones account of his life, was bustling and badly drained. Mudholes were everywhere in the streets. In one was a long pole with a hat stuck on its top, along with a sign saying No Bottom! But Lilias was there, and Andrew found her, and they went walking out to look at the prairie. Her family was a great help: Andrew found retail work. When the store burned down and his health failed, the Youngs invited him to stay with them on a farm they had just bought near the Ohio River. He went, and he stayed, earning his keep as a district schoolteacher—a teacher at one point sick with malaria and shivering under shawls lent him by some of the girls in his small class.

Andrew and Lilias married at the Young farm and returned to Chicago. She bore two children, both girls. He accepted a partnership in what was to become Carson Pirie Scott and Company, a department store big enough to compete with Marshall Field's emporium. Then, in the middle of an October night in 1871, he awakened to find the heart of the city in flames. He somehow found his way to Carson Pirie, rescued important papers, and managed to marshal enough wagons to haul some of the company's more valuable stock to safety. When he returned home the following afternoon, having neither eaten nor drunk much of anything, he saw his face in a mirror, "blackened and unrecognizable." "I remember," he writes, "giving way to the feelings called forth by this stupendous and awful calamity." I believe that was one of the few times in his life when he broke down, in public or in private.

In 1878, Lilias died. Three years later, Andrew married again, only to lose his second wife within months of the birth, in 1882, of a son, Bruce. In 1887 Andrew's daughters introduced him to a woman who had been their faculty adviser at Vassar. Her name was Martha Hillard. She was small yet striking, with a rich, low-pitched voice that needed little volume to reach and to influence her listeners. Andrew listened and was smitten.

Martha, "Patty," had just been appointed president of a seminary for young women, now Rockford College, outside Chicago. Andrew waited a week or so, then sent a letter to Rockford asking her to become his wife. Patty appears to have been quite calm in handling this tall and hasty Scot. She told him politely that she had other responsibilities. She may also have talked to herself about his being older by eighteen years. But Andrew was, to her, a "manly man," and she had her own sense of risking something to gain something. In the summer of 1888 she married Andrew. The minister was her father. The ring Andrew slipped on her finger was the same one worn by her two predecessors in his bed.

· · ·

All his life, Archie was taken by the Hillards. He used to say that he thought no one ever lived enough, but to him the Hillards did. He admired their fierce will, their granite convictions. They seemed to him to walk in history. Elder Brewster, the conscience of the Plymouth Colony, was an ancestor by marriage. Moses Hillard, Archie's great-grandfather and one of his heroes, was a sea captain at the beginning of the nineteenth century. Moses had been captured by the French in the Caribbean. He had brought back news of Napoleon's victory at Moscow and later agreed to bring the defeated emperor back to America in the false bottom of a water butt. The Little Corporal never showed.

Moses' son, Elias Brewster Hillard, the cleric who married Patty and Andrew, went out in the middle of the Civil War and found veterans of Valley Forge and Yorktown. He collected their hazy memories in *The Last Men of the Revolution*. Nothing brings home the youth of my country more than thinking about a relative only four generations removed from me sitting down with people who had been in on its birth. He asked one ancient what he would do if the Confederates got close. "If the rebels come here," he said, "I shall sartingly take my gun. I can see best furtherest off." Others talked to him about the Washingtons. Martha was "short and thick" and kind to her husband's men; the general was stern but not above showing his men how to "jerk," or throw, stones—possibly across a river or two.

Elias Hillard had a scunner against wrongdoing that might have stemmed from his father's habit of tanning his boys every time he returned from sea, on the theory that they must have done something to deserve it. The reverend's wrath and righteousness offended many, including some parishioners he accused of manufacturing shoddy uniforms for the Union Army. He moved often.

And then there was Patty herself. To be a college graduate and the head of an educational institution in her time was to make a certain amount of history. She associated with other women who were doing the same, including Jane Addams, the pioneer social worker and founder of Hull House in Chicago. She worked hard to find funding for the undercapitalized University of Chicago. (She once visited John D. Rockefeller in that regard. A family story goes that on the night train returning to Chicago, Patty suddenly saw a hand slipping through the curtains of her berth. The hand was John D.'s, and although he assured her he was simply looking for his own berth, she evidently suspected otherwise.)

Andrew and Patty chose a plot of land on a bluff overlooking Lake Michigan, in the northern exurb of Glencoe. Andrew named the house Craigie Lea, after a romantic Scots ballad ("And a' the sweets that ain can wish / Fra' Nature's hand are strewn on thee"). It was large, frilly, and, to my memory, so ugly it was beautiful. Andrew commuted to Carson Pirie by carriage and train, and Patty ran the place, conducted her extensive correspondence, and educated her children.

There were five all told, but the first, a daughter, died in infancy. Then came Norman (1890), Archie (1892), Kenny (1894) and Ishbel (1897). Norman was thought to be the most artistically gifted; Archie, the most combative; Kenny, sunny and funny; and Ishbel, loyal and accommodating. Patty raised them all herself. She talked with child psychologists and educators and distilled her own theories from what she learned. She read to her children almost every day: Bible stories, *Ivanhoe, Uncle Remus, The Jungle Book,* even Dante's *Inferno.* Reasoning worked well with Norman but not with Archie. Her second son, whom she found possessed of "tremendous force and will power" and "a high-strung nervous system, easily disturbed," required a more forceful approach.

After one spanking, Patty wrote in her memoir, "the yells of rage suddenly turned to a sharp cry of surprise. I picked him up, sat him on my knee and began talking of a bird on a tree outside. Suddenly he turned, threw his arms around my neck, and cried, 'Oh, Mama, I do love you.' My explanation was that he, entirely beyond his own control, appreciated the fact that I had controlled him." She also figured that the spanking had "drawn the blood from his head to a less vital spot and so relieved the pressure."

I know of no mother-son bond as strong as that between Patty and Archie. She trained him to pursue his purposes and supported him in that all her long life. The two could talk about anything from sex to politics. When he was in his thirties, he wrote to tell her that he yearned to be cradled in her arms. "I still feel not quite grown up, not quite responsible, not quite alone."

Andrew was fifty-four when Archie was born. He was of a generation of men who knew without thinking that they were masters of their houses. His sons called him Sir. He seems almost never to have been harsh with his children, just remote. The sole moment of intimacy Archie was able to recall happened one evening when Andrew's carriage was rolling up the drive. He suddenly spied his son and, leaning out, called to him, "Hello, Brownie." Archie's eyes were a warm brown, like his mother's.

My father talked to me sometimes about his father. He admired him greatly, he said—his probity, his ability to follow Emerson in keeping, in the midst of the crowd, that "independence of solitude." When my father died, we found this in his papers, unpublished, a cold poem for a distant parent:

> My father was a solid man
> And he was made of flesh and bone.
> I have the planet in my span
> And in my veins the stars are sown.
>
> My father walked upon the earth
> And with him would his shadow pass.
> I was rebellious at my birth.
> The sun strikes through me like a glass.
>
> My father knew Jehovah's face
> And would converse with him apart.
> I think he fears me for his place
> Is empty when I search my heart.

Archie stayed in Glencoe until the fall of 1907, when he was fifteen. He played with his siblings, fought with town toughs down by the railroad tracks. He learned so little at the local high school that he almost didn't make it into the preparatory school his mother had selected for him. Hotchkiss put him back two grades, which added to his miseries there. He was homesick. He felt out of place both in age and origins—a Midwesterner in a den of clubby Easterners, a child of new money thrown in with scions of old. He finally did develop the work habits he needed to grow and shine, but there was no joy for him in Lakeville, Connecticut. Not until he looked across his Aunt Mary's supper table at Westover.

. . .

I suspect that in dealing with the opposite sex, Ada was the more experienced of the two. She was her father's daughter, with a son's nickname, and she was at ease in male company. Archie seems to have had a devil of a time with puberty. His first hand-held lustings left him feeling soiled and sinful, and although he had a few sexual encounters fairly early on, he gives the impression in his notebooks that as a young man he thought the sex act left a good deal to be desired. But then, he was not known at Hotchkiss for his lightness of spirit. His companions admired his drive and his mind but found him excessively pessimistic, sentimental, and windy.

Ada opened this closed boy. A friend remembers them in late middle age as the "ardent couple," and the heat, for them, began at eighteen. They wrote each other almost daily, mailing off tiny envelopes with two-cent stamps. They even wrote to each other when they were together in her Farmington house. The courtship went on five and a half years, during which Mary Hillard set her cunning hand to derailing it, and Uncle Billy and Dinah sent Ada to Europe for a year, for her music and in hopes that she would find something else to think about. Neither scheme had the desired effect. Andrew and Patty reminded Archie that marriage was unthinkable until he had finished his education and found suitable employment. And in those days, sons, or at least establishment sons, tended to listen.

When Dean Acheson was graduating from Yale, his fiancée, Alice, looking through his yearbook, kept finding references to a fellow member of the class of '15, Archibald MacLeish: football player, captain of the water polo team, Skull and Bones, Phi Beta Kappa, poet, member of several cultural clubs, voted "Most Brilliant" by his classmates. Who was he? she asked. "Oh," Acheson said, of a man who later became his lifelong friend, "you wouldn't like him." Neither, I think, would I, had I met him then under the elms. Big Man on Campus, I would have thought. Insufferably superior.

Years later, Archie wrote to a friend and mentor, Felix Frankfurter, who had recently been appointed to the Supreme Court and was urging him to join the New Deal in Washington, "From the beginning of my more or less adult life, I have been plagued by the fact that I seem to be able to do more or less well things which commonly don't go together." Plagued indeed. Versatility brought him admiration and envy from others, and from himself a recurring and often keening indecision and self-doubt that pestered him throughout his life.

Well before he left Yale, Archie was agonizing over what he would do with himself. The faith of the Hillards, especially of his mother, pulled at him. He spent the better part of a night atop West Rock with a friend who later became the chaplain of Yale, trying to persuade the friend, and himself, that he was just the man for the ministry. He even wrote to Ada, who at the time was traveling with friends in North Africa, saying he might wag his pow. Ada's camel promptly ran away with her into the desert. Archie moved on to wrangle with friends over the comparative advantages of life in journalism, teaching, and the law—all of which he eventually sampled, while continuing to think of himself as a poet.

The law won, for a while. And it was here that Andrew came through for his son. Patty, I think, eased the way. She went with him to Yale, where Andrew talked with President Arthur Twining Hadley about Archie and received a shining report. "It seems," Andrew told his wife, "our son is a lad o' pairts." So saying, he told Archie he would stake him to Harvard Law School. And, he said, it was all right with him if Archie and Ada were married, provided they waited one year more.

They did, in a manner of speaking. Scott Donaldson, my father's biographer, says that in June of 1916, when they went to the altar in the old Congregational Church in Farmington, "Ada was pregnant, though she did not know for sure at the time." He may be right. I have learned that Ken, their firstborn, worried about that: he appeared a month early. Some part of me, the last-born, smiles at Archie and Ada's transgression, if that is what it was. Five and a half years without the possibility of intimacy is too harsh a sentence to pass on such an ardent couple.

Harvard shook the Yale stuffing out of Archibald MacLeish. He arrived full of honors and conceit and within days found himself pinned by far more experienced minds on the Socratic mats of the law school. That riled and excited him. By the time he was through with the school, which meant attending a special session for returning war veterans, he had risen to the top of his class and the editorship of the *Harvard Law Review*. And that, I have been told and told, is at the farthest remove from the small potato.

It is hard these days to keep on calling Archie's war the Great War; not after the tens of millions annihilated in its sequel (which itself is shrinking in younger eyes from the costliest carnage in history to something safely historic). But the First World War did do great damage to the most promising portions of a whole generation of males across Europe, and greater still to the ideals by which they lived.

Archie heard the guns of August and reacted predictably. "At first I hated the thought of enlisting," he wrote Andrew in the spring of 1917. "Now I can contemplate it with a certain grim joy. It means doing my part against a nation of madmen. It means giving my strength to tramp down an idea of government and society as abhorrent to me as are crawling lice or dead things. It means, also, a blow for world peace in order that this small son of mine, this grandson who will bear your name and carry on your mortality, may live his life in freedom of wars and lusts and lies . . ." He then added: "When convenient, will you send on our quarter's check?"

Married men were not then exempt from the draft, and Archie went looking first for something close to the fighting but not close enough to deprive his wife and son of himself. He went overseas with a Yale ambulance unit, but when that bogged down, he ended up in action—as a shavetail in the field artillery. In a later poem, he sees himself directing fire from the big French 155 mm guns. "The Marne side. Raining. I am cold with fear. / My bowels tremble . . . I am very brave: / Magnificent. I vomit in my mask."

Suddenly he was sent home—to teach French gunnery methods to trainees in Maryland. He never found out why or how he was picked for the job. Shortly after his departure, his unit lost half its strength to savage German shelling. Then at Camp Meade, influenza took a third of his men. And then there was Kenny.

• • •

Kenneth MacLeish was Archie's favorite sibling and Patty's favorite child. He could bring tears of laughter to a family not much given to lightening up. He followed Archie to Hotchkiss and then to Yale, as much in his own sun as in his brother's shadow. He did exceptionally well in water polo, indoor pole-vaulting, and the all-weather pursuit of appetizing young women.

Early in 1916, the spring of his junior year, Kenny and a group of Yale friends signed up for naval air training in Florida. On his first solo flight he fell in love with the air, chortling as the slipstream made his lips flutter, overstaying his time and finally drifting down through the dusk to a feather landing.

Kenny's unit went to France in October of 1917. As a combat pilot, his chances of surviving beyond two or three weeks were slim. Yet a year went by and he was still flying, still getting into hot water over buzzing his buddies and doing loops just above the trees. "There's no game like this in all the world," he wrote. "You're always taking such wonderful chances, and it's a grand feeling to get away with them."

Kenny and Archie ran into each other overseas. They got

tight and talked a night or two away. Kenny made sure his big brother was aware that "Archie" was flyboy slang for German antiaircraft fire. He was surprised by Archie's reassignment stateside and griped to his fiancée, Priscilla Murdock, that Archie had left before Kenny could hand him the engagement ring he would not trust to the mails.

On the eleventh of October of 1918, Kenny wrote Priscilla that he was going to fly over the front "to make one last try at really doing something. If luck is with me, all well and good; if it isn't—if there aren't any Huns in the sky or if I don't come through with a punch, then I'll give up and try my hand at something else." A few days later his squadron members saw Kenny making his run at doing something. He had elected to go after seven Fokkers by himself.

Six weeks after the Armistice, a Belgian farmer returned to what was left of his house and outbuildings near the town of Schoore. There, on a strewing of debris, he found the body of an American aviator, fully dressed. A couple of hundred yards off was a wrecked Sopwith Camel. Investigators came. They found Ken's papers neatly stowed in an inside pocket. They reported no wounds on the body, and no sign of the Camel. They took photographs, one of which was sent to Kenny's family. Archie and his half brother Bruce, who was by then climbing the executive ladder at Carson Pirie, decided not to show it to Andrew and Patty. Rats had taken the face.

No one knows just what happened. The Camel was a tricky flying machine. Its engine developed so much torque that it would often and unexpectedly jerk the craft to the right, and Ken could have fallen out at low altitude. Or he could have crash-landed the plane. If he had survived, he might have walked into an Allied gas attack; one apparently was in progress nearby on that day and at that time. The uncertainties must have been agonizing at Craigie Lea, but at least Patty and Andrew had definite word, after more than two months of waiting, that their son was dead and his body found. They decided to have Ken buried in a military cemetery in western Belgium.

Patty had sensed that Ken had wanted to talk about the possibility of his death and urged him to do so. He did. Some of what he wrote was engraved on a plaque mounted aboard the USS *MacLeish,* a four-stack destroyer named for him and commissioned in 1920: "If I find it necessary to make the supreme sacrifice, always remember this—I am so firmly convinced that the ideals I am going to fight for are right and splendid ideals that I am happy to be able to give so much for them. I could not have any self-respect, I could not consider myself a man if I saw these ideals defeated when it lies in my power to defend them."

The text on the plaque ends, "You must not grieve. I shall be supremely happy—so must you—not that I have 'gone west' but that I have bought such a wonderful life at so small a price and paid for it so gladly."

I feel like an idiot choking up as I read this. Only the young can say what Kenny said and believe it: I wrote roughly the same things to my parents when I was training for tank combat in the Korean War. I don't know what direction Kenny would have taken had he not gone west. A good many of the Yale friends in his unit went into banking, and he might have followed. I suspect that, whatever he did, the obscenity of the war would ultimately have sunk in.

I do know that it enraged Archie. When he was still with his battery in France, some of his men came up to him and asked why they were there. Because it's the best site I could find, he said. No, they said, why are we here? Archie answered—he shook his head in disgust telling me about what he said—"We are here to make the world safe for democracy." *Pace,* Woodrow Wilson.

On Memorial Day of 1924, Archie visited Kenny. He wrote to Ishbel about the ceremony, the speeches, his sense of "withering bitterness" at the absurdity, the silliness, "that that beautiful boy should be lying under the sand in a field he never saw—for nothing—for nothing." Out of that day came the poem "Memorial Rain." The ceremonies are in it, the speaking, the singing, march music, the feelings of futility and anger, a storm driving in.

> Under the dry grass stem
> The words are blurred, are thickened, the words sift
> Confused by the rasp of the wind, by the thin grating
> Of ants under the grass, the minute shift
> And tumble of dusty sand separating
> From dusty sand. The roots of the grass strain,
> Tighten, the earth is rigid, waits—he is waiting—
>
> And suddenly, and all at once, the rain!

There is another poem, date unknown. It is called "Family Group" and is built on two photographs. One is of Archie and Kenny together in France; a long shadow, perhaps the photographer's, stretches toward them. The other is of Kenny's body.

The faceless figure on its back, the helmet buckled,
wears what looks like Navy wings. A lengthened shadow
falls across the muck about its feet.

Me? I'm back in Cambridge in dry clothes,
a bed to sleep in, my small son, my wife.

Before, Though

ALL MY LIFE I HAVE WISHED I COULD HAVE BEEN with them then. The fogs of late summer lay on the Grand Banks, and the SS *Lafayette* sliced them, sounding her horn to warn the fishing dories. Archie thought the noise was like a heifer left at the pasture bars. And there they were, in the first week of September 1923, he and Ada, with Kenny, six, and Mimi, just one, and an aging Irishwoman to look after them, and, for once a figure in family history, Ada's mother, Dinah, along to help them settle. They had begun what I still think of as my family's greatest adventure. They were on their way to Paris, for a year, they thought, a year devoted to Ada's music and Archie's poetry. They stayed for five.

To me, a boy looking back to before, this was a hero's quest. It had started, as a quest should start, with false turns and doubts and dangers. The war was over. Archie had his Harvard law degree, along with a citation that said he ranked "highest in scholarship, conduct and character" among his classmates and gave "evidence of the greatest promise." Archie and Ada had a good life and good friends in Cambridge, among them Dean and Alice Acheson, the Harvey Bundys and their children, especially McGeorge, who was to become an adviser to JFK and LBJ. Archie's half sister Blanche Billings lived in a mansion at the tip of Manhattan. Her husband, Ben, came from Chicago wealth, enough of it to let him do things like throwing a dinner party on horseback in a swank New York hotel, each guest served by a footman with a tray at the stirrup (and, presumably, another with a shovel around back). So when things got dull in Boston, the young MacLeishes could whoop it up among the swells farther down the coast.

Archie's rational side fed on the law. He loved the competition, the verbal jousting, the strategies. He thought it the greatest indoor game in the world. He even taught it. He joined one of the city's prominent firms, Choate, Hall and Stewart. He knew, as the twenties rolled in, that if he stuck with it, he would probably end up at the top of the profession, rich enough to have a "huge and unheatable house at Manchester-by-the Sea," where the Brahmins bathed.

The problem lay in the sticking. Little in the law satisfied Archie's inheritance from his mother, that elevated sense of service to his fellow man. Less in it satisfied his central belief that he was born to be a poet. We are all, in some measure, attractions of opposites. Archie managed to fit more oppositions into his life than most of us: self-assertion and self-doubt; the pull of art and the draw of public life; teaching and writing; populist ideals and patrician prejudices.

He was a true agonist, just the sort of person to launch a proper quest. He began it in conversation with the moon, one of many during his long life with this, his most intimate companion. Archie was leaving his law office on State Street one February evening in 1923 and heading for the subway that would take him to Harvard Square. Something—the smell of stale air flushing from the entrance to the underground, the sight of the moon herself—kept him walking. He went up to Massachusetts Avenue and across the Charles to the square and on to his house on Coolidge Hill. I walked part of that way after fifty-five Februaries had passed. I had more snow than he did, and that probably slowed me, but just to get to Harvard Yard took me well over an hour and a half. Archie was as fast at walking as he was at everything else, except writing. Still, I don't think he could have made it in less than two hours.

When he was an old man, Archie recalled the memory of that walk and reworked it to make a prose poem. I came across it only recently and startled when I read the opening. I had asked Archie if he knew what I owed him. And here he was asking the moon, "What do I owe? For what? To whom?" He was telling the moon how hard he had worked, how hard it was to find time for his writing. Then this: "Why do you keep your face turned toward the sun no matter where the sun may lead you? Why do you blind yourself with sunlight?" And, at the end: "I had prepared, provided, made arrangements for a time to come, for work to come, for art to come: There is no art to come: there's only art—the need, the now, the presence, the necessity . . . the sun. It was the art I owed."

I share Ada's tendency to transmute fear instantly into anger. My guess is, therefore, that Archie's frighteningly late homecoming was lit by lightning. But once the air cleared, they began to talk, and they kept at it most of the night. Archie remembered that "she seemed to know what I would say before I'd said it," and that rings true. Ada knew her husband better than he did himself.

Patty MacLeish's story of the moonwalk dwelt more on her daughter-in-law. It was Ada, she wrote, on whom the greater weight of any decision rested. She was the one who had to "handle the family resources and meet the privations without much apparent return for herself. She courageously voted for the change, feeling that her husband's consuming desire to write must have its opportunity."

But Ada too had an art to owe—and even less time available than Archie had to honor the debt. She sang when she could, but she had a house to keep and two children to look after, as well as the "family resources." And she had locked inside her the memory of Brewster Hitchcock, little Brudie, befouled and dead in his crib less than two years before. The idea of going back to Paris, of getting back to herself as a singer, must have brought her face to face again with her own sun.

Becoming artists in their own country didn't seem a workable option to these two. Archie saw what was going on around him in America as a "terrible" time. It was "self-indulgent, it was fat, it was rich, it was full of the most loathsome kinds of open and flagrant money-making." It was, I think, surprisingly like our nineties. Both were times for Babbitts and their indifference to anything unrelated to profit. To stay in America was accordingly to practice art among hostiles and in the absence of mentors. To go was to follow Eliot and Pound and Frost east across the sea, to follow the wanderers to a city where art was life and the exchange rate was wonderful.

Archie went to work the following morning with the idea that he would talk to the firm's senior partner, Charles F. Choate, Jr. When he arrived, he found a message that Choate wanted to talk to *him*. Archie knocked, entered, and stopped in his tracks. Assembled before him were most of the firm's senior lawyers. They were there to witness and applaud Choate's offer of a partnership to the young man who stood stunned before them.

Archie had the extraordinary courage to say that he could not accept, that he had been planning to tell Mr. Choate that very morning that he felt he must leave the firm. He did not say that he was leaving the law to try to write poetry in Paris. Not then. That would have been asking too much of someone watching Mr. Choate's face take on the radiant red of a stoplight.

Thus the *Lafayette*. "Away they went," wrote Patty MacLeish of my favorite quest, "into an unknown future, burning their bridges behind them."

. . .

I am no stranger to innocence abroad. In 1954 my first wife and I went to Peru for a two-year fellowship aimed at studying village life in the southern mountains. Between us, we had about fifty words of Spanish. We moved first to the small city of Arequipa and rented an apartment above a police station. Our landlords stocked our kitchen with everything except a skillet. I looked up the word in our English-Spanish dictionary. It was *sartén*. I went across the patio and knocked on their door.

"Buenos días, Señora," I said.

My landlady, short and thick as Martha Washington, smiled and nodded.

"Necesito . . ." Memory flapped and faded. *"Necesito un . . . un . . ."*

The rate of nod accelerated with my stammer.

"Necesito un . . . sostén," I said.

The entire face began to jig and quiver. Clearly further explanation was necessary.

"Necesito un sostén para mis huevos," I said, enunciating as clearly as ever a green gringo could, making motions of breaking eggs into a bowl.

Our landlady fell back, gargling with laughter.

I turned and ran to, almost through, our door. I grabbed the dictionary. What I had said, slang and all, was: "Good morning, madam. I need a brassiere for my balls."

Archie had had four years of classroom French, but he was as tongue-tied those first days in Paris as my wife and I were in Arequipa. We would have heard from him about any lingual zingers: although Archie hated to be made fun of, he loved to make fun of himself. Several of his wilder dreams decorate the walls of familial memory, including the one in which Ada ran off with a man who swam through the sewers of Berlin playing a fiddle. The reason Archie got along as well as he did with Parisians had to do with the brilliant defensive work of his wife. Ada was way ahead of him in the language. She had the singer's ear for inflection and intonation that made a native of her within weeks. And she had that loyalist's instinct to run interference for the object of her loyalty when she could, and to make artful amends for him when she couldn't.

Ada, in fact, was the star. She studied with some of the best in Paris, including Nadia Boulanger. She sang at the Opéra Co-mique. She sang songs of Poulenc and Satie and of a young and gawky American in Paris named Aaron Copland. I have a folder of hers, labeled "Pieces from a Much Interrupted Past." In it is a folded and brittle playbill advertising a concert to be given by Ada H. MacLeish, "Cantatrice," singing Stravinsky, Ravel, Debussy. Critics called her a comer. A conductor of note asked her to go on tour with him, and when she said she'd have to check with her husband first, he went into a Gallic snit: "Go home, young woman. You are no good for a career in France."

Ada laughed to herself and went on singing. But she knew that she was caught in the cultural bind of any well-bred woman in the twenties who dared to take her talent to its limit. She managed a telling non sequitur to that effect in a letter to her mother-in-law: "I certainly prefer my babies to the greatest career in the world," she wrote. "But there is so much work ahead it almost fills me with despair."

Archie did not like what he was writing. It still smacked of the Victorian ideas of poetry he had absorbed at Yale. He looked to another American in Paris, the master of eccentricity, e e cummings:

> Buffalo Bill 's
> defunct
> > who used to
> > ride a watersmooth-silver
>
> > > > stallion
> and break onetwothreefourfive pigeons
> > justlikethat
> > > Jesus
> he was a handsome man
> > and what i want to know is
> how do you like your blueeyed boy
> Mister Death

"He's so good," Archie said, "I wonder why I keep on trying."

What Archie was trying for was a style made of "lucidity and concreteness." To get it, he took himself back to school. He stopped writing for several months and began to read. Even now, I don't know how he brought himself to do that, a man driven to write, a man fearful he had already waited too long to take up his art. He read Rimbaud and earlier French poets. He read the poets of England as far back as his English would take him. He read translations of Li Po and the other great Chinese poets. He taught himself enough Italian to follow Dante down. He wrote to the poet Amy Lowell in Boston, telling her about all this, and she wrote back in opposition to it: "Do not simulate experience, plunge into it."

Back in Westover, Mary Hillard, stung that Archie had deserted the law, was doing what she could to bring him to his senses by undermining the modest faith my parents had in themselves and their quest. She wrote warning that the children's health would be destroyed by unnamed Parisian effluents. She said she had asked her literary contacts about Archie's poetic talents and found none who would praise him. Archie first counterattacked and then ignored her.

Archie was to say later that he took up Dante's *Divine Comedy* "because Tom Eliot had read it to his great profit and because I was—as I remain—his devoted admirer. It did me, I am sure, no harm. But neither did it do me Eliot's good, for it was not my need that took me to it." It was Archie's need, though, that brought Eliot's influence to his early work. *The Waste Land* blew in the poetic wind then, and poets everywhere heard it. Archie made use of it and, when critics called him on his borrowing, noted that it was tough enough to be a man ahead of his time, as Eliot was, but tougher still to be the man following that man.

Pound, too, was a tough act. Archie didn't meet the dean of poetry he called "Ezry" (and once, in a letter to a friend, "that old turd") until 1939, but he did ask for and get early criticism from the crotchety genius who had helped Eliot and so many others. Learn Arabic, Pound told him, and later, learn Gaelic, the idea being to shake up his perspective. Archie did neither, but he did learn how to wean himself away from the masters.

After a while, Pound was saying to him, "one heave more, one more crunch of the teeth, and you ought to get through to your own."

He was right. New poems came with new breath in them. Swinburne, who had been pounded into Archie at Yale, receded, and with him went the inflated imagery of Archie's first efforts ("The tremulously mirrored clouds lie deep, / Enchanted towers bosomed in the stream, / And blossomed coronals of white-thorn gleam / Within the water where the willows sleep—"). Less than two years after his arrival in Paris, Archie completed the early drafts of a poem that would find its place in the anthologies. It appeared in 1926 in his collection *Streets in the Moon*. The poem was "Ars Poetica":

A poem should be palpable and mute
As a globed fruit,

Dumb
As old medallions to the thumb,

Silent as the sleeve-worn stone
Of casement ledges where the moss has grown—

A poem should be wordless
As the flight of birds.

*

A poem should be motionless in time
As the moon climbs,

Leaving, as the moon releases
Twig by twig the night-entangled trees,

Leaving, as the moon behind the winter leaves,
Memory by memory the mind—

A poem should be motionless in time
As the moon climbs.

*

A poem should be equal to:
Not true.

For all the history of grief
An empty doorway and a maple leaf.

For love
  The leaning grasses and two lights above the sea—

A poem should not mean
But be.

And there was the unanswerable question, the one about humanity's place in the universe—man naked against the stars; the cold visits of the moon; human awareness in an uncaring cosmos. The hidden eastward hurtle of the earth beneath him was more real to him than the bold thrust of the Eiffel Tower above him. Unlike Eliot, he looked for his cosmic metaphors not to the givens of Newtonian science but to the Einsteinian science of his own time. No clockwork there, just Einstein's mysteries of matter and energy, just the certainty of the uncertainties in his thinking.

The MacLeishes spent part of their second summer at Granville on the Normandy coast. Ada sang every day. One morning, a knock sounded on the door, and a young man asked, "Who is that singing Satie? No one in Granville sings Satie." His name was Christian Dior, and he was nineteen. Music was his passion then. Fashion would come later, and even in that unmusical pursuit he retained a soft spot for Ada. To her, he was "my Christian."

In Granville my family went to a traveling circus. Archie, who all his life worried about fire, took a look at the tiny tent and the lanterns inside it and crossed his fingers. Within a day or two, a rhythm started in his head that resolved into a prosaic phrase: "quite unexpectedly." The phrase became "The End of the World."

> Quite unexpectedly as Vasserot
> The armless ambidextrian was lighting
> A match between his great and second toe
> And Ralph the lion was engaged in biting
> The neck of Madame Sossman while the drum
> Pointed, and Teeny was about to cough
> In waltz-time swinging Jocko by the thumb—
> Quite unexpectedly the top blew off:
>
> And there, there overhead, there, there, hung over
> Those thousands of white faces, those dazed eyes,
> There in the starless dark the poise, the hover,

There with vast wings across the canceled skies,
There in the sudden blackness the black pall
Of nothing, nothing, nothing—nothing at all.

Paris was indeed wonderful, or became wonderful—for their arts and for them. Andrew again provided. He gave Archie the same allowance he had had during law school. Three thousand dollars a year then was something over thirty thousand now. The French franc helped by hovering at around sixty to the dollar.

Ada and Archie lived in luck most of the time. They started out in modest lodgings, but through friends moved up and up. They lived for a while in the pleasant suburb of Saint-Cloud, in the house once occupied by the great nineteenth-century opera composer Charles Gounod. And when a very rich couple returned home to the United States, they let Ada and Archie have their apartment. It was free, but maintaining the staff, butler and all, just about broke them.

The good living went to their heads and other places. Ada wrote that if they continued in their new eating habits she would have to hire a tugboat to tow her home. All this gave them what one waspish friend called "a champagne taste on a beer budget," but it also gave them the priceless sense that they were leading and not being led by their lives.

A few years ago, I stood on the Boulevard St.-Michel in front of the apartment my parents occupied early on and longest. It was a cold-water flat in a handsome building with a courtyard, four floors up. There had been a room above for the *bonne,* the maid. I thought of my father there, working mornings—always mornings—watching the roof leak under the gray winter rains and smelling the damp cocoa matting under his feet. I thought about my mother keeping house, instructing her servants, shopping, hoarding enough time for scales and songs. There was Ken, off to school across the park. There was Mimi, playing in the Luxembourg Gardens close by. The streets then were full of war wounded, begging or just sitting, and they frightened Mimi. I saw her clinging to her nanny, crying *"Je déteste les pauvres."* I walked away down the boulevard and within yards smacked into the present. There in front of me was a McDonald's. But before I could rise to righteous fulmination, I saw that even this importation of modern America's latest passion for efficiency and its deep fear of surprise had been gently altered by the French: on its counter sat a small dog, slowly and daintily dining on its Big Mac.

Archie would bridle late in his life when people asked him about running with all those other American artists in Paris. Paris, he said, was not an American phenomenon when he and Ada were there. It was not "Fitzgerald and soda—an escape from Calvin Coolidge to a hot spot on Montmartre—a jazz age in a gayer city." Paris in the twenties, he said, "was Picasso and the changing forms. It was Stravinsky back to conduct the 'Sacre' again. It was James Joyce, an Irish teacher from Trieste, with the manuscript of a novel called *Ulysses* which no one, it was said, would publish. It was Alexis Saint-Léger writing *Anabase* at the French Foreign Office and signing it 'St.-John Perse.' It was André Masson, the surrealist painter. It was Malraux. It was the most creative generation in the recent history of France or close to it.

"It was," Archie said, "a throng of gifted youngsters from every continent on earth. And those who came there in those

years—even the Scots—even the Scots with Yankee mothers
—were working in that city in those years as the young
worked once in Florence: under the shadow of the greatest
masters, judging themselves by measures they would never
match."

His poem "Years of the Dog" says it better:

Before, though, Paris was wonderful. Wanderers
Talking in all tongues from every country.
Fame was what they wanted in that town.
Fame could be found there too—flushed like quail in the
Cool dawn—struck among statues
Naked in hawthorn in the silver light.
James Joyce found it. Dublin bore him.
Could have sung with McCormack! Could he? He could.
Did he? He didn't. He walked by the winding Seine.
And what did he eat? He ate orts: oddities:
Oh he was poor: obscure: no one had heard of him:
Rolled on the floor on the floor with the pain in his eyes.
And found fame? He did. Ulysses: Yule Book:
Published to every people even in Erse.
(Molly Molly why did you say so Molly!)
Or the lad in the Rue de Notre Dame des Champs
At the carpenter's loft on the left-hand side going down—
The lad with the supple look like a sleepy panther—
And what became of him? Fame became of him.
Veteran out of the wars before he was twenty:
Famous at twenty-five: thirty a master—
Whittled a style for his time from a walnut stick
In a carpenter's loft in a street of that April city.

Where do they hang out now, the young ones, the
   wanderers,
Following fame by the rumor of praise in a town?
Where is fame in the world now? Where are the lovers of
Beauty of beauty that she moves among?

On that same Paris trip in 1993 I was taken by friends to the
Closerie des Lilas, in the twenties a refuge for artists and writers,
and now an expensive restaurant. I let it be known that I was in
Paris to see some of what my father had seen. Instantly, the
manager grabbed me by the elbow and propelled me through
the crowd to the bar. There, close to the beer taps, set in the
gloss of the wood, was a very small brass plaque. It read, in precisely cut lettering, "E. Hemingway." Seconds later I was back at
our table, sipping a complementary flute of fine and dry champagne.

Ernest Hemingway didn't see himself bellying up to any bar,
at least during his morning working hours, at least in his young
days. At the Closerie as at his other haunts, he could usually be
found at a small table with a café crème, or perhaps a good beer,
and a cheap notebook with blue covers. This is where Archie
found him in the spring of 1924. At Shakespeare and Company,
a bookstore near Notre Dame, Archie had picked up and read a
pamphlet of his short stories, published by a small press in Paris.
It was called *in our time,* and it got Archie out of his chair and
hustling along to the Closerie and to a friendship that started out
sweet and strong and then spent years souring and dwindling.

The closest I got to meeting Ernest was when he came to Peru
in the mid-fifties after big marlin to film for the movie of *The Old
Man and the Sea*. A friend of mine was flying back to the States on

the same plane, and I sent a note along with him. Ernest didn't reply, but my friend said Papa looked touched and talked with him a bit about good times with the MacLeishes. What I did meet as I was growing up was Ernest's influence. It lay below the surface of my family, lodged in behaviors. He was not often mentioned then, but now I see his afterimage.

Ernest, when Archie found him, was in his mid-twenties, bullnecked, broad shouldered, small waisted and two hundred pounds. He too was a middle-class Midwesterner. He too was competitive to the point of combativeness. His brother Leicester, younger by sixteen years, believed that Ernest always wanted and needed younger brothers around him, men he could "teach and show off to." I think my father, though Ernest's senior by seven years, acted that role, something I never saw him do with any other man. I also think he deferred as he did, praising Ernest's writing and his athletic prowess, because he knew that was the only way to be accepted by a man he very much wanted as a friend. Only rarely, as when they were bicycling in the country, would he unleash his drive and surge ahead.

Many other men deferred to Hemingway, with varying results. The strain began to tell on Archie fairly early. This, from "Cinema of a Man," written in the late twenties, was drawn from a trip the two took to Spain:

> He walks with Ernest in the streets in Saragossa
> They are drunk their mouths are hard they say *qué cosa*
> They say the cruel words they hurt each other
> Their elbows touch their shoulders touch their feet go on
>   and on together.

Half a century later, sitting on the west terrace at Conway, my
father looked back at his friend. Among the things he remembered was that nighttime was a terror to Ernest. He had to have
someone—a lover, a friend—in the same room with him to
stave off the terrible dreams. Archie thought they might have
been dreams of being wounded on the Italian front in the war.
Ada came and sat with us on the terrace. "I did a lot with Ernest
that Archie didn't want to do," she told me. "Archie didn't want
to go to the races, and he didn't want to go to the fights. And all
those things I did want to do, and I went with Ernest." Ernest
taught her to ski when they were all in Switzerland. At some
point, she said, he told her that she was about the only woman
he had wanted to sleep with whom he hadn't slept with. I was so
taken by that naked arrogance that I never asked what she said
to him in return.

• • •

The days, Ada wrote from Paris after they had settled in, gal-
loped along, "dragging us after them." She was the bubbling
one, at least in her letters. Archie, especially when the worry
over his work hit him, could be what one friend called "stac-
cato." But they had an enviable amount of fun. They drove out
to Chartres by moonlight one Christmas. They dined on pheas-
ant sent by a rich friend. Ada gave Archie a dinner dance. They
went to this concert and that opening. From restaurants to re-
ceptions, their only pace, from what I can make out at my remove, was a surge.

While living in their ritzy borrowed apartment, they invited
James Joyce to dinner. His eyes were bad enough so that he
mistook the butler for Archie and shook hands with him. By

then, Joyce was becoming fairly well known in the literary world, but his wife, Nora Barnacle, seemed to believe he had chosen the wrong career. Earlier, in Dublin, he had sung in competition and done well—well enough, Nora thought—to gain a steady income from his clear tenor voice. But he kept on with his stories and novels and his shaky finances. Nora would glance at him and growl to anyone within earshot, "James Joyce, the *writerrr!*"

But Joyce had never left music. He sang for his friends. He filled his writing with the songs he had collected, hundreds of them. When the pain and the blurred vision of his glaucoma permitted, he would come over to use Ada's piano, and they sang and sang. Two songs stayed with Ada. "Down by the Salley Gardens," a piece Yeats had tried to reconstruct from lines he remembered an old woman singing:

Down by the salley gardens my love and I did meet;
She passed the salley gardens with little snow-white feet.
She bid me take love easy as the leaves grow on the tree;
But I, being young and foolish, with her did not agree.

Ada taught me that one, and we sang it often together—that and "The Yellow Ale." I have never been more haunted by a song. "The Yellow Ale" has the feel of a translation from the Gaelic. It is a supernatural story of an old man with a young wife who meets an eerie stranger, one who was "no right man." The stranger asks if the husband will lend him his wife for "an hour and a day." The old man sings, "And I said I would do anything that was fair." Then he sings:

So let you take the upper road and I'll take the lower
O the brown and the yellow ale
And we'll meet again by the ford of the river
O love of my heart.

The young woman returns to her husband, telling him of what she did with the eerie man. And the old man sings, "When I heard her news I lay down and I died."

While they were living in Saint-Cloud, e e cummings paid them a visit. Ada suspected he came precisely because they never pestered him to come. "He draws as well as he writes, incidentally—a burning mind. Words come tumbling out, disarmingly foul-mouthed. Quite a drinker . . . We argued, discussed theories of art, of life." They met Scott Fitzgerald, whom, "oddly enough, we like very much." They met Sinclair Lewis, who is "more or less always drunk and when he is less is very amusing."

And they met "a lovely couple with three lovely children and tastes similar to our own." They were Gerald and Sara Murphy, both children of Long Island money, both in rebellion against it. They were committed to making lives that deepened their senses and those of their friends. In an age when heiresses would rather sell themselves on the street than draw on their capital, the Murphys spent whatever they needed to live those lives. Their investments were often in their friends; they loaned and they gave when a writer or painter or composer came up short.

Gerald was a couple of years ahead of Archie at Yale and a member of the same secret society. ("Ged'ld," a society matron once asked, "are you a Ba-own?") He was interested in art when the truly blue thought artistic pursuit somewhat suspect. In Paris he began to paint large, often huge, compositions whose precision tested the tolerances of reality. The French cubist Fernand Léger called him the best American painter in the city. Gerald, or Dow-Dow, or Dow, as his children and close friends called him, loved to act the dandy, cane and all. That and vastly exaggerated estimates of his wealth made him an easy target for those who called him a dilettante.

By some alchemy—I didn't get baptized until I was in my forties, and even then it didn't take—Dow and Sara became my godparents. They gave me wonderful things when I was a boy: books of old English music for my recorder, songs they had collected, books, stories; and themselves. I never spent as much time with them as I wanted, but each visit went straight to memory. They gave me my first raw oysters and with them my passion for shellfish. Their daughter, Honoria, ten years older than I, accompanied me to Broadway musicals courtesy of the Murphys. She was beautiful, but then they all were. Sara was exquisitely Nordic. Dow I remember as the Gilded Mick, so Irish in the face that you could laugh if it weren't for the sadness in the eyes.

The Murphys are forever remembered as the couple for whom living well was the best revenge. Dow, a voracious reader, may have happened on that phrase in the work of the English metaphysical poet George Herbert. He may even have used it himself. But when one of the Murphys' biographers, Calvin Tompkins, took it as his title, his subjects were not pleased. I think I can understand why. Revenge was never a part of their well-lived younger lives. Later, when there was ample reason for fury against the fates that had so wounded them, they took their tragedies with a grace that stays with me still

Archie and Gerald roamed all over the countryside, trying this wine, that cheese. At the wine caves near Beaune they were introduced to the art of tasting. All went well except for one oversight: they did not yet know that one holds each sampling in the mouth, experiencing its body and bouquet, and then daintily spits it out. They swallowed—and swallowed—as they moved slowly along the passageways. Suddenly, they heard music so beautiful they doubted they'd heard it. Outside again, they watched the moon and stars dance over them, and discovered they were hard by a cathedral. They were just sober enough to understand that what they had heard was the choir at practice.

Antibes, on the eastern Mediterranean coast of France, became the Murphys' summer home. Ada and Archie stayed there, along with Ernest and Scott Fitzgerald and their wives, and John Dos Passos, the writer who liked to approach his writing on foot, through the American South, Spain, Russia. I see Dos with his slightly popped eyes, I hear his famous stutter: "A-a-a-a-rchie!" and the stories from his walks.

Ada and Archie went sailing with Gerald. They ate lunches of new potatoes and bread and butter and white wine. They ate late suppers under the linden tree in the garden of the Murphys' Villa America, talking about what they were doing and what they were going to do. They took the sun on the beach with the Murphys' close friends the Picassos. Archie did elegant swan dives off high rocks into the sea and injured his back. He did half gainers and one-and-a-halfs off a local board, and Ada was there to watch the people watching her bronze boy.

T. S. Eliot has a line with a Latin beat: "Human kind cannot bear very much reality." Certainly not in that moonlight in those years, when the brass rings hung gleaming just above the candles. No one paid much attention to what was also there, the glints of what was coming to some of them. Not so much the Murphys, not yet. But Ernest's first marriage was foundering, and he showed early signs of a penchant for taking out his fears and angers on his friends. Scott was tight a good deal of the time. "When drunk," he wrote, "I make them pay and pay." Archie once took him aside to calm him down and got a punch in the face for his pains.

And then, in the spring of 1926, Archie himself took off for what was then Persia and is now Iran. It almost sounds to me as if he had gone AWOL. He left his work and his family and signed on with a group of diplomats looking into the possibilities of improving the country's sad transportation system, a tit for the tat of getting out of the opium trade. He was gone for three months or so. Maybe the caper had something to do with the fact that Dean Acheson had recommended him for the job. Maybe it was the challenge of the journey. My hunch, however, is that Archie had to get out. Ada had reported that his nerves were making him pole-vault at the ring of a telephone and blow up when the toilet paper ran out. All through their marriage, she dealt with that pygmy-shrew behavior of his, the one he passed on with only minor alterations to me.

Ada was worried that he was too "fine and sensitive" to stand the gaff of Persia and protocol, and she was right. Archie wrote telling her what an awful mistake he had made, how he was nothing without her. Never again, he kept saying. Never again? Many, many times again. Well after they had left France, someone remembered Ada saying, "You must think of Archie's life as that of someone who lives in a bustling port, all active and happy, and one day he looks up and sees a mountain, and thinks, 'Well, I've simply got to go up there,' and he does, and after a while he looks down at the bustling port and thinks, 'Now I've got to get back down there.'"

As the twenties aged and sagged, the franc gained ground against the dollar, and Paris became something less of an April city. The Lost Generation, the people caught in the metaphor Gertrude Stein spun out of a phrase she heard from her garage-man, found itself heading home. Ada and Archie spun like tops, trying to find a way to keep hold of their lives. Ada had to be within reach of Paris and, shortly after that, New York, to get the artistic exposure she needed. Archie had to be free from people, away from cities, for the next two or three years, a period he regarded as possibly the most important in his creative life. They thought of buying or renting an old New England farm for the warm months and returning to France for the cold. They thought of moving into a fifteenth-century house outside Paris and seeing what happened.

By something approaching pure luck the farm won out. Archie and Ada bought the place in Conway in the summer of 1927 and sailed back to France for what turned out to be quest's end. Ada had been talking about another child "for my old age," and that was arranged that fall. Then, in midwinter, Andrew, Archie's father, died. He had been long gone in his head, walking the halls of Craigie Lea whistling "Merrily We Roll Along." It must have been a strange death for Archie, the passing of a life so crucial to his own, and lived so far from him.

I have always felt that that death somehow merged with memories of those tedious days in Iran to produce one of the finest poems Archie ever wrote. He wrote it as he wrote few others, in one day. It was a farewell to Europe and to Andrew and to his apprenticeship. It evoked another Andrew, a poet who wrote about time as Archie wished to. He called it "You, Andrew Marvell."

And here face down beneath the sun
And here upon earth's noonward height
To feel the always coming on
The always rising of the night:

To feel creep up the curving east
The earthly chill of dusk and slow
Upon those under lands the vast
And ever climbing shadow grow

And strange at Ecbatan the trees
Take leaf by leaf the evening strange
The flooding dark about their knees
The mountains over Persia change

And now at Kermanshah the gate
Dark empty and the withered grass
And through the twilight now the late
Few travelers in the westward pass

And Baghdad darken and the bridge
Across the silent river gone
And through Arabia the edge
Of evening widen and steal on

And deepen on Palmyra's street
The wheel rut in the ruined stone
And Lebanon fade out and Crete
High through the clouds and overblown

And over Sicily the air
Still flashing with the landward gulls
And loom and slowly disappear
The sails above the shadowy hulls

And Spain go under and the shore
Of Africa the gilded sand
And evening vanish and no more
The low pale light across that land

Nor now the long light on the sea:

And here face downward in the sun
To feel how swift how secretly
The shadow of the night comes on . . .

So we came home, my parents with Kenny and Mimi and what would be me. Archie and Ada had both done much of what they had hoped to do. Voice and verse, each had scratched what Archie called "the itch of notice." Critics were taking him seriously. "I am a poet," he said. "The rest can wait."

It didn't.

Where Seldom Is Heard

THE MACLEISHES WENT THROUGH CUSTOMS ON their own front lawn in Conway, or so Ada and Archie told me. Everything came up from the boat, inspections were duly conducted of crates, boxes, and Louis Vuitton steamer trunks, and then five years of France were hauled into a Yankee farmhouse. What Patty MacLeish called "the long exile" was over.

Archie had a familial connection to Conway: the town was the last stop in the nomadic ministry of his grandfather, Elias Brewster Hillard, who died in 1895. In a sense, Archie had forsaken his father's city (Andrew had once hoped that he would eventually join Carson Pirie Scott) for his grandfather's village. When he and Ada arrived, there were still people around who had been married by Elias, and that helped break the hill-town ice. Ada and Archie went to church "downstreet" from time to time, and they made a stab at neighborliness by having a party. The trouble was that the guests arrived wanting very much to leave; Ada had set their arrival time for late afternoon, when most of them would normally be milking or doing other chores.

Eventually something resembling a mutual awareness developed, but it took some years to develop into mutual fondness. Ada and Archie were summer people and summer people were like swallows, gone during the hard seasons. I think many also picked up on Archie's ability to be at once outgoing and reserved. They left him alone and took their time to acknowledge him. In 1972, forty-four years after his arrival, they put him on the cover of the town's annual report. I saw how that satisfied his soul.

Shortly after they arrived on our ridge, I signaled my desire to exit Ada. I must have given proper notice, for she had time to travel the hundred and twenty miles from Conway to Massachusetts General Hospital in Boston. There, on what she said was "the hottest day in the world," she went into labor. Archie did not make it for the emergence—which is strange, since he usually arrived embarrassingly early for most arrivals and departures. He got to the hospital a day late, on August eighth, and thenceforth smilingly assured me that *that* was really my birth date.

Archie also said that I was born in Boston, but "otherwise you were born right here." Again, I never questioned that impossibility; I simply went by my mother's account of my birth. In adulthood, I even got myself a facsimile of the front page of *The New York Times* for August 7, 1928. Not much was happening. An Italian submarine had been rammed and sunk; President Coolidge was working on a federal budget that amounted to all of 4 billion dollars; the stock market was smoking up the grade on its way to the abyss; and the Gulf Stream, the object a half century later of fascination and study on my part, was said to have reversed course (probably the effects of a passing eddy spun off the main flow). I found elsewhere that I was coeval with Mickey Mouse and Andy Warhol and homogenized peanut butter and Shirley Temple and bubble gum.

Getting to Conway was a voyage as circuitous as any followed by my parents in those years. They started seriously looking for a summer place (winters, remember, would be spent in France) in the summer of 1927. They did their reconnoitering from Ashfield, just west of Conway, where Mary Hillard of the Westover School had a house. (Whether through changes of heart or in the interests of expediency, things had been patched up enough between the domineering aunt and her combative nephew to permit his darkening her door.) Uncle Billy Hitchcock kept his eye out for property in Connecticut, and that is where they made their first and silliest sally.

"We wanted two things," Archie said. "We wanted beautiful elm trees and a running brook." The first place they saw, in the hills of western Connecticut, had recently been a farm for the poor. It had neither elms nor stream. "So," said my father, "we bought it." Ada remembered the Connecticut place as "the last thing I wanted, but your father was in a hurry to start writing. I cried all the time, thinking about the poor farm." Archie, I later found out, was also sorry about it. He wrote to his friends in France, saying the house was cold and wet, that there was no one to talk to for miles. He invited the Hemingways and the Murphys to come build cabins on his land: he and Ernest, he said, could run for selectman.

"One day when I was busy crying," Ada said, "a friend told me about a house in Conway she had ridden by—she was quite a horsewoman—and it had a FOR SALE sign out in front with the *S* backwards. My friend said previous owners had put some things on it, but they would come off easily."

Archie and Ada looked the place over, peeking into the dirty and lovely rooms of a farmhouse that had probably been framed late in the eighteenth century. They saw beautiful mantels painted over and tin panels with angels on them covering the fireplaces. They looked at the real estate agent's sales screed, worked up perhaps a decade earlier, that went on about the town being linked to the Boston and Maine railroad by an electric street railway that had failed in 1921. The brochure describes "A Beautiful Country Estate at Conway, Mass. in the Berkshire Hills." It has a photograph of the house, taken from the road. There are elms on the lawn. You can see the south side with its pure New England front door. Around the corner to the east is a huge porch with fancy Corinthian pillars. A Southern family had lived there and tried to ease the northern lines of the house where and as they could.

The region, says the brochure, "has long been noted for its popular hotels, summer resorts and summer homes, as [its] climate is bracing, healthful and non-malarial. And the sweet pine groves offer their healing balm to the health of the summer recreation seeker." The house, it says, contained twelve rooms and halls, "originally of colonial design, forty by fifty feet, two stories, attic and cellar." It had been modernized and in the process its six fireplaces had been traded for steam heat. Water came by gravity from a spring, and there was a windmill nearby over a "never failing well."

Up the dirt road lay a barn. Forty-two by a hundred feet, it had stables for four horses and stanchions for thirty cows, a built-in silo and ice house. You could stand by that barn and look east along the ridge and see hills everywhere.

One hundred and seventy-five acres came with the house. There were two orchards. The soil, the brochure assured, was sandy loam, adapted to "the production of tobacco, onions, potatoes, corn, hay and fruits of all kinds." Valuable lumber was to be had from the woods. There was a brook (the brochure made no mention of the sizable pond the brook ran out of, because the Boy Scouts hadn't built it when the pamphlet went to press). All told, the property would be just right as a sportsman's club, "a private sanatorium, a select school or boarding house."

To the MacLeishes, it looked just right as their home. "So," my father said to me, "being very cautious and careful people, we proceeded to buy this house, too." That wasn't quite right. He neglected to mention that the purchaser of record was William Arthur Hitchcock, who, some three years later, transferred the deed to his daughter, Ada. The price for the entire farm was about $5,000.

Still, my parents would have had a sticky time of it if their Connecticut folly hadn't been snapped up by a man who had wanted it all along and had been hopping mad when they bought it out from under him. Then a friend lent them the money for the renovations they wanted in Conway. While Ada and Archie headed back overseas to close out the French phase of their lives, a contractor took off the porches and began work on a brick wing with a huge music room below, all set about with French doors, and servants' quarters above. "At that time," my father told me, "you expected to have servants." By which I assume he meant that *he* expected to have them.

Philip Hilts, who writes remarkably well about remembering, says, "The experience within us is not of the world itself. And our memory is not a memory of events themselves. Both are only the feel of neurons alight." Since I'm writing this in my seventieth year, I have come to believe that in me that light, rising to consciousness, passes through filters of age and attitude and is adjusted accordingly. Research for this book has added other filters, as have changing ideas of who I am and an imagination that even now refuses to be curbed. I wouldn't fully trust my memory for a minute, and that tends to add fictive wing to my story-telling.

Vladimir Nabokov claims to remember his crib; my full memory of my father begins somewhere around my eleventh year. When I told Ada this, she wasn't surprised: all during the thirties, she said, "he would just appear and disappear," as his commitments called. I see him down in the cellar, dressed in nothing but his drawers, stomping grapes in a wooden tub. That, of course, is nonsense—or rather a perfectly good story that someone told me about a time when I couldn't have been more than one or two. But I still see his purple shins and the smile of glee on him. The wine, I'm told, was undrinkable, just like the messes I made in the late fifties, when my own cellar was full of casks of grape juice whose fermentings sounded like a herd of bees.

There is also something in my head about a whippoorwill that got into the house in the middle of a summer night and sang, if that's the word, on the newel post of the main stairs. I recall it was so close I could hear the chuckle in its call, but I think that is a bit too precise to be acceptable. The big-mouthed birds are gone from these hills now, and I miss them and the metronomic insistence of their song.

I guess the melon moon comes closest to being the first true marker of my memory. I recollect being lifted from my bed in a little room at the top of the stairs and carried down and outside to the east terrace. There were several people there, friends up for the weekend or something, and they murmured. I looked up and saw my father's face above me in the moonlight. I was in his arms, seeing him and smelling him—all through my years with him I loved his smell. The moon looked like a melon to me. It probably had just risen, for it was big and deep yellow. And here I was, held up before it. I remember feeling very sleepy and very important. I suppose my mother was there, but I didn't look for her. No need. I was where I wanted to be. I must have been about three.

I yearn to believe that Ada nursed me. I think she nursed Ken and Mimi, and there was no reason why she couldn't have done the same for me. I have no memory of her ever holding me, but that may be because when I was older, she rarely gave me—or anyone other than Archie—more than a quick, hard hug. She was not demonstrative in that way, and, given her upbringing and her character, I don't see how she could have been.

Ada wrote to friends shortly after my birth and said that I did not have "the aristocracy of bone and modeling which has so far characterized our offspring," but that she was taken by my "little square paws." Several years later, though, she liked my looks well enough to have me Fauntlerized by a painter. I howled when I saw that portrait; I hated it right into adulthood. If I knew where it was now, I'd love to see it again. We'd make a fine couple, the Little Lord in his frame, in his fancy collar and brown velvet coat and masses of blond hair, and the old, bald man in his turtleneck.

I like to tell my younger daughter, Morellen, that I wouldn't have minded having her as a mother, or her husband, John, as a father. I see them with their one child, Ana. They listen, their interest is real. When they are firm, they always explain their firmness. Ana has choices I never had as a child, and she makes them and learns from them. The three of them beguile me: they give so much time to each other.

I think the bond between Ada and Archie, their need for each other and the pleasure they took in satisfying that need, made that kind of inclusion improbable for their children. They loved us, in different degrees at different times, but they could not and did not attend as Morellen and John do. A lot of their aloofness was generational and social: upper-class families of their day— and they were upper class—tended to prefer seeing rather than hearing their children, particularly in company. The Dr. Spocks of the time reinforced this behavior with admonitions to let crying children cry: if you went to them when they were in full voice, you would only end up spoiling them. (This kind of neglect actually goes way back. In colonial times, Indians used to laugh uproariously at the foolishness of whites leaving their children alone to wail.) Ken was a fretful baby. When he cried, Ada would sit at the foot of the stairs leading to his room and sing to him, often crying herself.

Archie had his own ideas about rearing children. I'm sure he didn't get them from his mother. In fact, Patty, who spent all that time learning how to raise Archie and the others, almost certainly must have been put off by his explanations of those ideas in an intemperate letter he wrote her from Paris in 1924. He told her that Kenny "irritates me when we are together and I often bully him." (Mimi remembers Archie chasing Ken, telling him that he was yellow.) Archie said he ought to "respect [Kenny] and advise him and let who will (and lots of them will) toughen him." What he would have liked to give Kenny was "himself. Not being able to give him that what I should do is prevent others from taking it away from him. And others will take it away from him not by opposition but by help. It is the easy tangents we slide off by. It is the friend who slightly directs you in the direction of your own genius who betrays you. It is those who go before and beat down the grass who lose you the way.

"I suppose," Archie continued, "what it all comes down to is the fact that you can't do much for a child . . . And too much fingering of children doth rot them young. Feed em, keep em alive, respect em and teach them to ask." This bit of psychological Darwinism could be Archie's rationalization for his own hands-off style of dealing with his children. But Ada, too, seemed to have had her doubts about how much she could do for Ken and Mimi during the Paris years. She wrote to Patty, "It is hard not to impose our wills on our children when we see what looks like trouble ahead. But it is no use."

I like to think that I can understand some of the friction between Archie and Ken, at least in the beginning. Archie had gone off to war when Ken was a baby and returned when he was a talking toddler. Ken and his mother spent much of the interim at Craigie Lea, where he did something Archie had never been able to do: reach past Andrew's remoteness and touch his heart. When Captain MacLeish came back, Kenny took one look at the stranger with the uniform and the mustache and said, "It is not a doggie." The son had had his mother all to himself for months, while the father had nothing but letters to ease his yearnings. The two males, small and tall, looked at each other and growled.

Archie's letters from France describe Mimi as captivating and elfin—a tiny beauty with a large will and the skill to use it. Ada ended one letter home saying that "Mimi is making demands for tea, with a face and a dignity so like Archie's that I find myself pushing the bell without a thought." Archie said he was completely under his daughter's spell, and he obviously wasn't the only one. She spoke French as well as or better than English, and that brought her notice. Ada told Mimi it was Maurice Chevalier who gave her the name she goes by. She had been born Mary Hillard MacLeish, but Ada and Archie seemed delighted to shift that gear when the occasion presented itself. The less to remind them of Aunt Mary, the better.

Mimi says that Ken "plagued" her in Paris, and I can believe that. I think he sensed Archie's devotion to her, and natural jealousy drove his protest. He kept telling her about things to fear, including feathers. They bit, he told her, and she believed him. Ken ragged her until Ada and Archie, on the advice of doctors, sent him off to a boarding school in Gstaad, Switzerland, noted for its ability to restore health to sickly little boys (Ken had been diagnosed as having had a mild case of polio when he was very young). It was a strict school. Ken was shoved into a closet when he forgot himself and spoke English instead of French. When Christmas came, Ada and Archie were permitted to leave off presents but not to see him. I'd like to learn more about my brother's time there; since the only surviving classmate I know about is Prince Philip of England, I don't think I will.

The fact that Mimi is really Mary has never bothered me. Ken was born Archibald—"wee Archie" to Andrew—and was renamed for his late Uncle Kenny upon his death. And I am Peter, after a kinsman in Scotland, one who did wag his pow. I became William as an infant, after Ada's father complained that with the death of my elder brother, Brewster Hitchcock MacLeish, there was no one left to carry on his name. I grew up thinking that Bill was a nickname for Peter, a belief strengthened by the fact that

Ken and Ada called me Bill, Archie called me Peter unless reminded otherwise, and Mimi steadfastly called me Pete.

It is one thing to make a mistake in naming: Andrew informed his children that a highly regarded academic in Scotland had told him he was a MacGregor, kith of Rob Roy and heir to the bloody history of that unfortunate and broken clan. He may have been, but when Archie checked the appropriate sources later on, he found that we were MacPhersons. And I think my parents sincerely believed that they lived on Cricket Hill—until they were informed that that prominence was located in another part of town and that they lived on Pine Hill. But given names carry myths and mysteries with them that, being given, can often shore up self-esteem. Peter does that for me. Bill does not.

"Mr. Stanley" is somewhere in between. My father began calling me that not too long after the melon moon. I don't know what happened to the tooth-and-claw views of fatherhood that had lathered him so with Ken. My older siblings may have worn a lot of it away before I came along. So here was I, a little boy doing his bidding and not scaring him. He started showing me around the place now and then, and he made the walks out to be explorations through savage country.

At some point I tried calling him Dr. Livingstone, but that name came off like a bad stamp. Archie loved "Mr. Stanley." He made the name serious and farcical, and he used it to call my attention to my world. He would stop on some woods trail and point out a shrub or a tree or some scat and tell me what it was and what it meant. He showed me the spot in the bend of our brook where Ernest had gotten a double on grouse, and thereafter I never forgot to salute the big man and his beautifully balanced shotgun whenever I passed that way. Later, when I was well into my teens, he pointed across a valley at a grove of pines and asked me what caught my senses about them. It was late afternoon, and the sun struck through the plumage of the trees to light up the boles. I told him that, and he put a hand on my shoulder and squeezed.

Once Archie saw me standing in the door of a bathroom where he was peeing. I think that was the first time I had set eye on his stream, and it, along with the means of its delivery, impressed me. "Ha-body noises, Mr. Stanley," Archie sang out. "Ha-body noises." He laughed, I laughed, and we both ended up bent with hooting over his nonsense. Late in his life, he signed one of his books for me "For Peter, Bill and Mr. Stanley, all three of him." He had it about right.

Mr. Stanley was my spirit of fun, and in time he made more of a traveler of me than the others could have. The struggle between Bill and Peter went on, with Bill gaining ground as I graduated to signing checks and legal documents and Peter standing pat on my birth certificate. When I was about fifty, I spent a week in northern Vermont, at a spot being developed as an Esalen of the East. My guru was Will Schutz, as effective a group therapist as I have seen. We went at it hard and long, exercise after exercise, so that by the end of the week I was getting pretty limber. The last day, I went running in the early morning, along a dirt road high among the hills. Lazing along a ridge, I saw a small boy in the bushes up ahead. He came out, running ahead of me. Then he slowed, let me catch up, and melted into my chest. I hollered "Peter!" and went leaping along, waving my arms, babbling, and blubbering.

The high lasted all that day and for a month or so more. I

began calling myself Peter. I changed my name on the mast-head of the magazine I was editing at the Woods Hole Oceano-graphic Institution. Some old salt asked me about it. "Peter!" he said. "What's it going to be in the next issue? Gertrude?" I went back to Bill.

Archie's sister, Ishbel, took some home movies of us at Craigie Lea in the late winter of 1929 and at Conway in the fall of 1930. There I am, hamming it up with my siblings. I can see what Ada meant: I made a perfectly acceptable baby, but my features certainly didn't approach the aristocratic. My square paws are much in evidence in the film, as is Mimi's love for me and mine for her. We were drawn to each other in the early years, and I suspect that at times she tried to be my protector. The movies show Ken kissing my neck and playing patty-cake with me, but that probably was at the suggestion of the camera-woman.

Finn shows up often on the screen. He was a large, pure-white German shepherd, named after the Gaelic hero Finn MacCool, and he taught me to walk. Archie had learned by leaning on his father's collies for support. I reached out and grabbed Finn where I could, often by the lips. He yelped, Archie told me, but he never bit me. Ever since, I have loved certain dogs just as in-tensely as I have loved certain people—at times more.

Perhaps it was the excitement and the successes of the French gamble that made my parents so willing to take, or to ignore, the risks that followed. They did not notice, until it was too late, that their new old house had not a shred of insulation in it. As cold weather came over the hills, the wind passed through the wall in my room and, barely slackening, blew my hair about as I lay in my crib. That was too much for Ada with her nightmares of my dead baby brother. The reason Ishbel made her movie in Craigie Lea was that we had spent the winter there with Granny Patty.

Archie went on from Craigie Lea to Mexico, there to do what he could to follow the path Cortés and his men had taken on their way to destroy Tenochtitlán. The journey gave him what he needed to complete his epic poem *Conquistador,* but it also took him through a part of the country that at the time happened to be—somehow unbeknownst to him—in full and open armed revolt. Archie received his first Pulitzer for the poem. If his layers of luck had been any thinner, he just might have received a bullet.

. . .

My parents bought their farm with about as much knowledge of how to run it as the courtiers playing peasant at Versailles. The place hadn't been really worked for years, and predators had the run of the ridge. Archie did some research on blackfoot, the bane of turkeys, and thought the risk of the disease was small enough to go ahead and buy some birds. They survived for a while, but other animals didn't. Some of it was plain bad luck. Finn scared a newly delivered cow so that she rolled on her calf. Archie got so mad he beat Finn with a chain—while the dog licked his hand. They got more cows, but contagious abortion ended that line of endeavor. They switched to sheep, but the village dogs got them. The foxes went after the turkeys and the chickens. Their bull, Johnny Fortune, kept getting loose and moseying down the road from the barn to the house, scaring hell out of everybody. And, I believe, blackfoot eventually did show up among the turkeys.

Archie always had a penchant for hurting himself—mashing his hands under rocks he was handling, cutting himself with an axe or a scythe. Some of the injuries came from his overconfidence in matters physical. Ishbel's movies show him and Ada at a misery whip, a two-man saw. They are doing everything wrong. They are pushing when they should be pulling, and the blade is bending dangerously at every stroke. A few frames later, Archie is axing a tree. His aim is very good, the kerf he cuts is clean, but again, he is going at a rate that is bound to burn him out in an hour—or, given his conditioning, two.

Slowly, my parents came to their senses. Neighboring farmers took over the barn and the pastures. After the turkeys went, Ken, Mimi, and then I took over the chickens. We had a couple of Toggenburg goats, but Archie and Ada were unable to keep goat hairs out of their milk, and the result was a taste that would gag a maggot. The goats went.

I hated taking little-boy naps after lunch, especially during the summers. I could hear the big people talking and laughing and doing things, and there I was, a wretched kid, bedbound. But in haying season there were wonderful things to listen for—the song of a whetstone on a long scythe blade; the click and stumble of horses on the steep grade just beyond Ada's garden. I waited for the voice of Bradley Bush, "Pa" Bush, riding his mower behind the team, bent forward by his arthritis. "Goddamyew!" he would shout. "Come up in they-ah." I could almost drift off in the heat and the humming after that.

Bit by bit, my parents turned their place into their stage. They built an extension of Ada's garden that ended at French doors just off the music room. They put a trellis over the junction. The idea was to have breakfast under the arbor, watching the grapes grow, looking down a brick walk lined with flowering shrubs to the roses and tiger lilies and hollyhocks in their ranks and clusters down in the old barn foundation. The food would be lowered to them in a basket. It was a fetching idea, but I don't think they put it to a test.

Ada's father had taught his daughter how to make her mark at auctions. Uncle Billy had been a master at getting what he wanted. Once during one of his Sunday drives in Connecticut, he spied a lofty highboy sitting out in the open on a front porch. It was crusted with paint, but he knew what lay under the mess. The woman of the house told him she didn't want to sell it. Well, he said, what *do* you want? A set of store teeth, she said. He bought them, brought them, and left with his prize. After his death in 1943, it appeared to great advantage under the high ceiling of Ada's music room.

Ada drove around the hills and down the valleys, from big auction to small. She would amble through the inventory, making her picks but showing no interest. When bidding time came, she would wait and wait and, when she was ready, make an almost imperceptible signal—the raising of one finger—and: "Sold!" I have a dozen fine champagne flutes she picked up for nothing. They were going as bud vases.

Ada had taken cooking classes in Paris, and her cuisine showed it. I don't know when I first savored her cheese soufflé, but I do know that it caused me to be seized by tingles of great joy. Archie had a wooden salad bowl the interior of which he polished with a heel of French bread rich with garlic. The lettuces were his own, washed and carefully dried. The dressing was vinegar and olive oil and closely guarded secrets. Cheeses were apt to be Vermont cheddars or imported Goudas or Edams, and they all enslaved me.

Archie's study, always referred to as his work house, was ready for him shortly after I was born. It was a one-room salt-box with walls of fieldstone, sited on a rise a couple of hundred yards beyond Ada's garden. Windows opened to the east and north. On the side facing the house, there was only the door and the long pitch of the roof to waist height. He walked there almost every morning a little after seven and walked back just before noon. Well after his death, I could locate the path he made across the hayfield by the way the grasses changed over it.

Unlike Robert Frost on his farm near Franconia, New Hampshire, Archie did not spend much time on poetry of place. I asked him once why that was, and he talked about Coleridge and Wordsworth and their tributes to their lakes. "They aimed at naiveté," he said, "and they achieved it. And although I like their work, I am a little bit embarrassed by the naiveté." A long pause, and then: "I think I will write about it. I think so. If only I could make the crossover."

He never really did. The one poem that in my mind does cross over is "A Man's Work," written in the 1950s:

> An apple-tree, a cedar and an oak
> Grow by the stone house in the rocky field
> Where I write poems when my hand's in luck.
> The cedar I put in: the rest are wild—
>
> Wind dropped them. Apples strew the autumn ground
> With black, sweet-smelling pips. The oak strews air,

Summers with shadow, winters with harsh sound.
The cedar's silent with its fruit to bear.

I listened to Archie reading his poems to Ada and, once in a
great while, to his friends. It came to me very early that I had
two singers for parents, the one working in song, the other in
stanzas. I don't think Archie at that time knew much about the
poetic traditions of the Gaels—in spite of Ezra Pound's advice.
But when his voice was in luck, he chanted and lilted with the
best of the bards. Not everyone liked his renditions as much as I.
Richard Burton, who visited the farm in the sixties with his then
wife Elizabeth Taylor, wrote in his journal that the poet
"moaned without sense or sound his own lovely verse. Elizabeth
and I listened in a tortured agony, . . . longing to smash the book
out of his hands and read it ourselves."

The sounds I heard from my father were wonderful to me
because I had not heard a human being use his voice in that
way. It was at once a flute and a drum, drawing me into his
rhythms and his augmented repetitions. It was a place I never
wanted to leave. It has stayed with me as a source of my being,
along with the smell of stone and storage down in the cellar of
the old house, and the feel of water in the pond, and the six
syncopated notes my parents whistled to call each other. They
were C, F, C-F-C, A.

The prospect of guests really turned up our temperature. New
sets were built and new lighting arranged. There were games I
couldn't play yet, like Scouts, in which you crept through the
woods trying to reach the stone wall at the end without being
seen by your opponents. If they identified you, you had to start

all over again. And on the lawn we played badminton and strange forms of croquet.

Feasting was my favorite, especially a clambake in an old meadow, unrepeatable and never repeated. Pa Bush and his people put it on, drawing on their own memories from Pa's natal Quebec. They had it all: a pit, hot rocks, piles of seaweed, lobsters, clams, corn, potatoes. I knew then what it was to eat my fill. After all of us had passed satiation, we staggered off and lay down. Archie told me years later that he remembered making it to a shady part of a stone wall bordering the field. "You came and lay on me with your head about here," he said, pointing to his rib cage, "and you passed out and I passed out." I must have been eight.

When guests came in my early years, I generally ate supper in the kitchen, but on special occasions I was allowed to go down with the party to the music room after dinner. There was a black bearskin on the floor by the fireplace, one of Ernest's trophies, and I lay on that and listened to the talk running full: loud and soft, clever and bawdy, never sad, never angry. Once I saw the elegant and famously reserved Dean Acheson, a risen star down in Washington, dance a dance of his own creation. It was the dance of the crocus rising into spring. The music, I believe, was *The Firebird.* The dancer started with his hands on the floor and, dozens of unbelievable undulations later, had them eight feet in the air.

I would listen with the adults to the Victrola playing the "Trout" Quintet or "Dinner Dance for a Pack of Hungry Cannibals" or "Mama Doan 'Low No Bass Fiddle Playin' Heah." ("She say it is a sin / To beat a swollen violin.") Archie's favorite at that time was a French comedian commenting on "Mon P'tit Ballet" in his versions of English, Chinese, German. I didn't understand a word but roared with laughter when anyone else seemed about to.

These were the evenings before I had learned how to hoof it myself in the Ada and Archie follies. In the best of them, I was completely forgotten in the fun. Then I could pull the pleasantry up around my ears and dig my fingers into the fur and breathe bear and be bear.

Uncle Billy

THE CRASH OF OCTOBER 1929 REACHED US IN bumps. The first came when my parents realized that dividends from Carson Pirie Scott were dwindling. (They would disappear in 1932.) That was bad news on our ridge and also at Craigie Lea; since Andrew's death, shares in the store had provided most of the wherewithal for his widow, Patty.

The second bump came when Archie started hunting around for income. There were no jobs in Conway or anywhere near it. Still, the downturn might be a thing of the moment—Mr. Hoover and a chorus of Micawbers insisted it would be. To mark time until happy days reappeared, Ada and Archie sent their friends advertisements for "Cricket Hill Turkeys" (this was before my parents finally realized they lived on Pine Hill), fed on "crickets and milk." They got enough response to load up their ancient Cadillac with dressed birds and haul them from one tony New York address to another. The enterprise netted them perhaps three hundred dollars.

We were facing pinched if not hard times unless something turned up, when Henry Luce turned up. He was a great admirer of Archie's, having followed him at the respectful distance of four years through Hotchkiss and Yale. He was about to add a new magazine to his stable, one devoted to a close reading of American business. It was to be large format, handsomely illustrated, and well written. Its original title had been *Power,* but Luce, perhaps because he had been brought up by his mission-

ary father to observe a measure of modesty, had lowered his
sights to *Fortune.* (*Power,* with its titillating overtones of aphro-
disia and corruption, would be a standout among today's zil-
lions of 'zines.)

Archie told Luce he didn't know anything about business,
American or any other brand. "That's why I want you," Luce
said. So they struck a deal, one that was to repeat itself often in
Archie's life: he would go to work, yes, but he would have
enough time to do his own writing. Over the nine years Archie
worked for Luce, the terms of employment shifted with the
needs of poet and publisher, from half time to full and back.
They helped to keep us going, and they kept us apart.

Archie started his new job within weeks of the Crash. Ada
and Mimi and I and a governess went with him to New York.
Ken was near Hartford, at a boarding school headed by a
woman whose tastes ran, even for those times, to the goofy
fringe of authoritarianism: she once arrived at the idea that it
would stiffen the spines of her boys if stocks were to be set up at
convenient locations where malefactors might sit in public
shame. She never followed through, but other evidences of ex-
tremism eventually caused a number of faculty members to set
up a more progressive school in Colorado. Ken would go with
them, and I would follow.

Within weeks, Ada decided that New York was no go. It was
city grit, she told me later. Grit kept getting into my golden
locks. The governess complained that idle men filled the nearby
park with themselves and their spittle, and she feared contagion.
My hunch is that Archie's nerves couldn't take this sudden com-
pression of his space, the sudden nearness of all those others. In
any event, Ada rebalanced her act and took children and gov-

erness to her father's house in Farmington, Connecticut. And that is where we spent the cooler months until the outbreak of the war.

I never thought of my grandfather Hitchcock as a generous man until recently. But then I never thought much about him at all until recently; I don't recall more than a dozen words he ever said to me or I to him in nine years of living together. There are few photos of the two of us. One, a tinted number, shows us outside in winter. He looks taller than he was, but that is because I am so small. He has something like a homburg on his head and a neat mustache on his face. He also has Saint Nick's belly, but that is hidden under his overcoat. I am dressed in a brown, woolly snowsuit and cap to match. I am reaching up to his hand, so far that the shoulder involved is about out of its socket. He is trying to smile. So am I, but the effort and the attire give me the look of a demented beaver.

All I really remember of the septuagenarian I called Grandy is his singing voice: low, rich, the perfect bass for the barbershop he loved so much. That, and how it made me hungry to watch him eat fresh tomatoes—the way the juice and the vinaigrette used to course down the grooves leading from the corners of his mouth to set his chin ashine. And how it comforted me to hear the mutter of his chuckle as he listened to *Amos and Andy* on the big radio in his room.

He slept on the second floor of the house. His windows opened on quiet air, for the big linden tree and a row of evergreens along the sidewalk took care of traffic sounds from Main Street. Behind the house the land sloped up past a goldfish pond to a few fruit trees and a chain-link fence. The boundary Grandy shared with a lovely estate up the street was open. The fence run down the other side of the property, past a small chicken house, past the garage with its own gas pump. It then made a beeline for the sidewalk, sealing off my grandfather from his less affluent neighbor down Main.

Just across the street was one of Uncle Billy's places of business, the Farmington Savings Bank, which I think he headed. The other place was a bank in Hartford, a half-hour's drive to the northeast, where he went from time to time to clip coupons and otherwise keep in touch with his worth. William Arthur Hitchcock was a gifted moneyman and was known for his talent. Others of his trade might be wearing last week's shirt or, in extremity, preparing to step out their office windows, but not my grandfather. His skills took him through the Depression in more than acceptable circumstances, and he took us with him.

I am now about the age he was when we drove into his driveway, rounded the circle, and started moving in on him. He had just lost his wife, Dinah, to cancer. He was handling that grief and that fear. And he was stepping into a life without a wife but with many close friends and, I believe, a romance or two. And then, here we came: his cherished Ada; children he didn't know and might well have preferred not to, at least just then; the governess; and, on odd weekends, the husband, a man who probably would have been able to keep his family together if he had stuck with the law instead of running off to write poems in Paris.

By now, Ada was something of a stranger to him. She had made a name for herself in France, and that had lifted her closer to her father's level than he might have found comfortable. She was no longer a small-town girl, and she showed it. In 1932, she went to the town hall and voted the Democratic ticket, while

Uncle Billy stood outside and bitched to his friends about the betrayal.

Ada settled everybody in and down. The governess was instructed in ways to keep us children from coming into close contact with the master of the house, and the governess took over. Ada spent a couple of days a week with Archie in New York. She gave some concerts. And she returned to Farmington, probably a lot more frequently than I remember. Yet what I do remember is the very strong feeling that I had just uncovered a deep secret: I was adopted. I must be, I said to myself, or why this? Complaint was not an option—far from it. I was afraid of complaint. I told myself that if I didn't behave, if I didn't play Charming Billy, I might get left by the side of the road. The governess must have tuned in to my inner conversation: if I was not a good boy, she would say gently, my parents wouldn't be all that eager to come see me.

After a while I accepted the confusion, as I tended to accept most things. I think I had heard enough about the Depression to know that I was sinfully lucky. I had all the toys I wanted, including a crystal set that could bring in WTIC in Hartford, with a man who kept ringing a cowbell and telling me that he had his pet cow, Bossy, with him in the studio. He had her moo from time to time. I had my own room on the third floor, opposite Mimi's room. The governess lived under a gable at the front, and an inclined corridor led up to a bathroom in the back. I had plenty of food, served by a maid with a blue front tooth.

There was a Ping-Pong table out on the enclosed porch, and when I got tall enough to see over the top, I played with Mimi or my governess. I rode with Grandy in the back of his Packard, to see the Christmas decorations in West Hartford or to drive out on some of his favorite country roads. The chauffeur's name was Fred, and it gave me intense pleasure when, on a clear, late afternoon, Fred headed west. Then I knew the sun would eventually find his jug ears and illuminate them in wondrous ways. That was a lot better for the senses than the smell the cushions gave off of smoke from hundreds of Grandy's thick cigars.

My problem was playmates. I could play on Uncle Billy's lawns as much as I wanted. I could play with a dog. But I could not roughhouse with a human my own age. That probably would have made too much noise to suit Uncle Billy—or Ada's ideas of what suited him. I went through the first four grades of the Farmington elementary school. The basement smelled of old clothes and older urine, but the classrooms were sunny, and in one of them a big map of the nation was displayed. I stared at it day after day until I saw it wasn't a map at all but a mutant udder, with Florida the one teat. I got to play with classmates during recess. I stayed after school with some of them and learned how to do a chicken dance for a play, but I couldn't bring anybody home with me.

There was a boy named Arthur who lived down close to the Farmington River, a lovely stream running through big fields of corn into woods of maple and ash and oak and birch. Once or twice I played with Arthur in and around an old grist mill. The millstones were still there, and what was left of a low dam across the river. Then the governess told me I couldn't do that anymore: Arthur, she said, was not of my station. So I ended up playing with a boy who lived on the other side of Uncle Billy's fence. We invented a village for the two of us, named it Doggietown, and we passed maps of the place back and forth through the chain links.

The ban on importing friends eased a bit later on, but while it was in force it riled me. I didn't show much of a continuous reaction, but every once in a while I would forget my vows of adaptation and throw a tantrum. The governess, or Ada, if she was there, would send me to my room. I would trash the place, ripping and snorting. During the ruckus, a noise would come out of me; at the beginning I wasn't sure who was making it. It didn't sound like anything in my supply of sounds, but later, when I was at a farm work camp in Vermont, I heard it often when they were butchering. It was the dying cry of a stuck pig.

. . .

The governess, who went by the name of C.—yes, just C.—would often clean up my messes if the piles of rubble weren't too high. I never have known another human willing to subsume the complexities of an entire identity under one letter of the alphabet. C. had been a nurse but had turned to nannying among the affluent. Once she drove me up to Maine in her Chevy coupe, complete with rumble seat, to see one of her old charges. He was tall and confident and could stand on the stern thwart of a canoe and pump it across the water by flexing his knees just so. I figured if C. had done that for him, she might be just the support I was looking for.

She came in close in many ways. She bragged to me about being a tomboy when she was young (she must have been in her forties when she came to us). She had a missing little finger to show for her youthful risk-taking. A baseball had crushed it, I think. She still had a pro's arm on her and did her best to show me how to develop one myself. The thing about her that took me a while to adjust to was her smile. It was quick and brittle, and there was no joy in it at all. And her teeth were quite small and shone like stars. C. took me roller-skating on the sidewalks of West Hartford. When I was nine or ten, I got my first gun, a .22 rifle. C. drove me to the local National Rifle Association range with it, where I earned medals for marksmanship and took courses in gun safety. Back then, the NRA was something I could and did love with a passion.

People regularly came to see Uncle Billy, and sometimes I was allowed to pass among them. When Ada was in residence, she often invited women friends in for bridge. The ladies sat around card tables and bid and trumped. Then they took to cooing over me and burrowing in my hair with their hands, and I hated them. They saw me as a pretty boy, the boy in that Fauntlerized portrait, and that gave me the pip.

Then Katharine Hepburn came to call. Her family in Hartford must have known my grandfather. I have not since been close to a woman as beautiful as she was on that day. She had been or was about to go riding, and as she stood in front of the fireplace in her jodhpurs and boots, leaning against the mantel, I got so excited looking at her when she wasn't looking at me that I started running in circles. I ran faster and faster until I threw up in the middle of Uncle Billy's best Persian rug.

He never said anything to me about it. Later, when I had grown from a little boy to a small one, he was remarkably low-key after the town police informed him that I had been hiding behind bushes along Main Street and bursting out to throw mud and stones at passing students from Miss Porter's boarding school. Since the school's reason for being was the production of "useful ladies," beaning one of them or messing up her camel's hair polo coat was not to be countenanced. Yet Grandy simply announced that he had had a talk with the chief of police and that I would not ambush the girls anymore. He didn't look at me. He talked to the air, to his tomatoes vinaigrette, to the maid with the blue tooth, but not to me. My compliance was immediate.

The only occasion I can recall when my grandfather addressed himself to me directly—and with fervor—occurred after a football game at the Yale Bowl. C. had given me some money, and I moseyed around trying to figure out what banner or plastic bulldog I could buy. I must have taken much too long, because when I got back to the Packard, there stood Uncle Billy with a red face and a raised cane. I will never forget C.'s scream. It was like a hawk's, but louder. She rushed between the old man and his target, and after a minute of stamping around, Uncle Billy calmed down, and we went back to Farmington.

My laggard ways were the proximate cause of the battery he contemplated, but surely his dudgeon was occasioned by how much we MacLeishes were hemming him in. Things had got to the point where he was ready to belt his namesake (who knows? perhaps I went from Peter to William Hitchcock to sweeten our acceptance in his home). If he had hit me, perhaps that would have broken through our wall and, when his remorse and my welts had healed, we might have moved a little closer. Perhaps not, but caning *is* a form of communication; others might have followed.

C. did not like little girls. Not at all. In particular, she did not like Mimi and her strong will. She told Mimi her parents didn't love her. She chased her and once threw a pair of scissors at her. She couldn't abide Mimi's slow eating: I once saw her get up from the table during lunch, stop behind Mimi's chair, and suddenly push her face into her hot soup. I saw Mimi come up spluttering and crying with soup all over her. I saw C. laughing behind her. I wanted to hit C., hurt her terribly, but what I did was laugh myself—and hate myself. Mimi was too frightened of C. to escape from her when she had a chance. She had been talking about her governess at summer camp, and the director heard about what she had said and wrote to Ada. When Ada asked Mimi what was going on, she refused to speak, and the punishment continued.

C. loved little boys, and, even though I knew what she was doing to my sister, I tended to love her back. One reason was the dogs. We had a succession of dachshunds around the house, and I played with them. At one point I had the elder dog hanging from a tree by her leash and only let her down when the thought struck me that I might not be able to explain away the corpse. Nevertheless, when the younger dog was run down in the driveway, I grieved for him all the way to the vet's. He died, next to C., on her front seat. When we got back, I ran to Ada's room to tell her. I could barely talk. C. was right behind me, crying. Ada looked at us both as if we were in delirium. "It was only a dog," she said. She was being honest: dogs were of little importance to her and a threat to order in her household. But something went cold in me. I think that was the first time I felt hatred for her and knew it and shrank from it.

C. grabbed me and took me out of Ada's sight, my head pressed against her side. That assuaged my grief, but the coldness came back. Six or seven years later, in Conway, I was out hunting one twilight when I looked in at a gate to the front lawn. I could see Ada through the bay window of the book room. She was sitting in her yellow easy chair, reading. Ten yards away from her on the lawn, eating, was a rabbit. I knew Ada wanted no plant-eaters close to her garden, so I hunkered down and put my sights on its head. It seemed too easy to kill it outright, so I moved suddenly to spook it and, when it ran, swung with it and dropped it. I stayed where I was for a minute with the gun cradled in my arms, and a picture formed in my mind. I saw Ada's head, and then I saw it over the blade and groove of rifle sights. I ran to the book room, told my astonished mother that I had shot the rabbit much too close to home, that I was locking away my gun for a week. And then I burst into tears.

C. never went after me to harm me, but the nurse in her determined that something was wrong with my digestion. I have no memory of problems. She saw them, probably in my refusal at the time to have bowel movements by the clock. She would intercept me, in my room, on the stairs, with a dose of citrate of magnesia. And, fairly regularly, she would give me an enema. I actually rebelled once. I stood before her naked in the bathroom and told her that enough was enough. "I'm not the type," I told her. She laughed so hard that I started laughing, or crying, or both. Then she whirled me around, bent me over the edge of the claw-foot bathtub, and drove her black plastic shaft home. Ada knew about these purgings and so must have approved. I still don't know why—probably because I never asked her.

I gave no thought in Farmington to the problems my parents were having trying to keep themselves and their marriage and their children together during the thirties. By the time I got around to talking seriously with Ada and Archie about these things, age had stepped between them and the way back. "I just tried to see the family as much as I could, do whatever I had to," is all that Ada would say. "It was not what you'd call a peaceful life, but it didn't occur to me at the time that it was unusual because too many people were in the same box."

From my vantage point at the bottom of the Hitchcock pyramid, I sensed strain in the house while Archie was there. It seemed strongest in the space between my father and my grandfather. Perhaps I merely wanted that tension, wanted to imagine Archie facing down Grandy over his remoteness from me. Whatever it was stayed around for a long time—until the early forties, when Grandy lay slowly dying of a stroke that left him half paralyzed, unable to say anything but "My-my-my-my!" When Archie went to see him, the old man took his hand and kissed it.

I was desperate for Archie. What I really needed was for him to take charge of me, to get me away from women, but even I could see he wasn't going to do that: he was wonderful, but he was just too infrequently present, too insubstantial, to bring off such a switch. I settled for the occasional weekend pass. When deadlines or research trips forced him to stay away, I ragged myself about my general unworthiness. My schoolmates helped me go farther down my well. They informed me that poets were sissies who couldn't pull their weight. A few of the older boys suggested that, since books were strictly for women, my father must wear skirts. And where was he, anyhow? Why didn't he live with us?

Christopher Plummer, who in the late fifties played a leading role in Archie's play *J.B.,* said something recently that fitted my situation in Farmington. He was talking about his daughter, Amanda. Neither he nor her mother, Tammy Grimes, were there for her when she was young, he said, and yet she came to love them both. "Maybe that's the best way to love a parent," he said, "to love it [sic] in the mind's eye and not the real thing." It certainly worked for me. I created an intimacy out of absence, drawing on memories reworked by fancy and on the occasional bit of hard news about the success of a book of Archie's, or an essay or a speech. This was enough to fill the long gaps between visits. Then Ada would go meet his train and bring him back to Main Street, and I would make the changeover, for a short while, from reverie to reality.

When Archie came, we got out of the house. We would go walking along the bed of the Farmington Canal, built in the early 1800s to take freight and passengers from the seaport of New Haven to Farmington and on up to Northampton, Massachusetts, on the Connecticut River. There was talk of extending the canal to the St. Lawrence and Canada, but the railroads soon superseded water transport, and, in a decade or two, the Farmington was filled with nothing but dead leaves.

We went kicking through those leaves. We went skating at night over at Beaver Dam. My double runners were too slow, so I stayed close to our fire on the bank. I saw others speeding across the silver floors of moonlight and heard all around me the singsong carom of ice shearing in the freeze. Archie and I often explored along the Farmington River, and I was Mr. Stanley again. Archie made an April poem for me: "The maple is red, / The elm is in feather. / Winter is dead, / Now comes spring weather." I set it to music.

That might have been what gave Ada the idea that it was time for some formal musical training. She or C. ferried me to piano lessons in Hartford. The teacher was impatient with mistakes, but we both hung in until I could play pieces well enough to love the instrument. I stayed with it for twelve years and then moved on to the guitar and the bagpipes. This teacher inadvertently contributed to my sex education. In her bathroom was a vending machine. I couldn't figure out what the vend was and so put a coin in, grabbed what came out, and, waving it about, went back to the keyboard. My teacher shrank back as if from an adder, but Ada, who was there to pick me up, told me it was a sanitary napkin and what it was for.

I now see some of what Ada was plowing through. She had, as she always had, the load of family management on her back. She eventually got used to running two or even three households at once; her lifetime total was something like thirty-two. But in the thirties, she was trying to juggle too many visiting rights. She was a visitor herself in her father's house, and it got to her. And she got to me. Once the woman who ran the town bookstore overheard me calling Ada "the old lady." She duly reported that. Ada bore down on me. My imagination was well into its Lord Nelson phase at the time, and she became a ship of the line training her bow chasers on the enemy child. When I saw her eyes, however, I instantly changed metaphors. She was looking at me as if I were a cocktail shrimp. I was sure she'd have my soul on a toothpick.

Things came to a head one day as I went walking with my parents along the Farmington River. It was winter, and the snow was right for snowballing. I fired off a round that happened to catch Archie in the nuts. He dropped, and Ada screamed. At some point during the scream I heard the words, "Get out of here," or something to that effect. So I ran, sobbing, not really knowing why I was running. Later, I decided that if it had been

just Archie and me, we would have worked it out a lot better—
once he had recovered the power of speech.

Ada loved to banter, and I found I did, too, and that things
between us went a lot smoother when we fed each other lines.
My radio was of great help. The man who owned Bossy was
funny, at least to me. I even began to make fun of my true
heroes, Jack Armstrong and the Lone Ranger. I parodied the
story lines of *Mary Noble, Backstage Wife* and *Stella Dallas,* seri-
als in which women always seemed to be getting pregnant, going blind or sailing off to China—sometimes all three at once.
One show outshone the others. It was called *Vic and Sade,* and
it was nothing but zany dialogue between a man and a
woman. They kept talking about friends of theirs with names
like Rooster Clark and Blue-tooth Johnson and I.I.Y.Y. Flirch,
and I kept stealing their stuff and making my mother laugh.

• • •

Shortly before the end of the family diaspora, Ada took me on a
trip. *Fortune* had sent Archie to South America to do some articles, and we—Ada and Granny Patty and myself—were going
to sail down and meet him in Chile. We left in January of 1938
and got back a couple of months later. I was nine.

Some shards of the journey remain: New York tugs pushing
us out into deep water in a snowstorm; the glory and the heat of
the Panama Canal passage; Indian blowguns dolled up with
feathers for the tourist trade in Guayaquil, Ecuador; shipboard
movie projectors that made Myrna Loy sound like Wallace
Beery; long lines of guanay, the birds that made a fortune for
W. R. Grace on the Guano Islands off Peru; the desert coast of
northern Chile; the dead-white flanks of Aconcagua volcano in

the mountains between Chile and Argentina; the black volcanic sand of the Chilean lakes. Discovery was unending for me. I tasted my first alligator pears in a surround of bougainvillea. I ate sea urchins and loved them. I drank wonderful wines in Santiago and Buenos Aires. I saw snakes in Santos, Brazil, and a mongoose killing snakes in Trinidad.

It was not just sensory joy. Here, Ada was different. She was different probably because she was away from the grinding cares of concern for Archie and Grandy and the children and for her life and time slipping away. She and I were alone together for weeks, sharing a cabin, sharing a voyage. She had evidently decided this would be *my* trip, though I don't think she ever told me.

I recently came across two of her journals. One covered several weeks in Japan with Archie in 1936. The other told me what she was thinking in South America. There are similarities of mood in these few pages that fascinate me. She cracked wise to herself in both journals, and she skewered people she thought substandard. An American woman in Tokyo looked "like a bad dream." Chilean women had fine breasts and "disappointing ankles." She ribbed herself: in Japan, she "spilled a drink and broke the heel off my shoe and altogether got an 'A' from Emily Post." On a stopover in Panama, she saw a frilly costume and resolved to have it, even though "it will make me look like a baked Alaska."

She kept an attentive eye on Archie in Japan—not because of the geishas (he "laid them cold" at one party) but because of his work. He never stopped. He wore himself out, and then his heart began missing beats and sending him other distress signals. When Archie received word from New York that a book of his was selling well, she made this entry in her journal: "I am so full of pride and so unable to express it." Praise would remain a stranger in our dialogue until she was an old woman.

Ada went everywhere Archie went in Japan—to parties, on train rides to nowhere. A Japanese photographer assigned to Archie's stories took them to see the best whorehouse in Kyoto. She also went places with me on our trip: down a white-water salmon stream that had me jumpy; up a mountain she would never have climbed by herself. She shut her eyes and boarded a small plane headed not over, but through the Andes to Argentina. She almost made it across, but when we ran into what were then called air pockets, the gallant traveler lost her lunch.

She found me friends here and there, including a lovely girl a year older than I who introduced me to the game of doctor. She noted that while I lacked the polished manners of the highborn Chilean youngsters I played with, I had a certain charm that made it easier for them and their elders to forgive my slips.

That charm slipped early and often. At dinner, in our hotel in Buenos Aires, Archie and I drank wine and started rearranging the furniture while rhumba, tango, and samba orchestras rose and fell on a huge elevator. I was sent to bed early so my parents could dance. I lay reading an English translation of Argentina's great gaucho novel, *Don Segundo Sombra* (Mister Second Shadow), by Ricardo Güiraldes. I followed the young boy as he left his town in the pampas to follow the Don into a life of herds and dust and adventure. I chafed at my ineluctable gringoness—so much so that I sprang to my window, forced it open, leaned out and roared, "Filthy American bastard!"

Five minutes later, footsteps sprinted down the hall, our door imploded, and in ran Archie and Ada and a flying wedge of security people. I have no memory of things being sorted out, but they were, and eventually silence and sleep descended. I still wonder, though, if the incident might have made the papers. Probably not. My voice would have to have been a lot lower. We returned to the United States shortly after that night, coasting up and around the bulge of Brazil and on to New York. Either in Rio or Santos, Ada and I fell in with a gay divorcée with whom, my mother later assured me, I flirted outrageously. It must have been the beer.

I didn't know it, but Ada left Buenos Aires feeling down in the dumps. Archie was staying on, yes, but there must have been other causes. The one I know about was her weight. She wrote that she could "fairly hear herself" getting fat. On the ship back home, she wrote, "From now on, this book will contain a daily confession of calories. I'm a sight." The calories for only two meals appear in the journal: "Sunday. Breakfast: Grapefruit, 100; coffee, 25. Lunch: cold chicken, 150; cold lamb, 100; tomato salad, 50."

She taught me songs on the way home, and we sang them. She told a friend later that our music kept her from going completely critical. As for me, not one jolt of magnesia, not one enema, the whole blessed time!

Fear Itself

IN FARMINGTON I HEARD ON MY CRYSTAL SET HOW the Depression was biting down. I knew a lot of people were out of work and drifting, and I thought that some of them might descend on Uncle Billy. I was worried about how they would smell: like the basement of my elementary school, maybe. In Conway, I learned how to look at what was really going on.

Archie's deal with Henry Luce gave him some time in Conway during the thirties. He even managed to survive for two or three days at a time in winter, the book-room fireplace gobbling logs, and the white dog, Finn, lying on the great hearthstone, sighing and farting. He was never lonely there, Archie told me. "You had the company of the house."

Each summer morning when he was there he'd be in his little stone house. I'd look over at his door, painted orange and black in broad diagonal stripes, and wonder what he was really doing in there. He never talked about that work, never read us any of it until it had seasoned in a drawer for a while. Much later he told me that he almost always started over from the beginning of the poem each day, spending two or three hours with it, advancing it, on good days, by a few lines. He wrote in script so small it looked like Morse code, on legal cap, with his beloved Blackwing pencils that "erase clean as time" while the mice peeked and pissed in the dark corners. His afternoons were for work around the place—in the big garden across the dirt road or in the fields with the Farmall tractor. The evenings were for talk or, later in the decade, when CBS and other broadcasters were developing their dramatic presentations and news programs, listening and then talk.

Fortune was giving Archie what he called a true education, sending him out to write story after story—over a hundred (by his count) in his nine years with the magazine—on farming and failure and the landscape of despair. When friends like the Achesons visited, I heard political talk on planes of intensity and commitment that seem alien now. Dean, moving up the Washington stepladder, told my parents how he thought Roosevelt was faring in Washington. Archie talked of how the New Deal was doing in Texas or Tennessee.

Twenty-five percent unemployment, bread lines, hoboes riding the rails, dust bowls, and Okies didn't mean much to me, at least not until the end of the thirties when I got a copy of *Land of the Free*. Then I understood what was happening. The book was a collection of photographs by Dorothea Lange, Walker Evans, Ben Shahn, and other artists, set to my father's poetry. I saw how the Depression stunned the country: women and children in dead doorways; men doing nothing. They speak in the poem: "We wonder if the liberty is done / The dreaming is finished / We can't say / We aren't sure / . . . We're asking." They are frightened, the wanderers:

Men don't talk much standing by the roads

Not in California:

Not remembering the vigilantes at Salinas:

Not remembering the bunk-house at Salinas and the
Silence when the shots stopped . . .

Not in Marked Tree, Arkansas: not often:

Not in Tampa where the flogged man died:

Men don't talk much standing by the roadside

All we know for sure is—we're not talking

All we know for sure—
                    We've got the roads
To go by now that the land's gone

Until I saw those pictures, my interest lay not in the terrible
times, but in how my father reacted to them. Ten minutes with
the news would have him airborne, and his opinions of conservatives in Congress, and ultraconservatives like Colonel Robert
McCormick of the *Chicago Tribune,* carried the muzzle velocity of
fury. He could not abide the colonel, and he could not abide the
stance of so many chiefs of industry faced with an economic rupture their theories of capitalism told them simply could not be
happening. "A sadder, stubborner, more timorous, whistle-in-
the-graveyard lot never before lived on earth," he declared. I set
about studying Archie's attack; it seemed like a pretty nifty skill
for a man to have when he needed it.

It wasn't as if he was always on the firing line. He laughed as
often and as hard as he argued. The laugh was a yodel, jumping
from baritone to falsetto and back. I have it. He used it when

Mimi announced that she was reading a Steinbeck novel called *The Wrath of the Grapes.* When I told him that the man to beat at the Little Big Horn was General Custard, he fell off his seat and rolled on the floor. "Mr. Stanley," he said, "you bugger me." I swelled with pride. Sometimes, out of the blue, he would dance a dance for us. His favorite routine was to mince around the room in time to some music from the radio, arms splayed, butt cocked and wagging. I couldn't believe then that he had a care worth mentioning.

It was only a couple of years ago, while going through research accumulated by his biographers, that I learned what Archie thought of his temperament. "I cannot remember a quiet period in the life of my mind," he said. "It was either anguish at the sense of sin, or it was intellectual doubt, or it was a sense of social rage. That is, rage at injustice not only in the American society but in every society. It led me to conclude that the world was a beastly place to be in." He was, Archie concluded, "a case."

A prime symptom of that case sits behind me on a shelf. It is a long poem Archie brought out in 1928. It lays open a modern soul. Originally, the soul's owner was fictional, one L. T. Carnavel. But Archie stepped out from behind that cover, and the poem was published as *The Hamlet of A. MacLeish.* It is more outspoken in its pain than almost any other work by this man whose vehemence led Gore Vidal to refer to him as "the dread poet" of the thirties. Archie's Hamlet is nothing if not alone; notes for the poem refer to him as "Hamlet without the murder, without an uncle, merely *without, without . . .*"

To the extent that this Hamlet can speak of what torments him—the memories of the butcheries on the Marne, of carrying his baby son to his grave—he speaks in something close to disgust for the world and himself:

> Why must I speak of it? Why must I always
> Stoop from this decent silence to this phrase
> That makes a posture of my hurt? Why must I
> Say I suffer? . . . or write out these words
> For eyes to stare at that shall soon as mine
> Or little after me go thick and lose
> The light too, or for solemn fettered fools
> To judge if I said neatly what I said?—
> Make verses! . . . ease myself at the soiled stool
> That's common to so swollen many! . . . shout
> For hearing in the world's thick dirty ear! . . .
> Expose my scabs! . . . crowd forward among those
> That beg for fame, that for so little praise
> As pays a dog off will go stiff and tell
> Their loss, lust, sorrow, anguish! . . . match
> My grief with theirs! . . . compel the public prize
> For deepest feeling and put on the bays! . . .
> Oh shame, for shame to suffer it, to make
> A skill of harm, a business of despair,
> And like a barking ape betray us all
> For itch of notice.

Reading this *Hamlet* now, I can say that since no one lives without bleeding, those who write about lives are apt to come upon some scabs. I can say that I, like most writers, hope for notice. I can say that I live in an age when the beans exist to be spilled, when scabs and self-indulgence are in—witness the televised shame session, the hot exposés of press and publishing. But that is mostly defensive play. Archie, in catching out his hero—himself—catches me. Or, rather, he catches a son's fear of showing anything resembling self-pity, in print or in person, knowing what his father thought of the poor-me posture. Henry Fonda is as dead as Archibald MacLeish, and that is why I am so taken by Peter Fonda's choice of a title for his memoir: *Don't Tell Dad.*

Even in its own time, the poem's blistering energy went beyond what a fair number of readers could deal with. And since it wore no clothes, it was easy prey for the satirist. Edmund Wilson, no admirer of my father's work, savaged *Hamlet* in *The New Yorker.* He called his takeoff "The Omelet of A. MacLeish," and he sent up everything he could, from what he took as Archie's excessive introspection ("And the questions and / questions / questioning / What am I? O") to the old charge of being derivative ("Nimble at other men's arts how I picked up the trick of it"). A long time went by, I recall, before my father allowed a copy of *The New Yorker* back in the house.

Archie called the Depression "the most humiliating period of years I've ever lived through; you were ashamed to have enough to eat." And angry. I think it would have been surprising had he not taken the national misery to heart, had it not drawn him out of the privacy of his earlier poetry and into the poetry and, increasingly, the prose of a more public man. The blood of Elias Brewster Hillard, that feisty parson, and of generations of Scottish sons of the servant of Jesus, had always flowed in him. With the Depression, he had found his pulpit.

He found it in *Fortune,* writing on housing in America. One of his leads followed George Follansbee Babbitt, Sinclair Lewis' rendering of the ultimate Rotarian, into his state-of-the-wallet bathroom. "There, surrounded by the glass towel rack and the glittering medicine cabinet and the flush plumbing of his American citizenship, he shaved." Babbitt was the privileged exception, Archie wrote. Thanks in part to crooked labor bosses and kickback contractors, less than half the nation's houses met even minimum standards. A large number had no bathrooms at all.

Archie's six-part poem *Frescoes for Mr. Rockefeller's City* used the mirrors of verse to set the loud exploitation of America in the Gilded Age against the honest promise of the land Lewis and Clark saw. The tycoons he ridiculed were no Babbitts. They were real capitalists, from banker Morgan to adman Barton (who held that Jesus Christ was the best salesman who ever made a pitch). In his essays, he attacked them and their political allies, the Republicans, for their "individualism which is all rights and no duties . . ." The rest of us, said Archie, "talk about our rights and our freedoms as if we still have them . . . but we are actually the least independent of creatures. We can do nothing for ourselves. If society should leave us alone, we would starve. We can eat and sleep and wear clothes only if we eat and sleep and wear clothes together."

Although communism interested Archie for a while at the beginning of the country's big slide, he couldn't get past its dictates, which he found at least as unbending as the commandments of capitalism. He and Carl Sandburg went to a party meeting in New York one time to get the lowdown, and what they heard was so far off their mark that they started to laugh— and kept on laughing as the comrades escorted them out to the sidewalk. American liberals of the thirties fared little better with Archie. They had given their movement its "characteristic tone of moral self-satisfaction, intellectual snobbishness and inability to act"—at a time when action to halt the slide was essential. Archie threw his bombs right and left in his public commentaries. If Bertie McCormick seemed to need enemies more than friends, so did his enemy A. MacL. The enemies returned the fire. Archie was an "unconscious fascist" to those on the left and a Red sympathizer to those on the right. The FBI started a dossier on him that grew in time to something over six hundred pages.

Almost the only glint of promise in the country that Archie saw was the White House. Americans, very much including himself, liked Franklin Delano Roosevelt and his New Deal because, Archie felt, "they are sick to nausea of the rich bankers and their economists on the one side and the wise revolutionaries and their economists upon the other, repeating over and over that the world is ruled by incontrovertible economic laws which it is not only blasphemy but idiocy to oppose, and which lead to certain fixed and inescapable conclusions."

Archie had experimented with repetition in his earlier verse, and he used it during the Depression and what followed to grab lapels: "The revolutionary party which can offer to restore the government to the people and which can convince the people of its sincerity in so offering, the revolutionary party which can bring to pass the great American dream of the commonwealth—the people's state—that revolutionary party will inherit the history of the country and change it into truth." If I read some of this prose silently, the words stick to the page, fixed there by their heavy insistence. I feel that the author is forgetting to breathe, that he wants to get to the reader before his words do. Reading it aloud, though, frees the rhythm and ring that Archie wanted. It worked for him then. I don't think it would work for us now; we are too intent on harvesting our amber waves of gain, on sidling up to celebrity, to listen to his kind of hortation.

I tell myself that I heard FDR's inaugural speech in 1933, that I took in the music of "the only thing we have to fear is fear itself." I didn't, of course; I was only four and a half. But the phrase kept echoing in our old Conway house until it slipped in between my ears, where it grated against what I had learned from what Archie was reading to me: Howard Pyle's *Men of Iron*, T. H. White's *The Sword in the Stone*. Chivalry poured early into my eyes and ears and out my mouth. I studied arms and armor. I made wooden swords and plunged them into our hay mow with the requisite "Scurvy varlet!" and "Yield, knave!" Archie and I memorized the opening verses of *The Ballad of Chevy Chase*. He would lead off: "The Percy out of Northumberland / And a vow to God made he," and I would sing out in my alto voice, "That he would hunt in the mountains of Cheviot / Within days three." And then both of us: "In the mauger of [in spite of] doughty Douglas and all that ever with him be."

Fear was something you curled your lip at in these stories. So when FDR went and made fear the nation's direst enemy, that put me in a tight spot. My problem was that I didn't know what to do about fear, and that ignorance dogged me far into adulthood. When I faked out a big bully chasing me across the schoolyard by suddenly sprawling and bawling about a nonexistent sprained ankle, I never thought of congratulating myself on my tactical smarts. I concentrated on kicking the daylights out of myself for being yellow, what the knights in my head would curse as craven.

Horses seem to like playing with fear; they can be standing peacefully in a quiet pasture and then suddenly roll their eyes and blow and bolt. I would probably be better off doing that, but I can't. Instead, the imagination I used as a boy to stave off fright seems to have turned on me. Now I use fantasies to populate my future with disasters until I freak out: I will die quite soon, of the most revolting disease reported recently in the *Times;* I will outlive my money. Thanks a lot, Lancelot!

Happily, the summer days of the thirties kept me out of doors a lot, away from the light and shadow shows in my head. I grew into jobs my siblings once held down: I mowed the lawns—front lawn, side lawns—kept free of plantains and other unmentionables by dint of scut work with old table knives. I loved it—the sweat, the sore muscles from the hours of pushing the mower up slopes, around the big elms, the sigh of the reel slicing grass.

Chickens were part of the family long before my time. Archie had raised them in Glencoe, for impressive pocket money. They would run to him when he came back from school and sit on his head (and presumably shit on his shoulders). The chickens whose care I inherited from Ken and Mimi were Leghorns, I believe. They were replaced by Rhode Island Reds, my favorites. I loved stroking their backs as I eased a hand under to capture a hot, brown egg. I loved eating their mash (this was before it was mixed with grit for their crops). Ken showed me how to hypnotize a hen. You tuck her head under a wing and whirl her in a wide vertical circle. When you set her down, she stays put for a minute or so and then comes to and stalks off, muttering under her breath.

Eventually, killing them fell to me, too. Archie had had trouble with that end of the business as a boy. I didn't seem to—or else I have conveniently buried the memory of the first kills. I do know that my mind slowed down considerably as I selected a bird, grabbed it, knocked it just behind the head with the edge of my hand, stretched its neck out on a short, thick maple log and reached for the hatchet. Once I was plucking and cleaning, I began thinking of breast meat and drumsticks, browned and savory, and the work flew.

By the time I was six or seven, I was haying with Pa Bush and his family, first as a tagalong, then with a pitchfork, folding the windrows into cocks. Finally, I grew up to men's work. I learned to put my fork in the cock just so, lift it, and pass it to the man making the load on the wagon. I saw that he paid attention to his corners, keeping them high so the mass would ride steady. The horses drew load after load to our barn, leaving fields looking like the cheek of an old man who wasn't that particular about shaving. The thick plank floor turned to timpani as the team stood stomping while the great hay fork swung down and up to dump clouds of dusty grass on the mow.

We smelled clover and timothy cooked in the heat. We drank switchel—well water and vinegar and maple syrup and maybe ginger—out of an old milk can. We saw what we had done to the hay-loving animals—the rabbits and the nesting bobolinks hopping in the stubble—looking for what had been. We raced thunderstorms to the barn, standing in the doorway to let the rain sluice chaff off our shoulders.

One of Pa Bush's helpers was his brother-in-law, Charlie Pair. When the hurricane of '38 was coming, Charlie and Pa's son Ray went with Archie to close the barn doors. The wind was already high enough to jam them open. "I think the barn would have gone," Archie told me later. "But Charlie got his back where he wanted it to be and gave a couple of shoves, and the doors moved." Charlie was blind.

Archie taught me to swim when I was three or four; I imagine but don't remember him holding me up, one hand on my belly, telling me how fine it was to be there. Archie was as graceful a swimmer and diver as I have seen. His crawl was perfect. So was his swan and his one-and-a-half, tuck position. He was proud of those skills. I remember the mortal look on his face when I over-took him in the lower pond. For a while he couldn't see that I was wearing fins.

We swam all the time, first in the upper pond, then in the lower. The upper pond was the Boy Scout pond, dammed be-low a marsh to form about an acre of water that left us feeling cool long after swimming in it. Neighboring farmers used our pastures, and we figured the cooling effect might come from cow pee.

Archie and the Bushes and their horses built the lower pond. It turned out to be shaped like a jug. I watched, a German hel-met from the war on my head, crouched behind a big maple, as the men blew stumps, and rocks and gravel and splinters flew by. With the lower pond came the pond picnic. The menu was a ritual: Archie's hamburgers, cooked over enough charcoal to stoke a small smelter, with a crust of brown and a core of red. They came with corn, usually our own Country Gentleman or Golden Bantam, then salad, then fruit and chocolate cake. Af-terward, we rested on the grass, looking up into stipples of leaves and light.

On hot weekend nights when my parents had guests, some of the company would pick their way down the path through the woods to the lower pond. Sometimes, if there was no moonlight, they would swim nude. Once or twice, when I was young and, it was thought, innocent enough to be acceptable, I went along and sat on a ledge above the pond. Archie would dive in and swim to the center; the women would ease in down the concrete apron, calling to him, telling him how silky the water was on their skins. I would look for the darkness below the bellies and at the points of breasts and yearn a bit. Ada would swim side-stroke to keep her hair dry.

Later in the thirties a new couple appeared at the lower pond, the Alexander Sloan Campbells. She was the former Ishbel Marjoribanks MacLeish, Archie's sister. Her father, Andrew, had borrowed the name from a Highland gentlewoman but evidently didn't bother to remember how it was pronounced; she suffered under *Ish*-bell (aka Squish) until some kind soul announced she was really Sha-*bell.* Andrew once told her, "Whatever you do, don't marry a Campbell." In 1936, when she was turning forty, she did.

The Campbell clan was resented by many Scots. Although the real reason for the opprobrium was their resounding success in the acquisition and exercise of power, the reason often given had to do with a massacre at the Highland village of Glencoe in the early eighteenth century. Few Campbells actually participated, and the massacre was but one of hundreds carried out by almost every clan in the land at some point in its history. Yet Andrew MacLeish of Glencoe, Illinois, was troubled by what had happened in Glencoe, Scotland: he believed that one of his own, a female MacLeish, had been killed there by the "Wry-mouths"—which is how the Gaelic of Campbell translates into English.

Alec Campbell was as gentle and as kind as Old Dog Tray. He had taught Ken English at two prep schools, Avon and then Fountain Valley, outside Colorado Springs. I never took a class with him, but I could see how he might sparkle as a teacher. It was enough for me that he and I could talk about anything, that he knew Gilbert and Sullivan backward and forward—having staged almost every one of their operettas—and that he had the bass voice our family needed to fill out our singing while we did the dishes on the servants' day off. He was especially good in "Green Grow the Rushes." Alec told me that he was put on earth to think beautiful thoughts. He had little taste for the practical and pretty much left that to Ishbel. She was a quiet woman, secretive in much the same way as Archie was. It took me years to discover how much she loved her brother, and how that love reflected on his youngest son.

Alec delighted in talking literature with Archie, the younger man often astonishing the older with his knowledge. With Ada, he loved to laugh and play the child. She much enjoyed the former and stiff-armed the latter. Once, when Alec was clambering out of the lower pond, he stubbed his toe. He called to Ada that he had cut it. My mother, tossing the salad for our picnic, neither paused nor looked up. "Don't bleed on the cement," she barked.

Ada and Archie had given Alec and Ishbel some ten acres of land on a bench a quarter-mile northeast of and below our house, well out of sight. The brook flowing from our ponds had cut itself a ravine there as it pitched into the valley of the South River. In the mid-thirties, the great Quabbin reservoir, some miles east of Conway, was beginning to fill with water for

Boston. Whole towns had been emptied and were being razed, and water was rising against the new dams. Alec and Ishbel found a school and a farmhouse there and had them dismantled and put together on their bench. The main room had exposed ceiling beams and buttonwood wainscoting. Wall boards in the shed carried carvings of cows made by schoolboys with their barlow knives fifty years before.

It was a summer house, heated only by a fireplace and a few electric heaters, and watered from a cistern near the brook and a shallow well up the hill whose contents often smelled a bit of fermenting frogs. Our place had gone from being Cricket Hill Farm to Uphill Farm, so the Campbells called theirs Downdale. I'd go there simply to sit and look off across the valley and hear the water rustling in the ravine. Then I would start thinking of where Downdale had come from and, when Quabbin was full, how the only things moving over the roads of those drowned towns would be spoons and feathers and deep-diving plugs.

• • •

In the spring of 1936 Archie and Ada celebrated their twentieth anniversary. They had always loved dancing together; once they were ejected from a ballroom for dancing the bunny hug. This time they threw a barn dance, and they had it in our barn. Uncle Billy came. In fact, he drove Ada to the dance in a rented buggy. Later, he strode out the back door of the barn without looking, fell three feet to the ground, and lay there for the time it took him to run through his considerable store of blue language.

Sara Murphy described the evening: "They had a country orchestra with a man who called out directions. We were all in invented peasant costumes made up of whatever there was." I believe I watched the peasants at their play from the hay loft. The Murphys' lives had turned terrible. They had lost one boy, Baoth, to spinal meningitis a year before the barn dance. Sara had sat beside him at the last, saying, "Breathe, Baoth," until he couldn't. The remaining son, Patrick, was wasting away with tuberculosis. I saw him once, lying in the big bed in our downstairs guest room, eating butter. He would die a year after the dance.

Archie said later that what had happened to the Murphys was "intentionally tragic, as if an enemy had planned it." Gerald wrote to Scott Fitzgerald about his loss. "How ugly and how blasting it can be and how idly ruthless." Sara cursed God; Dow made his room into a monk's cell. Yet they and their daughter, Honoria, endured and continued to give themselves to their friends—and to me.

It did seem as if something dark had lived in the bright sunlight of Antibes. Scott and Zelda Fitzgerald died not too many years after those magic summers, he of despair and drink and she of madness and fire. Dos and Katy Dos Passos visited Conway often. They and the Murphys bore bibulous witness to my parents' twenty-fifth anniversary, and next morning Dos appeared at breakfast with puffy eyes and a poem: "Gerald brought a jeroboam, / Very big and full of foe-um. / Went to everybody's doe-um. / Thank you, Gerald, glad to know-um." Six years later, Dos drove into a truck on Cape Cod. He lost an eye. Katy lost her life.

Archie's friendship with Ernest Hemingway all but collapsed in the thirties. My guess is that there wasn't enough gentleness left in either of them to blunt the aggressiveness between them.

Archie, remembering, said that "fame wasn't sitting well with Ernest. He was fed up with the world, and I was fed up with him." He was, off and on, but he also needed him. Being a journalist, even an extraordinarily successful one, was worse than hard. It was hard on his art. Only one artist he knew was earning enough from his craft to live on, and that was Hemingway. "Somehow," he wrote Ernest, "you make it all right for me to go on no matter how empty they make it on my side of the street."

That was the kind of admiration Ernest had to have and, perhaps sensing my father's dependence, increasingly resented. In 1951 he wrote to Arthur Mizener, a Fitzgerald biographer, "You know it is a horrible thing to be somebody's hero and have them attribute all sorts of qualities to you when you are a man trying to work at it as well as you can. If this is megalomania well make the most of it. But I was Scott's bloody hero for a while and Archie's and it was only embarrassing for me. They both got cured of it. One by death and the other—." I'd give a lot to know how he would have finished that sentence.

That attitude began to show itself early in the thirties. Ernest invited Archie down to Key West, and he went. He was taken by the Gulf Stream and the big billfish along its edges, but Ernest got on him for not giving the sailfish enough slack after they struck, and for generally acting too lubberly aboard the Hemingway boat *Pilar*. Although they never came to blows that I know of, they came close. On one occasion, reported by Ernest's younger brother Leicester, they got to arguing so heatedly that they decided to put ashore on a nearby key and work things through. Archie got out and was wading toward the beach when Ernest took off and headed for home. Only after his wife Pauline insisted did he return for my stranded, furious, and doubtless bug-bitten father.

The issue that damaged the friendship most could have been Ernest's charge that Archie had sold out by going to *Fortune*. When he bitched about it in Ada's presence, she marched off to the bathroom and when she came out told the bitcher where he could go. Archie was much more forgiving when I talked to him, but that was when he was eighty-eight. He said that Ernest had indeed been outraged by his signing up with Luce, "for reasons having to do with real affection." But Archie also felt that during his time at *Fortune,* he had "produced more good poems than at any other time in my life. So it was pretty hard for me to assume that that was selling out."

As the thirties unrolled, he was indeed gaining the ground he most wanted to gain. *Public Speech,* his book of poems that came out in 1936, was well received. *The New York Times* called him "the most influential poet writing in America today." Meanwhile, his give-no-quarter essays were earning him attention in a far wider sphere—and in another context.

· · ·

I began hearing the word "fascism" around the dinner table. I heard Archie saying "Hitler" as he would say "sonofabitch" or "lump of pus." Something was going on, something that spoke of a new fear. There might be war. Then there *was* war, in Spain. The loyalists were killing the goddamn fascists. That was too exciting, too righteously right, to be frightening to me. I knew my father was speaking out, not just about the relatively small war of the International Brigade and Guernica, but about defending democracy itself against the clear and present momentum of the

Nazis and their allies. He was speaking out with even greater passion than when laying into Bertie McCormick. By the time he was through, Archie had taken on the many Americans who thought that der Führer and Il Duce were none of their business. In particular, he went after the many scholars and writers who he thought were unwilling to save their country. He even suggested that people like Ernest and Dos had done the country a disservice by evoking the inanities of war with a clarity that poured cold water on patriotism. In his heat, he evidently forgot that he himself had done the same in his own earlier work.

Much of what Archie was really saying eluded me, but in the spring of 1937, CBS broadcast his verse play *The Fall of the City.* It ran opposite Jack Benny and his star power, and yet its audience was huge. "More people heard the message of a single poet and a single poem that night," a listener wrote, "than at any other time in history." I was one of them, guided into the story by Orson Welles—the Announcer:

We are here on the central plaza.
We are well off to the eastward edge.
There is a kind of terrace over the crowd here.
It is precisely four minutes to twelve.
The crowd is enormous: there might be ten thousand:
There might be more: the whole square is faces.
Opposite over the roofs are the mountains.
It is quite clear: there are birds circling.
We think they are kites by the look: they are very high . . .

I heard the noise of the crowd. The thousands were gathered to hear the voice of a dead woman resurrected. For three days, at noon, she had come to the door of her tomb and spoken. She speaks this fourth time:

> The city of masterless men
> Will take a master.
> There will be shouting then:
> Blood after!

There is word that the conqueror is coming, that he is invincible. Archie is using the story of Hernán Cortés and his conquistadors being peacefully admitted to Montezuma's great city of Tenochtitlán, the city they would destroy. In the play we do not know where we are or in what time, but these people too will not defend themselves, not with the prophecy still fresh, not with messengers egging them on to hysteria.

A general appears and commands them to fight, but they will not. And then the conqueror comes. The Announcer sets the scene:

> They cover their faces with fingers. They cower before
>   him.
> They fall: they sprawl on the stone. He's alone where he's
>   walking.
> He marches with the rattle of metal. He tramples his
>   shadow.
> He mounts by the pyramid—stamps on the stairway—
>   turns—
> His arm rises—his visor is opening. . . .

The crowd goes quiet. The Announcer waits, waits, then whispers:

There's no one! . . .

There's no one at all! . . .

No one! . . .

The helmet is hollow!

The metal is empty! The armor is empty! I tell you

There's no one at all there: there's only the metal:

The barrel of metal: the bundle of armor. It's empty!

And still the people do not see or will not see what stands before them. Then the empty armor moves again, and they leap to their feet. They are shouting, dancing. "You'd say it was they were the conquerors," says the Announcer, "they that had conquered." There comes a great roar:

The city of masterless men has found a master!

The city has fallen!

The city has fallen!

And the Announcer's voice, flat and final:

The city has fallen . . .

Less than a year later, the Nazis walked into Austria, and I thought of Orson Welles.

The Thing to Do

SOME MONTHS BEFORE HE DIED, ARCHIE AGREED to a series of interviews about his life conducted by two faculty members from nearby Greenfield Community College. During one session they asked him about a fracas in which he supposedly had been involved. The story was that a jackhammer had been at work for hours outside his office, and its blasting chatter had gotten him so steamed that he had to be restrained from going after the operator. Archie neither confirmed nor denied: all he said to the interviewers was, "Haven't you ever wanted to kill a man?"

Wanted? Me? Wished would be more like it. Much of the language I took from him for my own use was the language of violence—from "lump of pus" to "bag of meat." Since I never saw Archie as much as cock a fist, however, I had great difficulty understanding how a grown man would handle himself when called upon to lay an enemy low. As a boy he may have drawn blood down by the Glencoe railroad tracks. But in my own boyhood I saw my father as a warrior of the word. Although I admired him for his courage, it was not the kind I was after.

I despaired of ever gaining that treasured ferocity. Lacking ready opportunities to pit myself against other boys, I created my own confrontations in my mind. They last to this day. Do the high farts of speeding motorcycles shatter my silence? Instantly, fancy tautens a piano wire neck-high across the road, and I see helmeted heads tumbling on the pavement like semiskinned grapes. Even when I am doing my best to keep my imagination from kiting my blood pressure, the shriek of Jet Skis raping the serenity of a lake can entice me into a seizure of dangerous rage—dangerous because, being outsize, it can find no outlet to reality.

As I struggled toward my teens, these secret ragings were about as far as I could safely go. Any more overt evidence of my adolescence would have brought a gimlet stare from Ada and a stint in solitary. My safety valve was to play with Mimi. We got up games of hide-and-seek when we could muster a quorum. I see her, a beautiful and small sixteen, calling, "Still pine, no more moving." She had been my shield against the family, but I was looking for a sword.

I didn't think Archie could supply it. We went on walks as we always had; he read to me as always; we worked in the woods. Yet I sensed that he would not be the one to hand me up to my heroic version of manhood. He loved red meat, as my knights and champions did: he devoured steaks and roasts and hamburgers from T-Bone, Toothsome, Harold the Mere Steer, to name but a few of our beeves. What he could not stand was seeing them killed or in fact dispatching any but the most pestiferous creatures on the place. I believed he was simply too gentle, with me and for me.

That attitude probably was behind my telling Archie to go to the devil. We were up in the barn on some chore, and my hormones must have aligned in such a way that the words just fired out of my mouth. The explosion surprised and scared me. I expected Archie to cuff me or at least yell at me, but we finished what we were doing in silence and in silence walked home. I thought it was all over. At supper that evening, with the full fam ily as an audience, Archie described my delinquency. There was more silence. I believe Ada glared at me, shook her head and clucked a few times. Then general conversation resumed. I felt disgusted. I felt betrayed. My own father had let me down in what I held to be a matter of honor. In an affair of men, he had taken refuge in the bosom of matriarchy. Things would have seemed pretty tattered then, if it hadn't been for a countervailing circumstance: I had found Ken; or he had found me.

The linkup must have begun during the summer of '39 or '40. Until that time my elder brother apparently had seen little in me to get serious about. Oh, he had taught me how to play the recorder and to sing some of the songs he and his friends in the Harvard Glee Club had sung—things like "Spanish Ladies" and wonderful rounds like "Hey, Ho, Nobody Home." But as I was moving toward puberty, Ken crooked his finger, and I went with him.

I had been watching Ken closely ever since I could focus. I could spot his walk in a throng of walkers. He kicked out one foot just a bit, possibly as a consequence of his childhood polio. He was a little under six feet, lightly built, and strong and quick as an eel. His eyes were blue and foxy, and he could see what was moving so far away that I could only see movement there. His face had some of the sharp beauty of Ada's face, and he was well supplied with her edged wordplay. He could make his eyeballs jitter. He had lost his two front teeth at his Swiss school— knocked out during an ice hockey game by a boy, I'm told, who went on to become the Shah of Iran—and he would at times unhinge their replacements with the point of his tongue to give me a clown's gaping grin.

I dreamed of my brother a few nights ago and awoke with my

love for him and fear of him and anger toward him as potent as they were sixty years ago. I wasn't completely cowed by him, even then. I hated the way he ragged Mimi, something he did frequently and often cruelly. Once, at a pond picnic, he started in on her, trying to get her to believe that some bug or other was poisonous. I waited until he walked out to the end of the diving board, and then I ran at him and sent him flying on his back into the shallow water over the dam's apron. He emerged scraped but sound and within the minute I was trudging up the hill under maternal sentence to spend the rest of the afternoon in my room.

Ken and I made a pact that was never articulated yet almost always perfectly understood: I would agree to whatever he wanted. That was the same way I had felt toward Archie, but this time I was looking for a lot more action. I would sit grinning at Ken while he figured out some caper or other. Then he would put on his foxiest look and say, "The thing to do is . . ." and we would do it. I yearned to have what I felt he could give me. There were the chants he brought back from his days with the Hopis, along with rolls of their papery blue cornbread. There were new instruments to play—the guitar and, later, the bagpipes. And there were the guns, always the guns.

Ken had come back from some trip with a Kentucky rifle he'd spent days haggling for. Its flintlock hardware was original. The stock was of tiger maple with fittings of brass. To my dismay I found that I couldn't hit a barn with it. I'm left-handed. The Kentucky's lock was directly in front of my aiming eye; when the gun fired, the jet of smoke from the priming powder completely obscured the target during the split second before the main charge went off. I contented myself with helping Ken mold bullets for the flintlock. We used the little electric furnace my parents had given me to make lead soldiers. We would lean together over our work, watching the liquid lead pour from the spout, bright silver before the air darkened it, and smelling the hellish smells of what I now know to be an extraordinarily toxic metal.

I had better luck with Ken's other treasure, a scope-sighted Mauser .30-06 rifle that had once belonged to professional boxer Jack Sharkey. Its barrel was just long enough to satisfy the law. It had a beavertail forestock big enough to have settled nicely in Sharkey's enormous paw. I believe it had a hair trigger, one trigger to set the other so that it would release the firing pin if you breathed on it. Ken kept the wood bright with oil, and the steel smelled, as all well-kept barrels and receivers of the day smelled, of Hoppe's Number Nine solvent. If I live to ninety, that sharp, sweet stink will still call up my time with my brother.

Ken may have had the gun at Harvard to help him hunt seals in Boston Harbor for the bounty. I know he used it on a squirrel jazzing him from a stone wall across from the Conway house, because I was there. He deliberately creased the animal, putting his bullet close enough to kill it by concussion alone. He gave it to me, and it was my toy and my doll until the smell gave us away and Ada made me bury it.

Part of Ken's attraction for me was the profound confusion that lay between us. In musical matters, we were completely attuned to each other. We could begin something, some little figure, and then build on it, each going his way and yet complementing the other. That was our bond. Yet it was his insistence on destruction that I thought I most needed from him, his confidence in it, his insistence on having his way with it.

. . .

I suppose my earliest memory of Ken has him on the front lawn at Uphill Farm with a .22 automatic pistol. I must have been seven or so. He has a garter snake in a tin box. He puts the box on top of a fence post and empties the magazine into it. The stench of garter snake hangs around that post all afternoon. It makes me sick and excited.

Almost always, when I think of the snake, I think of another hot, quiet afternoon. Three people are on the lawn: a beautiful woman just shy of twenty; a graceful man a year older; a boy of ten. She is leaning back against a big elm, smiling at her lover. He is smiling at her as his throwing arm moves back and snaps forward. Something hits the bark by her waist and sticks. It is a dart. Ken is outlining the body of his fiancée, Carolyn de Chadenèdes, with darts. I am standing by. I remember nothing of what I felt; my guess is that I was trying to be like what I took him to be, all action, no affect. I must have had concern for Carolyn, for I loved her and lusted a boy's lust after her, but I forced myself to block that concern in my determination to be a man.

That scene has come back to me for years. After a while I began to comfort myself with the idea I had invented it. But then I talked about it with Carolyn a few years ago, long after she had divorced Ken, long after his death. It happened, she said. It happened during the time when she was still enthralled by Ken, willing to do what he would have her do. I told Carolyn I knew that feeling and began to think of when I had felt it strongly. There were the rainy days in the barn when Ken had us doing somersaults and other risky stunts into the haymow—and one rainy day when Carolyn hurt her neck doing that. I stood watching her crumple and cry, Ken holding her and talking gently to her. It was the first time I realized that this man I had given myself to could let his will play hob with his judgment. There was the time when Carolyn found Ken and me shooting each other in the buttocks with my air pistol. The victim pulled down his pants, turned around, and waited. The assassin taunted him with fake countdowns, used every invention he could devise to describe how horribly the pellet would hurt, then pulled the trigger. Pellet whacked into drawers and began raising a serious welt. After the howl, the roles reversed. Carolyn joined in for one round and then let common sense remove her from the torment.

In the early eighties, when I first began thinking of writing about the family, I asked Archie about Ken and his games. I remember that I took care to subtract my own eagerness to play them. "In some way," Archie said, "I can't tell you in what way, it was Ernest's sinfulness. Ernest had tremendous influence on Ken. He revered Ernest, this great bearded thing. And Ernest was very tender to Kenny, very protective.

"In Gstaad," Archie recalled, "Ernest would take Ken to the local butchery shop to watch animals being killed and cut up. I discovered that after it had been going on for quite a while. I think it was the hunter's instinct that was very strong in Ken, and partly the taste for blood that was in Ernest's self and in Ernest's work." And then he told me of how during a trip with Hemingway to the Tortugas, Ernest had maneuvered his boat to scare up seabirds. He shot down a number of them, simply to keep his eye in, and left their bodies in the water.

In Leicester Hemingway's book about his brother, I read how Ernest felt about quail hunting. Watching the birds flush and then reaching out and bringing them down again, he said, plea-

sured him "here," touching his crotch. I think it pleasured Ken
that way. I felt it *must* pleasure me. It appalled Archie. Ada obviously was attracted by it, or by something very much like it. I
wonder what young Kenny thought back in Paris when his
mother went off with his hero of heroes to watch men beat on
each other until their faces ran red.

I can't believe that my parents didn't know about what their
sons were doing with and to each other in Conway. Perhaps they
never knew about the dart game; we all kept mum about that—
and about the time Ken and I wounded a bat, took it up to the
house, stuffed it into a lamp socket and turned on the juice. Certainly they heard what was going on: on some afternoons, the
place could easily have been mistaken for a rifle range.

Ada could have stopped us with a word, but she didn't. She
knew what it was like to be a boy; her father had taught her that.
Perhaps she felt that our mayhem was simply something to be
expected. Archie did go through the roof when Ken shot a wood
duck on the upper pond. (We had told each other we needed
its plumage to make some trout flies.) His anger didn't last more
than a few days. Perhaps at the bottom of his feelings for Ken lay
some of the same fear I had of my brother. I also suspect that
Archie was delighted to see his sons pairing off. He was away a
good deal during those years and might have talked his conscience into seeing Ken as mature enough to be a surrogate
father.

He obviously wasn't, but he was perfect cover for me. When
we first began working with guns, I would think of how uncom-
fortable my father seemed around them. Pulling the trigger, I
could imagine how I was taunting him from within the safety of
the circle drawn by my older brother.

Ken taught me how to use the Mauser. Our first time out, he took me to the big pasture up by the barn. On the way, he taught me how to walk quietly, putting my weight slowly on the outside of my stepping foot and then rolling it in. It made me feel bowlegged at first, but I got the hang of it quickly enough to please my teacher. All of a sudden, Ken dropped behind the rubble of an old stone wall and pointed down the slope. I couldn't see anything. I swung my head slowly from side to side, pretending to scan, feeling foolish. He pulled me down, arranged me in something approaching a shooter's prone position, and gave me the gun, so heavy, so cold in the heat. After a while I realized that I could see through the 'scope. Ken moved the muzzle, and there it was, a woodchuck, bright and brown, sitting up on its haunches, a chinless old man looking at me. The cross hairs of the sight jumped and jittered with my heartbeat. The Mauser fired before I realized I had touched the trigger, and the noise packed my ears with hot sand. My first live target took off in a rippling sprint for its hole, to my instant shame at having failed and to my lasting relief that I had.

In time I would go out on my own, lying most fair evenings on some knoll, still as a stone, waiting out woodchucks. Their holes were a danger to horses pulling mowers or rakes or wagons in our fields, but that was not why I was there. I was there, I told myself, to root out the weakness that denied me the full joy in killing that I thought Ken took. Still, the best of times were when I forgot I had a rifle with me. Then, I was out for the sunset and the silence. I don't like calling back the other times: the porcupine I trapped in the vegetable garden and how his quills exploded as the pellets from my shotgun entered him; the kit fox lying at my feet, half his head shot away, whimpering himself to death.

Wallace Stegner grew up on a prairie farm in Canada, "trapping, shooting, snaring, poisoning and drowning out the gophers in our wheat field. Nobody," he writes, "could have been more brainlessly and immorally destructive. And yet, there was love there, too." I don't remember love being present when I killed. What I remember is the absence of almost all feeling. There was a coldness, a little like the frost that descended on me when Ada told me that my beloved dead dachshund was "only a dog." It was as if I were doing something that was breaking my circuits. It's plain now that in spite of young Bill's wish to be a man like Ken, there was far more of Archie in the boy than he knew or wanted to know.

· · ·

By the time of their marriage in 1938, Ken and Carolyn both had longbows, and that was fine, for it made me think of them as Robin and Marian. These were target bows, not powerful hunting models but simple workings of lemonwood and Osage orange. Ken seemed gentler around them, more patient in teaching me to handle them. I learned the art as it must be learned, in peace, and I loved it. What sank in was that everything is guided more by spirit than by mind: the placement of the feet; the steadiness of the arms; the wrist angle on the bow arm, cocked to let the string fly home without tearing up skin. The whole process—the draw, the anchor, the release—is based on doing everything precisely the same way, shot after shot. It doesn't matter if your arrows land ten yards to the right of the target as long as they land in a tight pattern. All you have

to do then is to move that cluster left, to the bull's eye. I still
think of the wooden bow as a stringed instrument. When all
parts of the process become one, the fingers relax. The loose—
the release—is almost unconscious; the archer knows it is done
when the bow sings. Only an archer in the present, right in the
middle of that most short-lived of tenses, can consistently hit
what he is looking at.

The three of us played archery golf at Conway, across pastures and fields and through open woods, the winner of each
"hole" deciding where the next would be. Sometimes it was a
clump of grass yards away, sometimes a rotten stump that took
five minutes' walking to reach. I still judge distance not in
straight lines but in bow shots.

The urge to shoot the sky is strong in archery. T. H. White
writes about this in *The Sword and the Stone*. The Wart, the boy
who will become King Arthur, and his foster brother Kay, make
the first kill of their lives, a coney. They salute the animal and its
taking in the traditional way: "The Wart watched his arrow go
up. The sun was already westing, and the trees where they were
had placed them in a partial shade. So, as the first arrow topped
the trees and climbed into sunlight, it began to burn against the
evening like the sun itself. Up and up it went, not weaving as it
would have done with a snatching loose, but soaring, swimming, aspiring to heaven, steady, golden and superb."

One late July afternoon Ken and I followed the Wart and Kay.
I shot first, watched the shaft until it was a dot and saw it fall.
When Ken shot, I missed the release and couldn't find his shaft
in the sun's glare. I figured the safest place for me then was as
close to my brother as I could get. But Ken had thought of another thing to do: he pretended that he, too, was running blind,

taking four steps this way, five steps that, with me hanging onto the back of his belt.

An arrow coming at you makes a dreadful noise. Put the middle of your tongue very lightly and loosely on the roof of your mouth. Then inhale so forcefully that the air hisses in and snaps your lips shut. That is what feathers tearing air sound like, and that is what I heard when Ken's arrow slammed into the turf a dozen feet behind me. Ken exploded in laughter, and before I understood just how much I had allowed myself to be suckered, so did I.

We proceeded apace to stalking. I thought the game was a new one, but I've since learned from one of Ken's friends that he introduced them to it when they were still in, or just out of, Harvard. The first thing is to locate some champagne corks. Given the holdings of Archie's wine cellar, that was an easy—and spiritually refreshing—task. Drill a shaft-size hole in the bottom of the cork and insert an arrow, minus its metal head. Then lay some folds of padding on the bulbous top and tape on the finished stalking head.

There were only a few rules: no charging, no shooting at closer than twenty yards. We would hunt each other along a course stretching from our lawn down the hill to Downdale. A few minutes into the game, I looked up from my covert to see Ken standing on top of Archie's work house, head turning slow and sure as a tank turret. I gave him the power to see me, though the only thing he could have seen was my eye looking back at him through a tiny chink in a stone wall. The conviction that I was a dead duck trailed me as I trailed him.

He took his time, stopping often, turning quickly to check his rear. When he reached the Campbells', he slid in behind a huge mountain laurel bush in an ell of the house. He was completely protected on both sides. Either I could call it quits or risk the open lawn in front of him. I waited and waited and then, desperate to avoid disapproval, ran yelling into the sunlight. When I was directly in front of the laurel, maybe thirty yards out, I stopped, whirled and loosed on it. I saw my shaft hit the bush and flash through before his hit me in the shoulder, spun me around, and put me on the ground. When I managed to stop writhing from the pain, there was Ken, bent over, staggering toward me, gasping, "No charging! No charging!"

I had nailed him! What a shot! I . . . and then the horror hit. Had the cork come off? Had it? But then I saw him straightening, still holding himself just below the sternum, where I had scored.

We argued about the charging. I thought I hadn't, but because he seemed so certain, I backed off. He started up the hill, so furious he was silent. I followed along, head down, scuffing stones on the dirt road, not sure whether I was glad he was alive or whether I wished I had done what we had only been pretending to do. By the time we got back to the house, I was mad enough to imagine how the laurel bush might have stripped the head from my shaft, how it then might have shot to and through the target, this older and bigger and crueler man who was always walking ahead of me.

But then, haven't you ever wanted to kill a man?

Poet on the Potomac

I HAVE THE LETTER FRAMED ON THE WALL. THE ink is still blue, but not the powerful blue it was when I first saw it more than fifty years ago. Dated June 6, 1939, it begins, "Dear Archie MacLeish: It is one of those curious facts that when I got your first letter I took to my bed with a severe attack of indigestion—and that when your second letter came I found myself able to rise and resume my normal life." I don't know what color ink the signature was written in. It's faded brown now, but the name is clear: Franklin Delano Roosevelt.

Roosevelt had read some of Archie's essays and articles. He knew him slightly, having given him and his boss, Henry Luce, a backgrounder a couple of years earlier. In 1939, he had a slot to fill, that of Librarian of Congress, and he thought Archie could fill it before breakfast and spend the rest of his time doing for the President what he was so good at doing on his own—jousting against what he saw as the tendency of so many powerful Americans to turn ostrich in the face of economic crisis at home and totalitarian threat overseas. So Roosevelt checked his idea with Felix Frankfurter, whom he had just named to the Supreme Court, got back a glowing response, and went after his man. "The President," Archie told me much later, "decided that I wanted to be the Librarian of Congress."

Archie didn't, or at least not all that much. Just the year before he had managed to extricate himself from Time, Inc., which was falling, he felt, into "awful commercialism." My guess is that he had fallen into a rut, the customary one of overwork and exhaustion. He told me that he had once fainted at his *Fortune* office and that the doctor had told him to slow down and cut back on his pipeloads of Balkan Sobranie.

The vehicle of Archie's extrication had been a precarious one. President James Conant of Harvard was looking for someone to run a new program, the Nieman Fellowship, which would bring journalists to study at the university for a year. Although the job was part time, paying less than a third of his *Fortune* salary, it gave Archie the opportunity to work with nine of the best young newspapermen in the country—and to gain a recognition at Harvard that would come in handy a decade later. The move also prolonged the family diaspora. Ada stayed in Farmington, along with Mimi and me. Ken, recently married and just starting graduate school in anthropology at Harvard, put his father up when Archie was in Cambridge.

It took two presidential shots to bag Archie. The first letter, and subsequent lunch at the White House, left him groggy but determined to claw off that coast. "I have never wanted to write as much as I do at the moment," he protested, "and have never had so many things which demanded to be written."

The President tried again, indigestion or no indigestion, and this time he succeeded. I don't know what the carrots were, but that June 6 letter hanging on my wall speaks playfully to one that had lured Archie in the past: "I am . . . very clear that you will be able to take 'time off' for writing, especially if you like travel to distant parts where you could also improve your knowledge of ancient literature. For example, as Librarian of Congress, you should become thoroughly familiar with the inscriptions on the stone monuments of Easter Island—especially in their relationship to similar sign writing alleged to exist on ancient sheepskins in some of the remoter lamaseries of Tibet."

I have a mental snapshot of Archie's return from his second conversation with the President. Ada had driven to the nearby town of Berlin to meet his train, and I recall the two of them standing by the Packard in Uncle Billy's driveway. They were talking hard, for the choices were hard. Archie didn't have the money to keep on at Harvard for more than another year or two. After that, he might be able to return to Luce, who had signaled such a possibility. But that would be hangdog. With Roosevelt, Archie had the chance to serve a cause he believed in passionately. And passion was his guide. Ada had been through almost a decade of living where she could. I can't imagine her being enthralled by yet another move, to a city she didn't know, with a man who seemed increasingly to be blocked from following the course he had begun so successfully, with her help, in Paris.

But, as usual, she opted for Archie. And so, in the late summer of 1939, we were bound for Washington. Ken had decided against a degree and instead signed up as a cultural anthropologist with the Department of Agriculture, so he and Carolyn also headed south. Mimi, having hated but finished Ada's finishing school, Westover, would head for her higher education in Chicago. Aging Uncle Billy would stay where he was, and C. would look after him. I had no idea who would look after me; my parents and I were all but strangers in that regard. I think that in the excitement about seeing all those monuments, I forgot to get overly anxious about that.

Archie's nomination was not particularly difficult. Some librarians didn't like the idea of a nonlibrarian running the nation's repository of writing. Some members of Congress didn't like the idea of a poet running it, and a few were outraged that the poet who had attacked their sacred capitalism would be, literally, their next-door neighbor. One congressman in particular, a gentleman from New Jersey named J. Parnell Thomas, had called Archie a "fellow traveler." I was surprised that my father was hopping mad about it. I knew he was a traveler. Wasn't I conceived in Paris? But why had he been traveling with Mr. Thomas?

I don't remember saying good-bye to the woman who had loved me and spoiled me and overnursed me from infancy on up. She just faded, as if I were clearing my memory for new impressions. Her image dissipated until there was nothing left but her shining teeth. When I tried to think of her, which was seldom, all I could bring up was Alice's Cheshire cat. I don't think I thought about Grandy at all when we were in Washington.

The heralds of war were on the radio as we got ready to leave Conway. I heard the voice of a man so angry it sounded as if he were squeezing his own throat. It was Adolf Hitler. We listened and watched the cows in our west pasture as they grazed around the juniper bushes and on toward the setting sun.

· · ·

Ada had found us a house in Georgetown, on Thirty-third Street between P Street and Volta Place. It looked small to me then and again when I walked past it three years ago. It is still beautifully proportioned, though now there is a sign outside advising the passerby that its beauty is protected by an impressive security system. We had none, except for a West Highland terrier named Angus and a police station around the corner that generated so much racket that within a year we moved across the street to a much larger house with a big backyard.

Georgetown was a wonder to me. It was part of a city yet felt to me like a village. It was full of green and flowers and the sly smell of boxwood. I missed the quiet of Conway, a silence so deep I could hear my ears. But there were new sounds—trolleys on Wisconsin Avenue and a line running along P Street. The whines and mutters of their wheels kept me good company. One trolley went out to Cabin John. I thought for a while the name had something to do with a privy, or perhaps an old hermit out in the woods. I still don't know where Cabin John is; not knowing is important to imagining it.

Dean and Alice Acheson were just across Wisconsin, and Felix and Marion Frankfurter not much farther away. Now that Felix was on the Supreme Court, Archie started calling him the "Li'l Jestiss." It fit. Felix was short all right, as short as Dean was tall. The two of them used to walk downtown to work on fine days, and from behind they could have passed for Mutt and Jeff. Felix was pure energy: he moved and thought in a field of it. He also had the cleanest glasses in the country. They sparkled like C.'s teeth.

According to one observer, Archie hit the library like the brush of a comet. Discovering that what he had been appointed to do had no real job description, he invented his own. It was clear that the library needed new energy to fit the times. Even basic functions such as cataloguing the flood of books, periodicals, papers, and films that poured into the place were missing some sprockets. And there were obvious needs. For example, a recording studio would make it possible for the library to augment its collections of American folk music and produce albums of in-house concerts and readings. There would be plenty more of those as the country's best poets were brought in on consultantships.

Then there was the clientele to consider. I heard Archie talking about how the American people should be "educated in their own culture," a phrase that the present establishment would think far too elitist to use. Archie went on to say that the library belonged to the people—another suspicious idea these days—and they should know more about it in particular and about libraries in general. They should know more about books and their power. And, since the library at the time housed both the Declaration of Independence and the Constitution, they should know about the power of the word in constructing democracy and in safeguarding it against such dangers as the rise of fascism.

I loved that kind of talk from my father. He was Buck Rogers, I thought, about to attain escape velocity. It made me think of him back in Conway, speeding behind the reel mower, shirtless, hatless, pouring sweat. Ada would come out the door, put on her sharpest frown, and holler, "Archie! Sto-o-o-p!" The pitch of the reel would rise a tone or two, and Archie would fly by, waving.

It seemed to me in those Georgetown years that Archie and Ada were giving or going out to dinner party after dinner party. The silver tray by our front door was never without a calling card or two. I liked the diplomatic ones best. When my parents entertained at home, I might get a gig as a kind of stand-up chameleon, switching from an old English tune on my recorder to a polka on an accordion I had trouble seeing over, to some

Yorkshire yucks memorized from my collection of Stanley Holloway records. "The Stick with the 'Orse's 'Ead 'Andle" was my first choice.

Ada sang sometimes. She had taught me "Dido's Lament" on the piano, and it did great things to my small soul to understand that if I were careful I could actually accompany her. Once, when I forgot a bar and froze, I was so eager to cover my mistake that I told her I had stopped because I thought her voice had cracked. I wince at that cruelty even now.

I must have been lonely, but I don't remember being so. By then, I guess, I had learned the MacLeish trick of denying simple sadness, let alone despair. All was well. Music helped the self-deception. One evening at the Achesons' house on Twenty-eighth Street, while I was in an upstairs bedroom practicing my recorder, Felix heard me and came bouncing up the stairs to ask if we could trade jobs. I shook my head as I played, and Felix laughed his electric cackle and bounced back down again to tell the dinner company that Archie's son would rather make music than hand down judicial decisions.

I had already been captured by folk songs, thanks to a spine-sprung copy of Carl Sandburg's *The American Songbag*, inscribed to my mother ("Ada: Sing 'em . . . And may your rare singing voice stay with you as long as you have wishes"). I was walking the streets of Laredo. I was goin' to Montan'. Then, through the door one evening came a real folksinger. Huddie Ledbetter was broad and strong and carried a 12-string guitar. Long into the night we listened to Leadbelly. He played "Irene" and "The Rock Island Line," and when he'd stop to work on a glass of warm gin and talk with Alan Lomax, the master folklorist at the library who had brought him, I started breathing again. Ada told me later that he had used the neck taken from a liquor bottle as a slide.

Carl Sandburg was in Washington off and on, speaking, doing things at the library. When Archie got a bad case of the flu, Carl came over with his guitar. He stood at the foot of the bed, fixed the peaked invalid with a hard eye and sang, "I Doan Wanna Be Buried in the Storm." A while later, Carl showed up on what turned out to be the wrong night, but that was normal for him. My parents had to go out, so they left him to me. I knew and loved Carl. He had sent me a copy of his wonderful *Rootabaga Stories* and written therein that he held me—Peter, to him—in high esteem. I had heard him reading aloud about Hatrack the Horse and about how Gimme the Ax goes to the station to buy a ticket that will "send us far as the railroad rails go and then forty ways farther yet," and about how the ticket agent says, "So far? So early? So soon?"

I knew how Carl could croon those words, holding on to the vowels as long as he could. But that evening instead of asking for what I wanted, I went for what I thought he might want. As soon as he had taken off his hat, I started in on him with the accordion. Politely, sadly, he lay down on a spindly French settee, wedged himself in, and went, or pretended to go, to sleep. I was left honking at a broad back and a head of silver hair.

Sometimes Archie let me come see him in the library. He had a magical office, tucked back behind a marble wall and guarded by his supersecretary, Thursa Bakey, on whom I had a considerable crush. Archie insisted on quiet in his workplace, and her gentle diplomacy was usually enough to persuade the most compulsive chatterers, myself included, to pipe down in his anteroom. Carl paid no mind to any of that. On an early visit to the librarian, he walked in unannounced, stood looking up at the busty Muses painted on the ceiling, walked around a bit, then turned to leave. "Over the poet's coco," he tossed back over his shoulder, "was rococo."

The original library was being cleaned and renovated when I last visited it a few years ago. Colors muted by grime when a smaller me had walked and run along those marble corridors all but shout from the murals now. The Main Reading Room, where I first smelled the smell of learning, today seems to have double the supply of sunlight in it because someone recently had the presence of mind to clear away the clutter in front of the windows high above the floor.

I never minded the dinginess, not while there were songs to be heard down where Lomax worked, not while hot on the track of a collection of volumes supposed to be bound in human skin (to my disappointment, I have recently learned that the leather came from another animal), not while leaning against a marble statue and trying to echolocate the flat crack of footsteps in some far corridor.

I spent two years as a day student at St. Alban's School up by the National Cathedral. All the best children went there, though I didn't know that at the time—perhaps because I made so few friends. There was one who lived close to Rock Creek, and he would call me up from time to time and ask me to come over and mess around. He and Matilda and her daughter Ellen, who ran the house for Ada, were about the only people I felt I could talk to when the need got particularly strong.

With some classmates I went to a store on Connecticut Avenue and shoplifted a fishing knife. I left with a gut tied in a sheepshank and a resolve never to try stealing again lying, yes, and taking change from Ada's purse, yes, but no more light fingers outside the house that might land the younger son of the Librarian of Congress in trouble. When trouble did surface, though, Archie's name usually pushed it under again. One day I decided to break rules and hitchhike downtown. The man who picked me up began to touch me. When he grabbed my hand and forced it down on what felt like an understuffed kielbasa running down his left pantleg, I mentioned my name. He let me out on the sidewalk in half a block. I have been searching for some post-trauma reaction to that assault, but all I remember is laughter.

There is also a faint memory about a nurse at the school taking a ruler or something to a boy's penis as it started rising during an examination. I can't vouch for that—as a matter of fact, I can't vouch for an unsettling amount of what transpired during my secondary education, from St. Alban's on. My own member was getting pretty active by the time we arrived in Washington. I rubbed it, I held it under a warm stream of bathwater. I looked at porn cartoons drawn on cheap paper. One showed a woman astride a man whose balloon said "Shake it, babe, I'm coming." I kept that pamphlet rolled up in the tube of a microscope Archie and Ada had bought me for Christmas. When we went back to Farmington for a visit, C. walked in on me while I was pleasuring myself in the old bathtub. She flushed and fled. I remained at my delight. About two years later, Archie gave me the shortest version of bird and bee on record, an oblique reference to emissions and a request that I tell him when I began having them.

The stalking game didn't seem to dampen things long between my brother and me. Fairly early in the Washington years,

Ken talked Ada and Archie into the idea of getting a boat. He then found them one, an old clinker-built cabin cruiser Archie christened *The Creeping Jesus*. My parents must have spent all of one night aboard. Thereafter, the craft was Ken's. He and Carolyn took her down the Potomac and into Chesapeake waters. Once, they took me with them. We were idling along, and I took a nap on the transom. Awakening with a full bladder, I lurched forward toward the head, only to knock first a blanket and then a pail into the open engine hatch. The blanket wrapped around the driveshaft like an Ace bandage, and the bucket went on next. It took Ken hours to cut, pick and tear the mess off the shaft. He never said a nasty word to me, and for that I thanked him silently all that day.

The President sometimes invited my parents along on his jaunts on the water. One hot afternoon they were out there aboard a Coast Guard cutter. FDR was aft, talking with Ada. Suddenly Archie spotted *The Creeping Jesus* creeping along. When he told the President, the order was given to come alongside the MacLeish yacht. Ken, looking out toward the channel, saw what he took to be the law bearing down on him. Evidently he had with him some armament that would bring trouble on his head, so he made for shallower water. Everything worked out in the end—no boarding, no arrest, just a hailing to the chief and pleasantries across the water—but during this Keystone chase, the President of the United States had himself a long and healthful laugh.

In the fall of 1941, Archie and Ada sent me to Fountain Valley, the boarding school in the shadow of Pike's Peak where Alec Campbell taught English along with Gilbert and Sullivan. I believe that I and my blossoming adolescence and my poor dion were simply putting out too much noise. FDR was asking Archie to help with speechwriting and encouraging him to play Horatio against the isolationists. Ada was running the household, giving concerts—with critical support from the likes of Eleanor Roosevelt. With all that going on, the Campbells and their school must have seemed to my parents to be the best solution for me.

Fountain Valley was wonderful fun for a thirteen-year-old. There was the horse wrangler, the small and strong Johnny Dole, to look up to. There were hideaways to build in the walls of arroyos. We called them kivas after the underground religious centers of the Pueblo Indians, but ours could hold maybe four medium-sized white boys. There were coyotes to listen to and kangaroo rats to trap. I probably improved my mind at Fountain Valley, but I know I improved my knowledge of and love for choral music. Friends and I liked to rework the lyrics to some of our songs. "Speed bonny boat like a turd on the ding," we'd warble, "over the pee cow pie." As Christmas neared, I heard one Sunday that the Japanese, the people Archie and Ada had visited only five years earlier, had turned around and bitten them and all the rest of us on the butt.

Before Pearl Harbor, I had heard Edward R. Murrow reporting from a London rooftop, bombs and ack-ack in the background, but I had seen nothing remotely connected to combat. That began to change during the spring vacation of 1942, when Alec and Ishbel took me to Phoenix, where we spent an afternoon in the control tower at a military airfield, watching little biplane trainers taking off and landing. On the drive across the country to Conway that summer, I was already memorizing silhouettes and performance details of warplanes that eventually

included Messerschmitts, Spitfires, Zeroes, and my favorite, the
split-tailed P-38 Lightning.

Ken had joined the Navy early on and would spend the war
flying blimps on antisubmarine patrols over the Caribbean from
a base near Miami. I saw and coveted the special Randall knife
he carried to cut himself free of the ship's skin if he crashed.
When Archie took me to a military show in Washington, I
writhed in excitement over the searing power of the flamethrow-
ers and the way strands of explosives snugged around telephone
poles could nip them like so many flower stems. I dreamed of
having a bazooka of my own, of killing Krauts and Nips by the
tens, by the thousands, and laughing at the screams.

I already knew about the Fascists, from their work in Spain.
Now, Archie was speaking out about how their psychological
warriors were playing on America's strong go-it-alone streak to
let air out of the war effort. Pearl Harbor had scared the country,
but people were of too many minds about how to react to suit
my father. The Selective Service Act had just barely squeaked
through the Congress. If Roosevelt's opponents were less bla-
tant about the British, and the Allied cause, there was still plenty
of subsurface anger in the country about America having been
dragged into the hostilities.

In speeches and essays, Archie identified those he saw as enemies at home: "the American defeatist who would rather lose
the war . . . than make the terrible effort victory demands; the
idle women whose dinner hours have been altered and who call
their country's struggle for its life 'this wretched war'; the slug-
gish men on the commuter trains who have never fought for
anything but golf balls in their lives." He argued that defeatism
could lead to a totalitarian takeover here, one that would have to

be exceptionally brutal to control a people who had for so long been free.

Roosevelt decided Archie should spend more time rousing the populace. He put him in charge of an odd outfit called OFF, for Office of Facts and Figures. When that succumbed to OWI, the Office of War Information, Archie stayed on for a while until problems at the Library forced him back to the job that had brought him to Washington.

. . .

After only a year at Fountain Valley, I was old enough to go to Deerfield Academy, about six crow-flown miles east-northeast of Conway. The town of Deerfield had fascinated me since I was old enough to toddle past the ancient houses along its main street. I knew all about the French and Indian massacre of townsfolk in 1704, and Ada had told me that a distant relative of ours had been taken captive during the attack and marched off to Canada. Also, somewhere in town you could still see a door that had been slashed by a tomahawk.

Frank Boyden was the academy's headmaster, and he was thought to be one of the best in the country. He was a small man who dressed in double-breasted suits. He had sad eyes, a giggle of a laugh, and the ability to control the rambunctions of his boys with one handclap. He sat in a large alcove in the main school building, always available, and there wasn't one of us who doubted that he could read our minds as we walked past.

Geometry excited me, and literature and French. Latin also held some interest, although this may have been because the name of the man who taught that dead language was Coffin. Sports were mandatory, and I went out for the usual seasonal offerings. I started as a back on the midget football team. God, we were small in our scratchy green jerseys, sweating and grunting and leaping through fall afternoons like manic leprechauns. Striding through his squad, red face gone purple, mouth like a gash, was a man we called (in his absence, of course) "the Oat." What I took to be unbridled fury, what consequently had me all but dampening my undermuslins in the first scrimmages, turned out to be Ralph Oatley's way of expressing bonhomie. It was his version of a smile.

The Oat helped me in two ways. The first had to do with a flinch reflex that accompanied me to Deerfield. It grew out of an accident several autumns earlier, when Ada was driving me to Conway. I had my head out the open window when I suddenly sneezed, smacking my mouth against the door. I then reached my hand across to her, opened it and showed her the better part of what had been my right front tooth. She pulled off the road, by a graveyard as I recall, and we both broke into tears. The accident gave me a distinctive appearance. A classmate told me recently that he thought I looked like a wild Gael fresh from some mountain moor. But as a midget footballer, I was so protective of my remaining ivories that I froze whenever an opposing runner headed in my direction.

The Oat didn't rag me. He waited until, in a moment of distraction, I forgot about my fear and brought down our star runner, whereupon he took the boy aside and whispered to him. Back the runner came at me on the next play, and again and again. In the end, I was tackling without thinking. I spent much of the following spring learning the lovely game of lacrosse, a small midfielder bouncing off large defensemen and all but inviting them to belt me in the chops. Over the years, I lost fragments of two more teeth to the sport.

Each weekday morning at Deerfield I walked to a remote Steinway and there labored at scales and then Bach and Debussy. But bullheaded adolescence began to win out over the ghostly beauty of "The Sunken Cathedral." Boys, I thought, boys who were going to become real men, didn't play the piano. They could, however, sing together. My freshman year, I had followed Mr. Oatley from the football field to an old barn, where several dozen of us opened our throats an evening or two a week as the Deerfield glee club.

The Oat not only made all of us one, he made all of us assume we were one. He kept us laughing and working, tenors and basses. We sang spirituals and classical pieces. We sang "Johnny's a Hand Organ Man" and a Russian rant that taxed us to the limit. We sang at Deerfield and at nearby schools, and once we had to leave one of our members, suddenly sick with the flu, in the infirmary of the Emma Willard School for girls in Troy, New York. If you can imagine the torture this engendered in our collective libido, you can understand why, decades later, I was so relieved to hear that coeducation had finally come to Deerfield.

I can't say whether the Oat knew of the dwindling of my pianistic effort. But just about the time when I had decided to give up the instrument, he asked me to play Bach's "Jesu, Joy of Man's Desiring" with the glee club. That excited me enough to produce a doubling of practice time. We performed the piece in the late spring of my senior year, and it was one of the most satisfying things I have ever done. I could feel the singers singing through my fingers. The instrument itself sang. When we were through, Mr. Oatley looked down at me with his signature smile. "You," he said softly, "are a musician."

I felt like one. I felt even more like one when I plowed through several days of aptitude testing a week or so before graduation. The testers scratched their heads and ruffled their papers and finally told me that I would be following my strong suit if I were to write musical comedies. To my regret, I have never tried my hand at it.

My contribution to the war effort consisted of a horse and buggy, bought to save gas. The horse's name was Jasper, and he sized me up quickly and correctly. Everywhere we went, we did things his way. Some evenings we would carry supper to my uncle Alec, who had volunteered to man the aircraft-spotting setup in a field across the South River from Uphill Farm. Jasper would boom across a covered bridge, and we'd climb a hill and trot across a field to a shack where Alec sat with binoculars, a phone, and a good book. We both knew our chances of spotting a Junkers raider were on the far side of zero, but it was pleasant where we were. We sang *Ruddigore* while the sun went down and Jasper munched.

Rationing got tighter. Ada and Archie had enough gas coupons to get from Washington to Conway, but the wartime speed limit—forty-five, I think—made a long fizzle of the trip. I went along once during the Deerfield years, and I remember the pang of pleasure that came with the sight of Conway in its valley as we topped a ridge and ran down in the dusk through Sheriff Parsons' excellent hayfields. I found myself with a familiar feeling, one of being in a place so beloved that I yearned for it even as I was traveling through it. I thought of the ghost farms, their cellar holes, their stone walls snaking through woods. I thought of the going farms like the Boydens' and the Totmans'. Farming was still important then; more than half of Americans were still on the land, as opposed to around three percent now. Farmers were my kind of people. They did what I wanted to do, and they did it all year round, in one place.

It got so we couldn't get enough mash for the chickens—let alone for myself. The only thing was to get rid of the flock. That meant killing and dressing about a hundred birds. Archie and Ken and I managed to do the deed in one day. Halfway through plucking, Ken got a bottle of warm vodka to ease things along. I was allowed several stiff pulls. On the first, I thought I was going to throw up. After the second, I didn't care if I did. I got to be so merry that I forgot about my birds lying in hot water to loosen their feathers. By the time I got around to them, they were parboiled. The feathers came off easily enough. The trouble was the skin came with them.

Archie always believed that the farm was ideal for his youngsters. He actually thought we had all the friends we needed there. But Ada brooded about that. I think she felt that if I were left to my own devices much longer, she would have to institute a regime of cold hip baths for me. So she sent me to the Putney Work Camp, up the Connecticut River Valley in Vermont. I went there for part of three wartime summers, and it was at Putney that I got to know and square dance with and be mystified by real live girls. I even kissed some—three would be my guess.

I also learned to be a passable logger. Charlie Gray ran the all-boy woods crew. He was a loner who required no more company than that of his fat blond cocker spaniel, Annabelle. There could have been no better elder for me than Charlie. He taught us all how to work with two-man saws, axes, wedges, peavies, canthooks. In his lumber truck, he and Annabelle would drive us through the hills to stands of hemlock and pine and maple and oak. Then the two of them would sit, close together, looking at a target tree. Charlie would study and study. After a while he would rise up, say, "Wal," and motion some of us over. He'd point out where he wanted the tree to fall so that its logs could be snaked out with ease. Then he'd show us where to make the kerf and, on the opposite side of the trunk, the saw cut, saving wood here, slicing into it there. One time, early on, we were convinced he had his calculations all wrong, but we did what he told us to do. The tree commenced to lean, and all of us novices hollered the manliest "Timberrr!" we could muster. The fall started out twenty degrees off the mark, but the tree corrected itself and landed bang on with a satisfying smash. We had factored out what Charlie had factored in: the effect of the wind.

At the end of the second summer I realized that of my closest friends at Putney, many were Jews. I liked their biting humor, their openness, their strong affection, easily given. When one of them, a massive boy named Moose, told me he was a Jew, I thought I heard self-deprecation in his voice. "So what!" I said, "I'm a Scot!" Moose told the woman who ran the camp about that, and she told me that she wanted me to come back for a third summer as a junior counselor. I told Moose that I wanted to be a Jew, and he said he would take it under advisement.

Most school-year vacations I spent in Washington. In the spring of 1943, when I was fifteen, Archie gave me a present: one week as a Senate page, courtesy of Senator Claude Pepper of Florida. I ran messages from the Senate floor to various office buildings and back again. The first day, or thereabouts, I was initiated. The other pages blindfolded me, took me out on a balcony and boosted me over the marble railing. Thinking I was still on or near solid ground, I struggled to get free—until the handkerchief slipped from my eyes and I looked down at a group of horrified tourists looking up. As I was hauled back to safety, I remember thinking that that was the day Archie was walking over to the Senate to present the library's budget requests. I could have fallen on him, I thought, as I straightened my clothing. Now, *that* would have made the papers!

In the fall of 1944, Archie wrote the President that he had done the reorganization that had needed doing at the library and would like very much to go home. He was by then chronically exhausted by unending emergencies, piddling and pressing. The latter included the day someone rushed in to tell him the Declaration of Independence, housed for public viewing in a glass vacuum case, was slowly and quietly tearing from an upper corner. Experts fixed it with paste and tissue fibers, but until it was repaired, Archie's stress level hovered near the rococo.

Nothing happened to Archie's request for a time. When the President did reply, he completely overlooked the home idea. Instead, he moved my father from a place where he ran things to a place where he had a relatively small part of the action. FDR made him assistant secretary of state for cultural and public affairs. By then, Archie had so many congressmen mad at him for his belligerence that he almost got voted down.

• • •

"When the President asks you to do something," Archie told me later, "you do it." He took on more chores than ever before. He worked long and hard on the development of the United Nations. He traveled often. Although I took vicarious pride in his journeys, I also allowed myself a vengeful snicker when I heard of the way Archibald MacLeish had left a navy ship while carrying out official duties—somewhere in the Caribbean, I believe. It seems he had disembarked fully, stepping back one step too far and shooting into the sea. He was fished out forthwith, and when I heard the news I relished the thought of all that suddenly sodden importance.

By then Ada and Archie had a house and a half. It was on Orinoco Street in Alexandria, across the Potomac, the boyhood home of Robert E. Lee, which is now open to the public as a museum. There were two drawbacks to this house: when the wind blew from a certain direction, it carried the perfumes of a fertilizer factory; and no matter how the wind blew, Archie had next to no time to enjoy his mansion. Mimi, who had finished her studies in education, did manage to get married in it, to a naval ensign named Karl Grimm, but no one seemed to have enough time to sit down and make the place a home.

Early in 1945, Ada and some of Archie's friends finally prevailed on him to take a break, and he did, with typical reluctance. We and the Murphys traveled by private rail car to the Homestead resort hotel in Hot Springs, Virginia. The hills were just greening up, and Dow and I rode horses through that beauty. He and Archie and I cooked in various waters. On close to the last day there, we were eating breakfast on the balcony outside our rooms, looking at a rising hawk. It kept testing a thermal with its wing, almost as a hand tests bathwater. Gerald walked over behind my chair and, facing Archie but not looking at him, began to recite a poem I had never heard. It was Gerard Manley Hopkins' "The Windhover":

I caught this morning morning's minion, king-
   dom of daylight's dauphin, dapple-dawn-drawn Falcon,
     in his riding
   Of the rolling level underneath him steady air, and
     striding
High there, how he rung upon the rein of a wimpling wing
In his ecstasy! then off, off forth on swing,
   As a skate's heel sweeps smooth on a bow-bend: the
     hurl and gliding
   Rebuffed the big wind. My heart in hiding
Stirred for a bird,—the achieve of, the mastery of the
     thing!

Brute beauty and valour and act, oh, air, pride, plume,
     here
   Buckle! AND the fire that breaks from thee then, a
     billion
Times told lovelier, more dangerous, O my chevalier!

   No wonder of it: shéer plód makes plough down sillion
Shine, and blue-bleak embers, ah my dear,
   Fall, gall themselves, and gash gold-vermilion.

I remember that I didn't need to understand the words to feel
them. I hear Gerald now, the accent of wealthy Long Island altering the *r* in "bird." I see Archie on the balcony, looking out at
the green, looking very sad. He had been five and a half years in
Washington, five and a half years away from his art. I now know
that Gerald, in effect, was returning Gerard to Archie: it was my
father who years ago had brought the songs of that great poet to

my godfather. Amanda Vaill, who recently published a fine biography of the Murphys, says that Gerald's gift was "a reminder
of [Archie's] essence, a reminder that he had to return to it to
survive." A year later, Dow sent me my own copy of Hopkins,
beautifully bound, inscribed in his perfect hand.

Two months later, Franklin Delano Roosevelt suffered a massive cerebral hemorrhage at Warm Springs, Georgia. Archie
wrote the proclamation of his death. "The courage of great
men," he wrote, "outlives them to become the courage of their
people and the peoples of the world. It lives beyond them and
upholds their purposes and brings their hopes to pass." That
fall, he left Washington.

Now, with my father eighteen years dead, I think about how
Roosevelt's letter followed on. After recommending that the
librarian-to-be consider traveling to Tibet, it continued, "If you
do go on such a trip, I would like to go along as cabin boy and
will guarantee that I will not interrupt the Muse when she is flirt-
ing with you." It wouldn't surprise me at all if Archie has taken
him up on that. I can see them together, a president and a poet
on the roof of the world.

Making the Bridge

I KNOW ARCHIE HEARD JOHN FITZGERALD KENNEDY speak at Amherst College on October 26, 1963. He sat beside the President on that occasion, the ground-breaking of the Robert Frost Library. There is a photograph of the two of them, turned to each other, smiling. I look at Kennedy's grin, his handsome, cocked head, and think of what a bullet would do to both only weeks later, in Dallas.

I'm fairly sure Archie heard what Kennedy had to say about power and poetry: "When power leads man towards arrogance, poetry reminds him of his limitations. When power narrows the areas of man's concern, poetry reminds him of the richness and diversity of his existence. When power corrupts, poetry cleanses, for art establishes the basic human truths which must serve as the touchstone of our judgment." Here was a poet who had experienced the narrowing of his own concerns listening to the world's most powerful politician reminding him of that experience. Archie told me that leaving government had "raised hell with me." He had acquired enough power to want more. Afterward, he said, "I knew I had to make the bridge and get back to being myself. I knew I had to take time over that, but I suffered during those years."

He was like a diver going through decompression, stopping over and over on his way to the surface. First he tried exercise. During the fall of 1945, he cut brush behind the house until he could barely swing the brush hook. He outworked me the few

Sunday afternoons I could get free from Deerfield Academy to help him. Once he tried to burn some of what he had cut, but it was too green. That was the way he felt, he told a friend, too wet at the center of what had been his art to do anything but smoulder. That was not entirely true: even then, he could write a good poem. Here, from *Actfive and Other Poems,* published in 1948, is "The Learned Men":

> Whose minds like horse or ox,
> Dispassionate in the stall,
> Grow great in girth and wax
> Beyond the animal,
>
> While mine, like country hog,
> Grows leaner as I age,
> Chivvied by flea and dog,
> Baited by love and rage.
>
> If mind by God was meant
> To grow and gain in girth,
> Swelling in sweet content,
> I cease I have no worth:
>
> But if it was God's will
> That mind, no wish refused,
> Should waste by wanting still
> By God I am well used!

Archie spent a couple of years doing this and that, earning the money we needed (the postwar boom hadn't yet revived the family finances). Then, in 1949, Harvard asked him to be Boylston Professor of Rhetoric and Oratory. I was delighted by the perks of the appointment, one of which permitted him to pasture a cow on the Boston Common. He spent thirteen years in Cambridge, teaching young writers with names like Donald Hall and Edward Hoagland and Robert Bly and Jonathan Kozol. Well after his retirement, Archie said he was sorry he never had John Updike in his writing workshop. According to Archie's biography, Updike had applied for admission, twice, and been turned down.

I went to Yale three years before my father returned to Harvard. I think I applied elsewhere, but only as fallback. My trips to the Yale Bowl with Uncle Billy (the cane episode notwithstanding) had predisposed me to root for the Blue. My grades at Deerfield had been good enough to satisfy the gentlemanly academic standards of the times, though they probably wouldn't get me into a decent community college now. My name didn't hurt. Neither did the fact that I could and did boast of being the seventh generation of the family to come of age in New Haven.

My great good luck was not Yale per se but the Yale class of 1950. It was huge, something like fifteen hundred men and boys. More than half had served in the war; a good many could not have afforded Yale if it hadn't been for the GI Bill. We were a demographic anomaly in more ways than one: a few months after my seventieth birthday, I read in the alumni magazine that a classmate of mine had recently died—at the age of eighty-six.

It didn't take long for me to realize that the old Yale of Dink Stover was not only dead but beyond memory. The vets in the class were late for their lives in the civilian world, and they were expert at playing catch-up. They helped us set academic records that stood for years, and they helped me outgrow my boyhood constructs of chivalry and painless glory. One in particular took me aside when I confessed my envy of his combat record and shame at my lack of one. Don't give me that shit, he said, and then went on to relate just enough of his experiences in Europe to convince me—well, to move me toward the conviction—that I was an exceptionally lucky kid to have missed the terror of war and should fall on my knees and give thanks to the stars for that luck. Even so, the sorrow over not having killed stayed with me right through Yale.

I went there almost bereft of self-awareness and burdened by the disguises cobbled together over my boyhood to gain favor within my family and protection without. These I updated with a pair of white shoes and a raccoon coat that had belonged to Ada's great aunt, Sarah Garlick. Sarah must have been a giant of a woman: I had to get a tailor to lop a foot off the bottom to enable me to hop on the running boards of the trolleys that took Elis out to football games at the bowl. Yet gradually, through gaps in all this frippery, I began to recognize outlines of someone who might eventually turn out to be me. Now that singers like Burl Ives and John Jacob Niles were showing me new ways to sing it, I was drawn more strongly by folk music. True to Uncle Billy's tradition, I took up barbershop.

I had no idea of myself as a writer—that would have been overreaching, especially now that Ken had entered the field by going to work for *Life* magazine. But I had been writing little pieces since the age of nine, when I made a poem for Mimi. (Its title was "Oh World, I Wonder.") In the summer of 1945 I heard a train whistle going crazy down in the Connecticut Valley: three shorts and a long, three shorts and a long, on and on, warbling with wind, rising and falling with the Doppler effect. Everyone knew what that meant. It meant *V,* and it meant Victory. That is how I learned the war was over. I wrote a piece about that, and the Deerfield paper ran it. What really opened the petcock though was a course at Yale called Daily Themes. We worked on assigned topics that got deeper and tougher as the year went on. I remember laboring over a piece exploring the nature of horror. I had a little boy in haying season running beside the mower and falling and losing a leg to it. The story excited me so that I kept adding horror on horror until the story itself lay down and died.

Daily Themes had me reading my work to my classmates, editing their work, swimming in writing. What I learned there I took into other classrooms. Yale was experimenting then with what to me were wonderful majors, expansive strokes of learning. The one I chose was Literature, Philosophy and the Fine Arts. I have to laugh as I write this, thinking of how modern academe, downsized and outsourced, would deal with such breezy endeavors. I was free to study and translate French literature, read the Russian novel, Chaucer, Shakespeare. The university insisted that its brightest faculty lights brighten undergraduate classrooms. I took a course in astronomy with Lyman Spitzer, in geology with Richard Foster Flint, and in philosophy with the great Paul Weiss.

On weekends, I made the required trips to Vassar, where little more than fear of females awaited. After a while, I found safer ground with Ken and Carolyn and their friends, playing guitar and singing with Artie Shaw and the puppeteer Bil Baird. Bil and I traded songs, which means that I stole his—including two versions of "One-Eyed Reilly," a ballad about a wandering Irish penis.

. . .

My parents added to my education in their own way. Ada had been a hit in wartime Washington. She had sung at the White House, she was honored and envied as a hostess. She served as director of domestic camp and hospital programs for the Red Cross, at one time informing General George Patton that he was being too hard on his troops. I don't know what therapies she undertook to help her recover from Potomac fever, but they couldn't have been easy. Despite all this, Ada set about giving me a strong dose of music right after my freshman year. She arranged for me to go to Tanglewood, summer home of the Boston Symphony Orchestra. I was, among other things, to resume piano lessons. It turned out that no teacher there was interested in taking on such a piker. So I sampled everything. I sat in on Leonard Bernstein's classes and once joined other students on a wild ride with him to have lunch in Lenox, all of us having at a Bach chorale at the top of our lungs.

Ada herself came over and took me to the house of Serge Koussevitzky. I had known since an early age that my father and my mother knew everyone it would be fun to know, so I wasn't surprised. I sat watching "Mr. Koo," trying to reconcile his small size with his huge presence, and listening to another guest, the violist William Primrose, enchant the afternoon.

If I couldn't play the piano, I could sing. Robert Shaw was at Tanglewood, with what was to me a staggering agenda. He proposed to lead his singers in performances including Mozart's Requiem, and the Beethoven Ninth, the "Choral" Symphony.

We performed the Ninth late in the summer, on a hot night that was almost unbearable for us, tucked, as we were, into risers behind the orchestra at the airless end of the huge music shed. We sweated through our evening dress within minutes. Mr. Koo grew redder in the face with each passing sweep of his baton, and a good many of us feared for his life. The soloists dove and soared. Then came that ending, the incredible cliff-falls of that ending, and we stood there panting, laughing, weeping, roaring. Mr. Koo applauded us. We applauded him. We applauded the audience, which seemed for a while to be climbing over the chairs to get closer to what had been a miracle. I know Ada and Archie were there, but I don't think they joined in the clambering. That was my first exposure to communal ecstasy, and it never really went away. If you happen to be driving through western Massachusetts and see a bald old man behind the wheel of an aging Toyota pickup, waving his arms and his head, obviously crazed by what is on his radio, you'll know who it is and what he is listening to.

The next summer Archie was the one who sent me off, to a gigantic wheat farm in the middle of Montana, run by a man Archie had written about in his *Fortune* days. A friend and I spent weeks up on top of big Holt twenty-foot-cut combines, keeping eyes on cutters and reels and conveyor belts and the great spouts of grain pouring into the hoppers behind us, smelling of fertility. It seems to me we drank about a gallon a day from canvas water bags. The only relief from the sun was the occasional thunderstorm charging in out of the west. We would wait until the last minute and then dive under the bellies of the machines. We would lie there, scratching ourselves,

watching the gale roll through the standing wheat, flinching and
hollering at the lightning.

Ada and Archie together sent me off at the end of my junior
year on what came close to the young gentleman's grand tour of
Europe. Two classmates and I bought a Citroën and drove the
streets of Paris, then headed south to the Pyrenees, east along
the Mediterranean coast, back north through Belgium, Holland,
and Germany to Switzerland, and then down to Rome. We paid
dutiful attention to museums and operas and architecture. We
paid a different kind of attention to the leavings of war. This
cathedral stood with its great glass intact, that one showed us its
holy bulk against an evening sky and its gutted nave the following morning. Rotterdam was largely rubble mounds of temple
size and endless stretches of the greenest grass. The harbor entrance at St.-Tropez was plugged with sunken yachts, and the
pines stretching on to Antibes, once the sheltering place for the
Murphys and their friends, were splintered by artillery and
small-arms fire.

We were welcomed in France. In Germany, four years into its
defeat, people looked through us as if we weren't there. Standing before the open door of a cremation oven at Auschwitz, I
found myself wishing that the Germans weren't there, that we
had liquidated them as they had tried to liquidate the Jews. I
came to my senses in a few days, but hatred remained for years.

As I moved through Yale, I knew I was sailing on Archie's
wind. Some faculty people had known him as a student. Most
students knew about what he had become in the thirty years
following. I was elected to the Pundits because Archie had been
a Pundit. All I remember of the honor was that it enabled me

to sit at table in Mory's, drinking Green Cups and watching James Thurber draw priceless doodles—including, I think, a barefaced lie—on the tablecloth.

One spring afternoon, a fellow member of Yale's lacrosse team invited me to drive back to town for Tap Day. I was a junior and therefore qualified as a proper sheep for the ceremony. I knew I had neither the academic nor the extracurricular credentials to get tapped. But I went along and stood making cracks about my friends milling in the courtyard of Branford College while secret-society members, all seniors, leaned out upper-story windows in search of their prey. I was just about to let loose a zinger when something hit me very hard on the shoulder from behind. It was a hand. A voice behind my left ear roared, "Skull and Bones! Do you accept?" I bleated. The owner of the large voice must have taken that as an affirmative, for he roared again. I thought for a stunned instant that he had been coached by Ada. What he said was, "Go to your room!"

I sprang off to Davenport College, all but whimpering with delight. Within a hundred yards, I was walking again. Nothing had changed; I had not gone from average to outstanding in the course of one afternoon. I had been tapped because Archie had been tapped. I felt safe and I felt sorry. Oh well, said the small, dull voice of the adapter, it's the price you pay: better a legacy than a loser. I think that realization explains why by midlife I had blotted out the name of the man who spoke to us on the night of my initiation into Skull and Bones. It was, a clubmate recently assured me, Archibald MacLeish.

During my senior year, I tried to figure out what I wanted to do and be. Archie kept out of my deliberations, saying only that whatever I settled on should be the reason for living. I should be best at it, he implied, or—a distant second—I should be the best I could be. Music tempted me. But music made no money. Besides, Ada had pointed out that although music brought joy to my life, it was almost certainly not my life. She, the professional musician, knew about the hours, the sacrifice, the tenacity required by the art, and she knew from experience that I was too easygoing for that muse. I took Ada's point—too easily, but I took it.

Geology flirted with me for a while. I loved the science, the field trips, the chance to work and play at the same time. But I feared the requisite immersions in physics and other foreign disciplines. No. And then I entered a competition for those who wanted to become Time, Inc., editorial trainees and, as I thought I would, made the grade. Off I went, following the tracks of father and brother, to New York for a few introductory weeks, and then on to *Time's* Dallas bureau.

That summer the Korean War started, and I spent less than two months in Texas before being called home to deal with the draft. They were happy weeks, learning the trade, coming to love the beauty of the Big Bend country, eating so much barbecue that I developed something akin to scurvy. The bureau chief had a weekend retreat, a decrepit former stage depot where I met folksingers and painters and writers, and one rummy moonlit night, an armadillo that walked up to me and suddenly leaped several feet into the air. I still am not certain that armadillos can jump, but in the interests of my sanity I hope they can.

• • •

My draft board was in Greenfield, Massachusetts, and it happened to be headed by my former headmaster, Frank Boyden. I asked for and got a reprieve while I tried to get into flight training. The air force put me through some tests, told me I was too dumb to be a pilot, and, months later, that I might be intelligent enough to be a navigator. By then I had decided that tanks were the thing for me. They had rifles at least an order of magnitude larger than anything I had ever fired; perhaps I might shine with them. So I applied for officer training at Fort Knox, was accepted, and let Frank Boyden know I was ready for the army. One fine and cold October day in 1951, I showed up at the train station in Greenfield and there accepted from Mr. Boyden a very small Bible whose covers were fake leather over steel. It was a relief to know that the Great Speckled Bird might intercede between me and a North Korean bullet, but I never had occasion to slip it into my shirt pocket.

My trainers were always adequate and sometimes—I think of the black master sergeant at Fort Dix who took my company through basic training—superb. Several of my commanding officers were of Scottish descent, and when they learned I could play the pipes, sent me to go get them. My battalion commander at Dix, upon seeing me cleaning pots on KP, even ordered that I be freed from that onerous duty so that I could have more time to practice "The Forty-second" and "Blue Bonnets Over the Border."

I got a kick out of barracks humor, the bitching, the groans and expletives when a noncom roused us at dawn with, "Drop your cocks and grab your socks!" But below that a brand-new affection was growing. My life was being controlled as never before, but the controllers were men, not women, and I was responding well. I knew I would have no trouble with weapons, and I didn't—except for my being left-handed in right-handed situations: I discovered, with considerable pain and subsequent hearing loss, that it is not a good idea for a southpaw wearing a steel helmet to fire a submachine gun from the hip: the noise goes directly from the ejection port to the steel pot, where it intensifies and destroys the ears. But I also discovered I could do quite a few things I had been given to understand I could not do. My mechanical abilities, which Ken advised me were minimal, turned out to be above average. So, to my great surprise, did my ability to teach men, and, when in the proper frame of mind, to lead them.

Basic training for sixteen weeks, leadership school for eight, and then Fort Knox for six months of officer candidate school. Fort Knox, just west of Louisville along the Ohio River, was home not only to those who wanted to learn how to be tank commanders but to those who had spent their lives commanding armored units right on up to combat command and beyond. Guderian, the German tactical genius, was studied there, and Rommel, the "Desert Fox" of the North African campaign, along with American heroes like George Patton.

Tanks were everywhere, creeping along the paved roads, tearing across the rolling terrain, and throwing rooster tails of red dust into the air. From a distance, the chittering of their tracks sounded like a very large body of mice practicing mouse songs. Close-up, the crack of their 90 mm rifles compressed the body and shut down the mind. I still remember the drill inside the turret as it swings, the tank commander identifying the target, the kind of shell he wants used—armor-piercing for enemy tanks, high-explosive for personnel—the loader slamming home the round with a cry of "Up!" and the gunner squinting through his sight, flying the "geese" of his rangefinder, and hollering, "On the way!"

Modern tanks, like those used in the Gulf War, are obviously much more sophisticated, much faster and deadlier; I have read that it usually took only one round or, at the most, two, to kill an Iraqi tank. But even ours could regularly topple telephone poles a thousand yards away with shells covering almost a mile in one second. What worried me was the fact that the Korean mountains were terrible for tanks. On top of that, the North Koreans had Russian tanks that could do pretty much to us what we could do to them—turn us into tomato soup.

I thought of myself not as some fuzzy hero out of my fancy but as someone present and accounted for. I did write passionately to my parents about my aching need to serve my country. Perhaps I had read some of Uncle Kenny's letters written just before he had been shot down; I don't remember doing so, but when I compare my letters with his, the similarity is indicative of a little light plagiarism. Still, the emotion itself was honest enough. I can remember standing at attention in a December dusk at Fort Dix, listening to the breaking voice of a trumpet playing Retreat, and watching the flag come down and weeping. But along with patriotism came, at long last, the realization that I didn't much want to die. I told myself I was prepared to do so, but when my orders came, my demeanor lightened visibly.

I was to teach small-unit tank tactics to the trainees pouring through Fort Knox, some on their way to untankable Korean terrain. That I did for a year, explaining maneuvers in the classroom and running a field course that I hope gave a small taste of what tank crews would face in combat. For the final six months of my duty, I served as a flack—a public information officer for my division, the Third Armored. I left Fort Knox in April of 1954 as a first lieutenant.

In the army, I had begun to read Archie's work as work rather than as emanations from on high. I was aware that the length and contentiousness of his public service had distanced him from the literary world. Critics had all but ignored a collection of poems published in 1948. Yet "Years of the Dog" was in it, and so was "Winter Is Another Country." I felt and feel about "Winter" as I do about "You, Andrew Marvell." Death gave energy to both, the death of Archie's father in 1928 and the death of his mother, Patty, in 1947:

> If the autumn would
> End! If the sweet season,
> The late light in the tall trees would
> End! If the fragrance, the odor of
> Fallen apples, dust on the road,
> Water somewhere near, the scent of
> Water touching me; if this would end
> I could endure the absence in the night,
> The hands beyond the reach of hands, the name
> Called out and never answered with my name:
> The image seen but never seen with sight.
> I could endure this all
> If autumn ended and the cold light came.

With the war safely in the past, Archie's old friend J. Parnell Thomas and his associates were busily blowing their horns for a national foxhunt—a red foxhunt. Archie went into action, and this time I knew enough about the matter to fly into my

own dyspeptic fury at the Republican ultraconservatives—
something I've managed to repeat on far too many occasions
since. I kept saying to my mirror that I couldn't understand
why Americans, having faced down an attempt to impose ideology overseas, were in the main content to ignore an attempt
to impose ideology at home.

That was an idea borrowed from Archie. In an essay published in 1949 under the title "The Conquest of the United
States," he wrote, "Never in the history of the world was one
people as completely dominated, intellectually and morally, by
another as the people of the United States by the people of Russia in the four years from 1946 to 1949. . . . [A] people which rec-
ognizes its unity only in its opposition to another people, which
understands its purpose only in its resistance to another purpose, is not a people which has a unity or a purpose of its own.
And it is not a great people whatever its power or its wealth."

Archie was well positioned to take on Joseph McCarthy,
Thomas' successor in the foxhunt. His *Collected Poems,
1917–1952* won praise and prizes, including his second Pulitzer
and the National Book Award. He was gaining renown at Harvard, and his public recognition across the country was remarkably high. In 1952, Archie made McCarthyism the subject of a
verse play called *The Trojan Horse*. Twenty-five years later, when
Houghton Mifflin reissued the work, Archie wrote a new pref-
ace for it. The country, he said, had "believed in itself. It believed in its institutions, its form of government, the human
freedom for which it had fought. And yet, when an insignificant
and unrespected member of the United States Senate launched
an attack on the integrity of the American government, he was

supported by so large a body of American opinion that even his bravest and most admired opponents in the Senate were silenced for a time. . . .

"The whole thing, seen now in retrospect, was a patent fraud—a fraud as obvious as the Trojan horse itself with those armed Greeks hidden in its belly. But even so, there was a mystery in one as in the other. Why had the Trojans taken the huge horse in, breaching their own walls to let it pass? Why had our deluded generation of Americans accepted McCarthy's enormous fabrication, made not of wood but lies, and set it up in the hearing rooms of the Senate to threaten not the communists but the country?"

McCarthy's censure by the Senate so excited me that I couldn't understand why Archie seemed so unmoved by it. I think now that he was simply exhausted by the fight and that he saw what I did not see—that the censure was part of a cycle. He had seen the wave crest and recede before and knew it would come again. He was right.

. . .

At Yale, I had developed a powerful yen for a beautiful young actress. We kissed exactly once. I told her I loved her. I then reflected on the fact that I was a college kid and she, though younger than I, was already well out in the world. It seemed ridiculous to me to keep on trying. We never saw each other after that kiss. To say that as a young adult I was inexperienced with women was to be euphemistic. I was flat ignorant. Ada and Archie could be bawdy with me, and they were fairly relaxed about nudity, but nothing about their relationship served my purpose. To hear them talk, Archie could do no wrong, and Ada was literally above reproach: Archie had put her on a pedestal, declared his inferiority to her in matters of living wisely, and gone about his own business.

It was a performance I was unequipped to duplicate. I can say in hindsight that, lacking a memory of being held and nurtured by the woman who bore me, I naturally was backward in the arts of holding and nurturing a woman I yearned for. Then there was the matter of an education almost totally lacking in female schoolmates after the fourth grade. In their absence, I spent my adolescence in the presence of males fully as horny as myself, many of whom convinced me that they were getting it regularly, thus adding to my lust and to my despair and self-loathing.

My sexual circumstance was by no means unique among young men of my young manhood, but I didn't know that. At twenty-one, I was about as accomplished with women as your average twelve-year-old today. Dancing? I was a master of square dancing and round dancing, but in the matter of more sophisticated navel maneuvers, had nothing to offer but what I could recall from six lessons from the Arthur Murray salon in Washington, D.C. Ada did try to push me into joining the young set by arranging for me to attend a Junior Cotillion ball in New York. All atremble, I entered the hall, which for some reason reminded me of the nave of a cathedral. And there, leaning against a column, gorgeous beyond description, was Jackie Bouvier, the future Queen of Camelot. I took one look at the pack of swains preening before her, any one of whom seemed far ahead of me in matters of dash, and I ran. I ran out of the cathedral or whatever it was. I haven't the faintest idea where I ran to, dressed in my first and last tuxedo, but it would surprise me to learn that it wasn't a bar.

In desperation, I had nodded to a passing prostitute in Rome
during my coming-of-age dash through Europe. All I remember
of that episode is a bidet full of used condoms and contortions
ludicrous enough to bring us both to laughter. By the time I received my steel-jacketed Bible from Frank Boyden, I had slept
with perhaps a half-dozen young women. I had relished each
encounter, but remained a total stranger to the arts of intimacy.

And then, on leave from my training, I met a woman who
went straight to my mind. She was lovely, she was lively. But
what drew me most was her intelligence. It was at once deep
and inviting, and I accepted the invitation. I started out as her
Sunday lunch date, moved in a few months to Saturday night
and, a few months after that, invited her to marry me. I knew I
had serious competition, and the thought I might lose her led
me into duplicity. I described in some detail the kind of life we
would have together, a fabrication that almost herniated my
fancy. Selfishness has always been one of my strong suits, but
never more so than then. She must have seen through my rosy
constructs, but she didn't let on. She agreed to my proposal.

Ada and Archie wanted us to be married at Conway, where
Carolyn had married Ken sixteen years before. My affianced
dressed, as Mimi had, in Sara Murphy's pearl-armored wedding
dress, and I wore my dress pinks. Ken piped the "Highland
Wedding." As we marched out of the church, I suddenly caught
the glint of tiny, pearly teeth. There was C., looking at me with
such love that I walked the next dozen paces as a small boy
wondering where he was going.

We spent the first days of our honeymoon on Nantucket and
then went back to an Uphill Farm vacated by Archie and Ada
for the occasion. My new wife seemed radiant to me, and that

put me in retreat. My love was hopelessly entangled with my lust. I was also a husband, and in the fifties a husband was still looked on as protector and provider. I didn't know how I was going to provide for myself, let alone her. The victim in me could not have been more delighted. You, it said, are now a prisoner.

Perhaps I was acting on precedent. In my copy of Roy Winnick's *Letters of Archibald MacLeish,* Archie writes to a close friend while aboard the ship taking him and Ada to a honeymoon (with cockroaches) on Bermuda: "I have not yet realized in consciousness what change it is that has struck across my life, but my soul knew Wednesday afternoon that there *was* a change and, joyous as it was, I yet felt a certain ache of memory of dear days that are now dear shadows." His friend and he "are now men and the world expects grist of us. No longer may we lie in elm tops and nurture sweet fantasies of suicide—we are now pebbles in the eternal sack set to polishing to the end of time. God shield us all say I." I do not know what either his bride—or mine—was thinking.

I returned to Fort Knox, we found a place to rent, a glassy cabin sitting on a bluff looking north over the Ohio River, and I started thinking about what I might do after the service. The idea of civilian life scared me enough that I was tempted to stay in. But my wife had the good sense to see through that defense. Somehow we found out about something called the Institute of Current World Affairs in New York. It was devoted to sending selected young men overseas to become area generalists. The idea was that they would dive into their chosen culture, meld with it, and write about it in newsletters sent to a small readership in government, academe, and the press.

In late April of 1954, a couple of days after I had left Fort Knox, we were in Chicago having dinner with a very tall and aged man. He wore glasses that magnified his eyes, and he kept flapping one hand at us as he talked. His name was Walter Rogers. The net effect of that and several other discussions was that in June we boarded a Grace Line passenger freighter bound through the Panama Canal to Lima.

We knew enough about learning Spanish to settle in a place where English was rarely heard. That was Arequipa, the political rebel of the south, where it was up to us to begin what we had come for, up to me to understand the difference between a skillet and a brassiere. The city on the Chili River, a green gorge running down the tan slope of the desert, was high for us—7,500 feet—but almost a mile below the altiplano and puna, where we would be spending most of our time. It was the perfect base camp, a mix of coast and sierra, of white elite, the mestizos of the middling classes, and the masses of Quechua and Aymara people drawn from the highlands by what they saw as a better life.

We made friends with *arequipeños,* traveled with them to the cold sea at the foot of the desert, to the wide, still streams of the altitude, where American rainbow trout gone native grew to twenty pounds and more and, here and there, took on the color of the mountain sky on the brightest day. We walked along the river, looked up at the high volcanic peaks east of the city, and learned to say, *"Somos buenos arequipeños, porque no hay malos."*

And we learned to live with a moving earth. There were hundreds of temblors in a given year. Some were mere tickles in the night; the bigger ones sounded like a train overhead. The chickens and dogs kept on the flat roofs of the city heralded them. We would then sprint to stand under what seemed to be our best-built doorway and wait in total helplessness. One afternoon, driving back to town, I topped a rise and saw it seized by one of the train tremors. I was too far away to feel the customary lateral jolts playing with my feet, but Arequipa suddenly seemed slightly out of focus, and a fine, white dust rose to fill the streets like mist.

Shortly before the summer solstice, we left our base camp and drove into the mountains toward Lake Titicaca, past salt lakes filled with hundreds of flamingoes. We turned north between the great ranges of the high country and drove across plains of yellow *ichu* grass, where the air was so thin that the wind was silent and a man with his llamas seemed like a minute away when he was a mile off. Late in the night, we reached Cuzco.

Every few years tourists die in Cuzco. They fly in from Lima, on the coast, and wheeze as they walk streets more than two miles above sea level. On their way to see the glorious ruins of Machu Picchu, they climb even higher before dropping down almost a mile. Then they return in the dusk to a stroke or infarction. After months in Arequipa, my wife and I ran a smaller risk of that. Soon we were able to walk most hills. Sometimes we went up with friends at night to the Incan fortress of Sacsahuaman to sit among perfectly cut and fitted boulders, drink Pisco brandy and watch the moon shadow slide across walls the color of moonlight.

We both wrote newsletters for the Institute of Current World Affairs, but Walter Rogers was not about to give women equal billing in that department, and after a while my wife gave up on him and concentrated on her journal. I have just finished rereading my efforts, wincing at the innocence and obvious discomfort of the first ten, nodding at the slow advance of command. I never did very well on economic conditions. I was better at looking at landscape and the ways of people in it. Ada wrote me at Cuzco that Archie had taken to reading bits of my work to guests at Conway. He had never done that before to my knowledge, probably because there had been next to nothing to choose from.

We had a pickup we called the *"burrito azul,"* and we drove our blue burro all over southern Peru: up and over the cloud line to the east, and down through the "eyebrow" of the jungle into the jungle itself, along mud roads tracked by tapirs and jaguars and sheeted with the wings of living butterflies. Then west, past rocks lacquered with minerals, and down, jagging through switchbacks to the coastal town of Nazca and along the Pan-American Highway to Lima. My wife was new to driving, so I took the wheel. Sooner or later, the mountain roads would run along the rims of river-cut gorges hundreds or thousands of feet deep. The rules of those roads said that ascending vehicles had the right of way, that at night all oncoming vehicles had to take turns illuminating the roadway with their headlights. On our early voyages, we screamed as I braked in the gravel to avoid a truck or one of the rocks a trucker had used as a wheel chock and left where it was. After a while we stopped screaming—except when we thought we might be on the verge of going from area generalists to general aerialists. We never went over the edge, but many did. Their passing was noted by crosses, by thigh bones, even skulls, used as markers. Not much could be done about the kill rate when it was the custom of truckers and bus drivers to save money by turning off their engines, putting their transmissions in neutral, and placing themselves and their cargo—much of it human—in the hands of higher beings. Even my relatively careful piloting was too much for the blue burro. Upon completing a weeklong trip, I was informed by a mechanic that there was but one bolt holding bed to body.

We were so far from family, so much on our own. We danced the mountain dances. We rode horseback into remote country to see people wearing tunics that hadn't changed since the Incas wore them. We laughed and we loved. Halfway through the second year of our fellowship, my wife discovered that she was pregnant. I dropped into the kind of fear that erases love and reason. Mr. Rogers had been talking about a three-year fellowship, but that was for two people, not three. I was counting on him to give me what I needed to earn a living in Latin America. The question, in the grip of that fear, was not what we were going to do but what I was going to do.

The doctors in Lima told my wife that for health reasons she would be better off in the United States. She then gave me the gift of insisting that I stay to finish up the second year, and I didn't hesitate to accept it. I went back to the jungle. I took my only trip into the northern mountains, through the most beautiful valleys I have ever been in: green, terraced land, eucalyptus trees, a river, and, rising to over 22,000 feet, giant Huascarán. In July of 1956, I flew home. I felt as though I were leaving home for a foreign country.

My wife was staying at Uphill Farm. I was still so captivated by life there that I had thought it a splendid idea. It was not. She was caught in the clockwork of house schedules. At a time when she needed simple kindnesses, she received almost formal attention. Ada was the perfect hostess, which made my wife a guest.

She decided to fly back to her own family home to have the baby while I looked for work.

Nobody seemed interested in Latin America, not even the people in Washington whom Archie wrote to. At the end of my rope, I contacted a family friend at the CIA. I had heard a good deal about the agency in Latin America. I knew about its role in the overthrow of the president of Guatemala in 1954, and thought it had been immoral and stupid. Many of my friends in Peru had thought I was a spook. Going back as the real thing wasn't something I looked forward to. But at least I'd be where I wanted to be.

I was all but ready to mail application papers to my friend when an offer arrived in the mail. It came—I could not believe it—from *Fortune*. Working there would be walking right back onto my father's turf, but if I were going to be a family man, I said to myself with something short of resolve, I'd better act like one. And as soon as those words were out, I heard Ada's voice toughening me, as she always did when she spied a tremble in my lower lip. "Poor boy," she would say in comic concern. "Poor boy, far from home."

Show Me My Guilt

ON THE NIGHT OF DECEMBER 11, 1958, AT THE ANTA Theater on West Fifty-second Street in New York, Christopher Plummer and Raymond Massey walked out on a strange stage to begin the prologue of a strange play. There was no curtain. Above them was a reach of canvas, part of a circus tent. Stairs rose to an open landing and then up and out to a kind of crow's nest. Below that was a small circular floor holding a bare table and some chairs. That was earth. A construct of balls or bulbs on wire orbits hung over the table, representing the cosmos.

I'm pretty sure something like that set had been in Archie's mind for decades, certainly since the day in the twenties on the coast of France when he and his young family had gone to that rickety circus and he had left with the words "quite unexpectedly" nudging him toward "The End of the World" and "nothing, nothing, nothing—nothing at all." At the ANTA Theater that night, the tent would disappear, leaving nothing but Archie's constant archetype: one man alone and naked under the stars. The man's name, and the play's, was J.B.

Young Plummer and old Massey played failed actors, staying alive by hawking, respectively, popcorn and balloons under a not very big tent. The show, Archie wrote in introducing a recording of *J.B.*, "has traveled through the towns and cities of the earth, year after year, time out of mind, playing the Old Testament story of the sufferings of Job.

"Dissatisfied, as actors often are, with the interpretation of the story, they make up their minds, late one evening when the show is over and the tent empty, to play it themselves as they think it should be played." Massey, "Mr. Zuss," decided he would play God, leaving Plummer, "Nickles," with no choice but Satan (Nickles had hoped to play Job). "The two," Archie writes, "take on themselves the wager of the Book of Job: Satan's wager that if God will strip Job of everything he has, Job, the perfect and upright man, will curse God to His face."

Mr. Zuss and Nickles messed around on the stage, afraid of what they wanted to do, cracking weak jokes to hide the fear. They talked about the play rather than playing it. Mr. Zuss mostly took the higher and, to me, duller ground. There was not much there to work with at first but pomposity. Nickles was the more interesting. He had been around, had seen the human condition of our mid-century, with its wars and other obsceni-ties. He knew how to look. He was the one who riddled the rid-dle of God and good:

> I heard upon his dry dung heap
> That man cry out who cannot sleep:
> "If God is God he is not good,
> If God is good He is not God;
> Take the even, take the odd,
> I would not sleep here if I could
> Except for the little green leaves in the wood
> And the wind on the water."

When they finally began, some voice offstage snickered at them. That shocked them, got them poking around in old prop trunks for the masks the regular cast used. They found them: the

Godmask, hairy, ancient, wild-eyed; the Satanmask, staring, its agonized mouth in a cruel rictus. They tried them on and this time the offstage voice guffawed. More alarums. Finally the time came when the masks themselves spoke, in huge voices:

> *Godmask:* Whence comest thou?

> *Satanmask:* From going to and fro in the earth . . .
> And from walking up and down in it.

> *Godmask:* Hast thou considered my servant Job
> That there is none like him on the earth
> A perfect and an upright man, one
> That feareth God and escheweth evil?

Plummer and Massey disappeared in darkness. Light poured down on the table, on J.B., his wife, Sarah, and their five children, about to sit down to a turkey dinner. I sat there in that packed house, hearing nothing—no coughing, shifting in seats, no breathing. I was part of a collective quiet Christopher Plummer talked about years later: "That's, I suppose, the greatest feeling in the theater," he said, "that they're so with you that they're silent."

Archie's Job was a businessman, a banker, not the proprietor of camels and sheep. His wife was Sarah, named for Sara Murphy and her sufferings, not the nameless woman of the Bible whose only purpose was to bear Job's children. His disasters were all around us in the world outside the theater: the son killed in a war, the son and daughter killed by a drunken driver, the daughter raped and slaughtered by a junkie, the daughter crushed by a nuclear blast. His comforters were our comforters: the priest, the political ideologue, the therapist. His boils could have been biblical boils—or the sores of radiation sickness.

Archie, speaking three years before *J.B.* opened, in the church where he and Ada had been married, said God "had need of the suffering of Job—had need of it for himself as *God.* . . . Which means that in the conflict between God and Satan, in the struggle between good and evil, God stakes his supremacy as God upon man's fortitude and love. . . . Our labor always, like Job's labor, is to learn through suffering to love . . . to love even that which lets us suffer."

I was not sure the audience walked away pondering that difficult lesson. I was, as I had always been, moved more by Archie's song than by his moral, and the lyrics I wanted for my memory were Nickles'. As we made our way to a cast party at a basement Chinese restaurant near the theater, I wondered what the critics had thought. New York was in the midst of a newspaper strike, and no one was sure if enough positive reaction could get through to keep the show going.

It was a tense party, for tense people: Alfred de Liagre, Jr., the show's producer; Elia Kazan, the director; the playwright and family and friends—including John Steinbeck, carrying a bull's pizzle as a cane—and the cast, minus one. Then Christopher Plummer appeared. My memory says he made his appearance undoing a kind of cape. He walked straight to where Archie sat at a small table, went down on one knee, and flared the cloth before him in a gesture Gerald Murphy would have admired. A great shout went up. Plummer had heard the news from a radio or television station. The reviews were good. Brooks Atkinson of the *Times* had written, "Looking around at the wreckage and misery of the modern world, Mr. MacLeish has written a fresh and exalting morality play that has great stature. In an inspired performance on Thursday evening, it seemed to be one of the memorable works of the century as verse, as drama and as spiritual inquiry." *J.B.* would play for a year in New York, another on the road. It remains in production somewhere around the world to this day. It would earn Archie far more than the rest of his works combined; the book has sold more than one hundred thousand copies in English alone. The play garnered Archie his third Pulitzer. It won a Tony award, as did Kazan.

· · ·

J.B.'s cast gave Archie a present he mounted on a wall in Conway, a photograph, taken at rehearsal and signed by everyone. It showed the playwright alone in the banks of empty seats, listening, his head in his hands. The caption is Job's cry: "Show me my guilt, O God!" I needed no one to show me my guilt: I had been fired from *Fortune* a few months before *J.B.* opened. I had thought I was doing fairly well at the beginning of my short stay there. The managing editor had commended me for a couple of pieces. But where I missed the mark was in the corporate story, the meat of the magazine as it was then. It seems I couldn't find the formula for turning the business decisions of company managers into suspenseful copy. That was no surprise to me; as a capitalist tool, I had no edge. I had grown up hearing my father rail against corporations and corporate executives. I had seen enough of the depredations of foreign interests in Peru to develop my own dislike for business as usual. I knew it, and the

Andrew MacLeish as an old man.

Martha (Patty) MacLeish and *(right to left)* Archie,
Kenny, Norman, and Ishbel.

Archie *(right)* and Kenny in France in 1918.

Uphill Farm, looking west across Ada's gardens.

Archie and Ada on the east terrace, late thirties.

Mimi at thirteen.

Uphill with Archie, just before World War II.

The bowman brothers, a year or two before the stalking.

MacLeishes at Yale: a '15 and a '30.

Weird Hall in winter.

Upping the volume.

Morellen *(left)* and Meg.

Archie with JFK, weeks before the President was shot.

Elizabeth can say the most unusual things.

Archie as an old man.

knowledge made the eighteen months of misplacement seem
like a hundred. It was no comfort to see many of my colleagues
struggling under the combined weight of tough deadlines and
tougher editing, their stress manifested by the sharp rise of flush
rates in the lavatories as closing times drew near.

My toughest task, next to telling my wife of our plight, was
telling Archie. I needn't have worried: he was quiet and kind—
mostly, I think, out of love, but also because of his intense dislike
for the way he felt the patriarchy at Time, Inc. had grown so at
odds with individual creativity. He put out his feelers as I put out
mine, and he hit pay dirt first. A friend of his was backing a
Latin American newsmagazine called *Vision* in New York and
Visión from Mexico south, and there was an opening. As it happened, I knew the managing editor. I talked with him and joined
up, whereupon Archie wrote expressing his delight and suggesting that I become the best American reporter in Latin America.

I was back where I wanted to be, at about the same salary. It
was a gift, but I was in no mood for gifts. After all, I had but
recently been working for one of the jewels of journalism. *Visión*
by comparison was helter-skelter, a collection of people from
all over the hemisphere. We had a courtly Argentinian and an
Uruguayan who wore no underwear and had once lived in a
working windmill outside Montevideo. We had a Spaniard and
a Mexican. We had a clutch of Cubans. They probably knew
more about what Fidel was up to than many in our federal intelligence establishment—and almost as much about what the anti-
Castro forces had in mind, including the imbecility of the Bay of
Pigs. We had names that translated as Fortune Bald and Sweet
Mary Sardines. It was a rich mix, but for an embarrassingly long
time I remained too hangdog to see it. What got me was the ob-

vious: I had failed my father. Just because he didn't curse me for being fired from *Fortune* was no reason I shouldn't curse myself.

After a while the self-flagellation mutated into hypochondria. When the stress of deadlines went to the stomach, a favorite residence for MacLeish stress, I read the result as cancer. A couple of belts of barium later, my doctor told me all was well, but I wouldn't believe him. One day at the office, I stood before a mirror and stuck out my tongue as far as it would go. Dear God! Lumps back there in the dimness! I was hysterical by the time I phoned for medical help and described what was obviously my terminal condition. There was a long pause. Then came the verdict: "Mr. MacLeish," a tired voice said. "Those are your taste buds." The silliness went on for a couple of years more before a physician suggested that I seek psychological assistance. I didn't take his advice for another twenty years.

I rose in *Visión*'s ranks to become special projects editor. That meant that I wrote long reports—on Latin American land reform, tax reform, common market maneuvers—which appeared in Spanish in the magazine and in English in little pamphlets whose distribution strategy remained a mystery to me (copies even reached Mac Bundy at the White House). When I was selected to go along on good-neighbor tours of Eisenhower and then Kennedy, I found the travel anything but broadening. We in the press plane were hermetically separated from all reality except handouts and various photo and spin ops.

I did end up as pool reporter for Ike's parade through Montevideo, during which the police, responding to a few protest demonstrations, soaked the route with enough tear gas to cause The Man to plop down on the seat of his open car and whip out his handkerchief. I related this trivial event to my colleagues and found myself being grilled for details as if some fiends, obviously communist fiends, had snatched Ike and borne him off. I never did get to tell them about how he had walked into the reception in his honor blowing his nose, mopping his red face, and grinning one of the best grins in American presidential history.

In August of 1961, in Mexico City, doing research on my land-reform piece, I boarded a plane bound for Guatemala. We had just reached cruising altitude when the left wing dipped and we turned east, over the Yucatán peninsula and out to sea. A stewardess came down the aisle with the news: there was a man in the cockpit with a gun, and we were going to Cuba. That was one problem. Another was that we were heading for José Martí airport outside Havana, and there appeared to be some doubt as to whether the runways there were long enough to accommodate our 707. Yet another was the nature of my research: I had some pages in my bag that were quite critical of the Castro model of land reform. These I disposed of in the chemical toilet aft and returned to my seat with a light dawning: the fear that so often threatened to undo me was fear of what might happen; I had much less trouble with fear of what *was* happening.

The landing was one of the smoothest I've experienced, and it took up every inch of runway. We saw the hijacker being led off under arrest—we heard later that he was an Algerian who had decided he could best protest French activities in his country by commandeering us—and we were then led to a waiting room. We sat and stood around for hours before word came that we were reboarding for a flight, not to Guatemala but to Miami. It turned out that our departure had been hastened by the presence on our plane of Colombia's foreign minister, later its president, Julio César Turbay Ayala. He had been taken into Havana for a chat with Fidel, who came back to the airport with him to see him back on board and give our pilot an *abrazo*. That done, the Cubans loaded each of us down with an armful each of gladioli (immediately confiscated in Miami as possible agents of biological menace) and a bottle of Bacardi in a carton that proclaimed: LET'S GO TO CUBA, THE INVITING ISLAND NEXT DOOR.

Having decided to fly to New York to write up the hijacking, I called Conway to reassure everyone. I talked with my wife, then Archie, then Ken—who said he'd been about to fly down to Havana to rescue me. I told him I didn't think the Cuban Air Force would have welcomed him. What I wanted to say to him, what kept jigging in my mind all the way home, was: stick to your own goddamn adventures.

. . .

Home was by now a smallish old house in northern Westchester County, New York, with a huge oak tree and a brook out back. My wife and I had moved in about six months after our daughter Meg was born and two and a half years before the arrival of our second child, Morellen. I thought it was perfect then, but now wonder how I could have been so deluded. My wife, having come through a difficult pregnancy and birth, settled into a kind of life diametrically opposed to what she had enjoyed before. Instead of places to go and articles to write, she had diapers to change. I helped on weekends, but during the week, I was out of the house by seven-thirty to catch the Ossining train to New York. Sometimes at *Fortune,* and more often at *Visión,* I had to stay late, getting home well after the daughters were in bed.

That didn't seem to bother me. I may have screwed up on my

first try, I thought, but I'm still working in New York, the biggest of brass rings. *Visión* was getting to be fun; the hijacking had given me new cachet there. Besides, all around us, young comers were living precisely as we were. Most of the men I knew seemed to accept the crowded trains as a symbol of their success: we were kings of our road; we knew how to fold our newspapers so we could read them in the jam and arrive in the city bright with knowledge. Weekends were for blowing off the accumulated steam. That, at midcentury, was the good life, the divided life that was to catch the imagination of novelists from Sloan Wilson to John Updike.

In the Andes we had learned to live at intimate scales, within observable distances. In Westchester we lived at the small end of a great electronic ear trumpet, deafened by reports, forecasts and analyses of events, and often unable to devise reactions that made sense. In 1962 I spent days carefully cleaning and stocking our cellar to shelter us from Russian missiles based in Cuba, knowing that we would be about as safe, tucked under the beams of our old wooden house, as our elder daughter would be under the old wooden desks of her school—her assigned station in the event of attack. When Kennedy was killed a year later, the first thing I did when the shock had worn off was to cancel my subscription to several periodicals published in Havana. For a time, news accounts had me convinced that the assassination was a reply to the Bay of Pigs invasion, and I was afraid of being caught reading enemy propaganda.

The following spring, something new came into my life—a visiting delegation with employ in mind. They were from Cornell, and they wanted to launch some sort of yearlong program to point up the university's strong ties to Latin America, and they needed someone to head it. I went up to Ithaca, looked down at Cayuga Lake, long and deep, stood on bridges over gorges filled with falling water, and itched for the job. It would take two years—one to plan and help raise funds, one to manage the results. My wife liked the place and the plan, so we made the third of nine major moves during our marriage.

It took some time to adjust to the surprisingly fierce politics of a university, but in the end there was sufficient cooperation among key players to make a success out of the Cornell Latin American Year. We had conferences and concerts and we topped everything off with an exhibit of contemporary Latin American painting at the Guggenheim Museum in New York. The art critic Hilton Kramer was not pleased. For all I know, he may have been right, but I loved the show.

The first and closest friend I made in Ithaca was an ecologist with not a gram of interest in things Hispanic. We fished together for river trout and lake muskellunge, and I grew fascinated with his ability to see nature whole. I asked for books to help me understand the process, and my friend gave me Aldo Leopold and Rachel Carson and then pointed me at the university library.

Everything but my ego knew I had found my work. I began to explore how I could stay at Cornell, earning my keep somewhere in the administration and building a competence in what was still called conservation. But when another group came knocking at my door, this one headed by David Rockefeller, I laid *Silent Spring* aside and headed back to New York. I would be the first executive director of the Center for Inter-American Relations. I would wear suits and bright shoes, and I would associate with the best people. I would be one of "David's multipliers." And in little more than a year I would realize my mistake. It turned out that my major responsibility lay in refurbishing the Center's building on Park Avenue, a Stanford White structure whose previous tenant had been the Soviet mission to the United Nations. I spent most of my time with a decorator, shopping till we dropped in one pricey antiques store after another. In a year and a half, I was in David Rockefeller's office telling him I was not the right man for the job. David was, as always, kind and sympathetic. He said he hoped I hadn't been wasting my time.

Yale needed someone to handle its foundation relations. Yale also had a Forestry School renowned for its ecological studies. So I took what I had begun in Ithaca and went to New Haven. Within months, someone was at my door again. Yale's president, Kingman Brewster, wanted me to help run his office for him while his regular chief of staff was completing the planning for the school's switch to coeducation. I protested that I didn't know anything about the university, that I was bound to leave a mess for him to clean up. He said he wanted me. I agreed to give it a try. The press release made me look like some sort of Renaissance robot, capable of handling anything while needing nothing in the way of sustenance or sleep.

• • •

By the time I went to work for Kingman early in 1969, Archie and Ada had turned their life from a carefully scripted play into something approaching a Broadway production. There was less spontaneity, less fun. Schedules were tighter. Parental opinions became pronouncements. More and more, we were told that there was only one university and that was Harvard, only one poet or politician who made their grade. Judgments came so

firm and fast that at last we understood what was never said—
that there was only one way of doing things, and that way was
theirs.

Uphill Farm was still such a sanctuary for me, a place where I
could be so well served, that I all but refused to judge the effects
of my parents' judgment on others. My elder daughter, Meg,
had the honesty to fill me in years after damage had been done.
As a child at Conway, she said, she saw me acting more as Ada
and Archie's son than as her father. As a result, "the little kid in
me [still] sees you as an extension of a family that . . . scared the
pants off me."A lot of the grandchildren had similar reactions, I
think. Alec Campbell once overheard a snippet of conversation
between one of Mimi's young sons and a friend. "But how,"
asked the friend, "can you pee on Archibald MacLeish when
you don't even know where he lives?"

In the summer of 1962, CBS filmed Archie in conversation
with his close friend Mark Van Doren. They roamed around
Uphill Farm, breakfasting above the garden, walking over to
Archie's work house and down to the lower pond, talking and
talking. I have a copy of the film. After thirty-six years, it jumps
a little and the sound wanders out of synch now and then, but it
brings back that time and those two retired teachers and working poets. The film catches Archie at seventy. *J.B.* and Harvard
are behind him, but he still has almost twenty more years to go.
His face is young, his voice is young. (It is always, when I hear it
in recording, higher than the voice I remember.) With Mark
there, Archie is more relaxed than he would be in solo performance, yet I can still catch his assertiveness. He sits on the prow
of his chair, leaning forward, stroking his hands, making circles

in the air with them. The underarms of his shirt are wet with sweat.

Mark is quiet, mindful. He says he likes to do nothing some days. That's beyond my power, says Archie. Mark says he loves the monotony of passing time. Archie says the one thing he can't stand is monotony. Then Mark says something I love. He says he likes to remember that "the day is more important than you are." Mark sits still and stands still. Archie moves, he shows off. He fly-fishes for trout in the lower pond, trout stocked only weeks before, courtesy of CBS. His technique in casting for and landing the docile fish shows he is a beginner at the art. At the end of the film, he dives in and swims, and there his expertise is instantly obvious. "You're crazy if you don't come in," he calls to Mark, knowing full well that Mark is not a water man. I watch him and see the origins of my own penchant for performance.

Conway certainly helped keep Archie's persona in fighting trim, but his main training camp was at the Mill Reef Club in Antigua. He and Ada built a house on that lovely Leeward Island early in the fifties. It sat on a small point, where you could feel the air, and watch the Atlantic blow by into the Caribbean basin. They called it La Desirade, after Columbus' favorite landfall in the New World. For a while, Mill Reef was peopled by the merely affluent. In time, though, what had happened to the Murphys' Antibes happened to the MacLeishes' Antigua: the truly wealthy came and saw and moved in. They were there by the time I saw the place in 1957, and in greater strength when my wife and I made our second and last visit in 1964. We left our children home both times, since my parents said they took alarm at the thought of youngsters toddling about that close to the sea.

Archie didn't seem to mind the rich at all, which at first surprised me. I still carried his image of the tycoons in one poem of *Frescoes for Mr. Rockefeller's City,* published in the early thirties: "You have just beheld the Makers Making America: / They screwed her scrawny and gaunt with their seven-year panics: / they bought her back on their mortgages old-whore cheap: They fattened their bonds at her breasts till the thin blood ran from them." I remembered the Mr. Mellon of the poem ("Mister-Mellon-is-represented-as-a-symbolic-figure-in-aluminum- / Strewing-bank-stocks-on-a-burnished-stair.")—and met his descendant on the island, along with a Gould and the CEO of General Electric, who played a form of killer croquet with Archie. I liked them all very much, but could never rid myself of the idea that they were copies and that the originals were back home making more money. I now think Archie liked these people because he and they were successful and because success, perhaps more than misery, loves and needs company.

In fact, Archie actually studied the rich on Antigua. They became characters in a short verse play, *This Music Crept by Me upon the Waters.* To Archie, they were after "a New World Capri or Antibes where they could build their houses off beyond the winter and play golf and bridge and meet for cocktails every evening. What they found was something altogether different— beauty of a kind they could not always bear: deep-water islands blazing with high veils of light . . . islands they knew they could not live in, could not leave."

A couple of years before he and Ada discovered Antigua, Archie wrote to Ernest Hemingway that Conway was fine, but

"It's water I want and I never see water. Somehow I seem to have buggered my life up that way and I don't see what I can do about it." Archie found his water. He lived by it, off beyond winter—but only during the winter months. Lived, and drank. As far back as I can remember, alcohol was Archie's divine emollient. It lubricated sprightly discourse at the dinner table and out on the terraces and down by the lower pond. He would, on occasion, slyly "slug" a male guest to see how he could handle his booze. I never saw Archie out of control, and he expected his children to follow his example. He laughed more and used his hands more when he was working on a martini, but that was about it. I never saw Ada even approach anything demanding control: she drank sparingly, not wanting, she would say, to get "flushed and chatty."

The drinking at Antigua was a form of dueling. The weapon of choice was rum, slightly lightened by simple syrup and lime juice and dusted over with grated nutmeg. It was delicious and devilishly mood altering. I bid my second farewell to the island hung over and dry and with a left leg that seemed a trifle numb. In time, I came to connect the bibulous life of Mill Reef with a string of ulcers Archie suffered, at least one of which was of the serious, bleeding kind. Archie attributed his initial attack to the aftereffects of his fight with McCarthy, but I believe it was more a reaction to Mount Gay rum.

Just before I went to New Haven, Archie told me he was working on another play, this one based on his friend Stephen Vincent Benét's story "The Devil and Daniel Webster." Four years later, I sat on a slope behind the Conway town hall and watched local actors put on Archie's *An Evening's Journey to Conway, Massachusetts.* The play brought the town alive through the eyes of a teenager who thought it was dead and worth leaving. Archie told me it was one of the most satisfying things he had done, and I thought the new venture might be in the same league. But I soon learned that it wasn't going to be a verse play. It was going to be a musical, and Bob Dylan was going to write the music.

Dylan did write some songs, but apparently they didn't fit. So what was to be a musical became a conventional play written by a poet who by his own admission was not a conventional playwright. The result, *Scratch,* opened in New York in May of 1971. It began, as *J.B.* had, with a family at table, in this case a bounteous New England table, and it moved into the fable of Webster helping a neighbor get out of a bargain with the Devil. As I had rooted for Christopher Plummer as Satan, so I rooted for Will Geer as Scratch. He was funny, he was sly, he was what I secretly liked in myself. Webster was passionate, yes, but his heat tended to do odd things to his gravitas.

No Chinese restaurant for this cast party. We went to the top of the Time-Life Building and ate and drank and looked out at black air. I had brought my pipes, and somewhere around midnight Ken and I stood on Sixth Avenue and took turns skirling to the thinning traffic. No Brooks Atkinson the next morning. The *Times,* in the person of Clive Barnes, dumped on *Scratch.* The review was vituperative. The writing was pedestrian, Barnes said, the issues of the play "pseudo-moral," the construction of the work "simply deplorable." Twelve years later, a few months before Archie died, I went to Dartmouth for another performance of *Scratch,* which was not played but read by actors sitting on high stools. It read beautifully.

The morning after the New York opening, I was lying in bed
in our hotel, inventing punishments for Mr. Barnes. Archie
knocked and opened the door. His face looked cheerful, his
voice was quiet. He wanted us to know that the play would close
in a few days. He sounded almost relieved, and perhaps he was.
I think he had known almost from the beginning that the play
was a mistake, the odds of the gamble too long. And yet, closing
on eighty, he had to try Broadway once more, to persist. A few
years before, he had brought out a thin book called, after Yeats,
"The Wild Old Wicked Man" and Other Poems. There were poems
to his friends, to Mark Van Doren, living close by, and to Ernest
Hemingway, dead by shotgun suicide. And there was this title
poem:

> Too old for love and still to love!—
> Yeats's predicament and mine—all men's:
> the aging Adam who must strut and shove
> and caper his obscene pretence . . .
>
> And yet, within the dry thorn grove,
> singer to singer in the dusk, there cries
> (Listen! Ah, listen, the wood dove!)
> something conclusion never satisfies;
>
> and still when day ends and the wind goes down
> and not a tree stirs, not a leaf,
> some passion in the sea beats on
> and on . . .
>   (Oh, listen, the sea reef!)

Too old for love and still to long . . .
for what? For one more flattering proof
the flesh lives and the beast is strong?—
once more upon the pulse that hammering hoof?

Or is there something the persistent dove,
the ceaseless surges and the old man's lust
all know and cannot say? Is love

what nothing concludes, nothing must,
pure certainty?

      And does the passionate man
most nearly know it when no passion can?
Is this the old man's triumph, to pursue
impossibility—and take it too?

Circling the Square

I HAD SPENT JUST EIGHT MONTHS AT YALE WHEN Kingman Brewster invited me to transfer to his office. During that time, I had learned which departments and schools of the university needed what in the way of foundation support, and I had helped to bring in a bit over a million dollars toward those ends. My friend McGeorge Bundy had left the White House for the Ford Foundation, and I sent on several proposals to him and his colleagues, singing to myself, "Fordy Fundy's / Got Mac Bundy. / Ain't that keen? / All that green? / To ease our hypertension / Let's ask for a subvention. / Gee, Dave Bell! / Thanks, that's swell."

I didn't think I'd have too much trouble dealing with the president's office; all I needed, I said to myself, was time to grow into the job. If self-satisfaction hadn't blinded me, I might have seen that time was the one thing I couldn't have. Schools all around the country were disintegrating. I knew that. The racial explosions of Watts in 1965, and Detroit two years later, had gone straight to student sensibilities. So did the savage mess of Vietnam. Berkeley had blown up a couple of months before I went to Yale. A couple of months after my arrival, I was startled to see a photograph of Steven Muller, the man I worked for during the Cornell Latin American Year, walking step for step with a young black man carrying a shotgun. Steve had been mediating a settlement in the takeover of the university's administration building.

In January of 1969, the front page of the *Yale Daily News* carried a photograph of a man looking older in the pate and younger in the face than his forty years. The headline read NEW ASSISTANT MACLEISH OVERSEES EXTERNAL AFFAIRS. Immediately below the photograph was a story about black students taking over a building at Brandeis University and shutting down its switchboard. Just prior to their sit-in, the *Daily News* said, the Brandeis protesters had been visited by veterans of the student takeover at San Francisco State the previous May.

Time? What time? As it turned out, about a year—a year of middling troubles building toward a couple of months of the real thing. My own trouble during most of the interim was that I couldn't bring myself to pay attention to what Yale students were thinking and doing. Student activism in my day had meant cheering at football games. Nineteen years later, it meant organizing, serving on committees, pressuring authority to change.

I see now as I didn't then that these people, these *young* people, were doing what Archie repeatedly had told me to do when I was young. They were living their lives. I was the one who was letting my life live me, who was clinging to unclingable stasis. Faced with Vietnam, racism, the excesses of capitalism, the assassinations of Martin Luther King and Bobby Kennedy, I raged when no one could hear me and otherwise limited myself to well-mannered argument. I did not act, either alone or in concert with others. I considered confrontation beneath me, which is to say that I was afraid of it and condemned it in others as a threat to the thin veneer of civilization in the country—my civilization. And, of course, it was a threat, one far more potent than I imagined: what was demanded in the streets and on the campuses of the sixties—less emphasis on tradition and reason and more on experimentation and the emotions—has become part of the national culture of the nineties. Now, in turnabout, it is the radical conservatives who are calling for social conflict to set things right.

I started out thinking that Kingman Brewster would most likely lean toward defending the established faith. He had trained as a corporate lawyer, had taught law at Harvard before moving to the presidency of Yale. A handsome, fleshy man, he was only nine years my senior but infinitely more polished. He could don or doff the patrician mask to full effect and with perfect timing. He was full of humor. Yet although he could be zany, there was a gravity—no, a purpose—to him that was always evident.

I had never met anyone who was so involved in his place of business. He loved it and so knew it with a special passion. He walked Yale as a watchman might, noticing, noting. He could explain the Yale corporation and faculty to me so I thought I understood them. He treated students neither as subordinates nor as equals, but as fellows in one of the world's most important undertakings. He wanted things his way, and very often he had them. Speaking to male undergraduates about the females soon to join them, he said, without a hint of a smile in his voice or on his face, that in the days before coeducation Yale "had been a gay place." The young men hooted and sniggered, but the president faced them down and went on with his talk. "Gay" was a word he was not prepared to yield entirely to its new usage.

A classmate of mine was provost of the university, and when I was stumped by an academic problem or process, I talked with him. But when I wanted to feel the fire that moved an increasing number of students, I went to William Sloane Coffin, the university chaplain. It was Bill who was advising students on the draft, who talked to them about what was wrong with the country and right with their souls, who talked about them to Old Blue alumni in a way that flared their nostrils and reddened their faces. I could say to Bill, as I often did, that as an amanuensis to the president of Yale University, I made a good cook. He would look at me and give me a grin of encouragement, or understanding—or, quite possibly, agreement.

I kept my footing for a while. The alumni magazine needed a new editor, and I managed to persuade William Zinsser to take that on. I figured out who were the president's strongest supporters and most effective detractors on the faculty. I handled the less important portion of Kingman's mail and helped him keep his impossible schedule. Once, when he had wedged in a meeting with a leader of New Haven's black community just before he was due to catch the train to New York, he asked me to barge in, his bags in my hands, at precisely twenty minutes to the hour. This I did, with a breathless you're-going-to-be-late admonition. Whereupon Kingman's guest slowly swung his head to look at me. "Hello, flunky," he said. I like to think he didn't know how right he was.

Military training on American college campuses was drawing more fire every month, sometimes literally: ROTC facilities were being threatened and, before the crisis had subsided, some would be destroyed. Kingman decided to call an informal meeting at Yale's new indoor hockey rink to give feelings a chance to blow. I heard him tell someone he wanted no media coverage. Hours before the event, as I was tearing around the office trying to solve logistical problems, Yale's public information director showed up with a reporter from CBS and asked if the network could cover the meeting.

Assuming that Kingman had changed his mind about coverage, I gave the go-ahead without checking. When I told Kingman, he yelled something about people not doing what he told them to do. He didn't yell at me, he yelled at the wall—and that was all he ever said about the matter. In an instant, he was joking with me, which merely made me feel like more of a dolt. I stewed until dinnertime, then went looking for Kingman to offer my resignation. He was busy with his own plans, so I waited.

More than two thousand people showed up at the hockey rink—students, faculty, trustees and administrators. I sat up near the roof, contemplating my sin and my fate. I paid more attention to the CBS camera crew than I did to the speeches and protest songs going on down on the floor. A vote on the continuance of ROTC at Yale was called for, and I winced. Undoubtedly the protesters would have the edge, and I would be the one to have opened the process to the public.

Tally takers went up and down the aisles. When the totals were passed up to the presiding faculty member, he paused as if confronted by enormity. I shut my eyes. Then he said he couldn't believe what he was about to announce: the vote was 1,286 for continuance, 1,286 against. Kingman doubled over in laughter. The crowd hollered and hissed and whistled. My blackened soul revived. Here was something I would never have expected from that evening. Here was, for the moment, comedy trumping the tensions of confrontation and response. Here, for the delectation of late-night viewers, was a certifiable bright moment from the famously troubled American campus, courtesy of my mistake.

The trustees decided to end ROTC activities at Yale anyway, but that didn't seem to dampen the general infatuation with unrest. A certain surreality set in. Demands increasingly replaced requests. Instead of corresponding with the president's office by mail, student groups took to marching over to Woodbridge Hall, assuming postures of ire and defiance, and all but nailing their theses to the door.

On one occasion I was selected to deliver something, I can't remember what, to a vociferous delegation from the School of Art and Architecture. It was decided that I needed some protection, which was provided in the form of several husky campus policemen. They formed ranks behind me in the narrow hall, and in so doing pushed me flat against the door. When one of their number reached around me and pressed the latch, I shot out into the sunlight like a cake of soap squeezed from a wet fist. I gathered up what dignity remained to me, but it didn't do anyone much good. The students, as unprepared as I for my airborne arrival, couldn't help themselves: it's hard to be militant and mirthful at the same time.

Truly serious trouble blew in from Chicago as the winter of 1970 turned to spring. Bobby Seale, cofounder of a four-year-old movement called the Black Panthers, had been in court there along with other dissidents hauled in for leading street confrontations during the Democratic National Convention of 1968. Seale was extradited to New Haven to face charges, along with a varying number of his colleagues, of having tortured and murdered one of his associates near the city. The trial would be held in a courthouse just two blocks from the Yale campus. Hardly was that news out than the Black Panthers organized a defense committee to aid Seale and his codefendants. Spokesmen spoke, in the kind of hyperbole specifically designed to pester honkey ears: the trial was trumped up by whites to keep the black community on its knees. All power to the people!

This was catnip to the dissidents in the Yale student body. Some were active in the civil rights movement in the South, more were supporters. Here was their cause come home. Here was injustice next door, far more accessible than the obscene war half a world away. Excitement grew as the rest of the nation began to focus on New Haven. Within weeks, radical students on dozens of campuses made plans to attend a rally on New Haven green on the first of May, May Day, to express their support for Seale and their anger toward their parents' world. A few suggested that while they were about it, they might as well burn Yale down.

Push had come to shove, and I still couldn't figure where to take my stand. My head supported the civil rights struggle and condemned the Vietnam war, but my guts still held out for order and what I regarded as the proper way—the gentleman's way—to handle disagreements. What, said my innards, would become of us when decent conduct had sunk beneath these waves of obscenities, repeated to the point of pointlessness? What would happen to a society in which so many heaped so much abuse on those charged with protecting it?

Kingman was calling in the best talent he could find to help him. Henry ("Sam") Chauncey dropped his coeducation planning to devise tactics for May Day. Sam knew what we had taken to calling the Blue Mother from the top of Harkness Tower to the bottom of the deepest steam tunnel. A former assistant secretary of defense took over external affairs. My titles kept dwindling and changing; at one point I was assistant to the president for education, but no one, including Kingman, knew what that meant. On bad days, I saw myself as an embodiment of the Whiffenpoofs' poor little lamb—not yet sufficiently familiar with his place of employ to be of much use in its coming difficulty, not yet sufficiently open to what was going on to even understand that difficulty.

I went to a rally for Bobby Seale at the Ingalls indoor hockey rink. There was David Hilliard, the Black Panthers' chief of staff, at the rostrum. In front of him, arms crossed on chests, eyes deadly blank, stood several Panther security people. I sat facing them, one of several hundred whites. Hilliard lashed at us, and at first I couldn't understand why. He was among, if not friends, then fairly sympathetic souls. What did he want? To turn us against him? The answer was that Hilliard was talking to and performing not for us but for a national audience of blacks. He was showing them precisely how a black revolutionary in America could kick white ass and do it among the spires of the white establishment.

Hilliard got to the standard bit about going after authority, white authority. He was starting in on the absolute necessity of killing police, offing the pigs, when some brave white person booed him. Hilliard stopped. "Boo ME?" he yelled, and called us all racists. Some of us laughed at him, shouted at him. I don't remember what I yelled—it wasn't racist, but the anger hurling it most assuredly was. A white student suddenly started scuffling with the bodyguards, trying to get up to the speaker's platform. They let him through, and he just stood there beside Hilliard. A senior faculty member, a psychologist I knew, went to the student, talked to him gently, and began to lead him away, saying that the young man was obviously in some trouble. The student said something I didn't hear. It was reported later as: "I'm not in trouble. I think it is you who are in trouble. I think it is all of you." If that is what he said, he was closer to being right than anyone else in the rink.

· · ·

During my first year working at Yale, I had driven the hour or so to and from Bedford, New York, where we had found a house looking over a steep slope above the Mianus River. It was full of fireplaces and picture windows and uncontrollable levels of moisture in its nethers, and we cherished it. By the late spring of 1969, though, Kingman was suggesting it might be better all around if I moved closer to my work.

I was still reasonably optimistic about a future at Yale; if pickings got thinner in Woodbridge Hall, there was always the possibility of working something out at the Forestry School; I had been sitting in on classes over there and had gotten to know many of the faculty. My wife, who once again was living in relative isolation after two years of university life at Cornell, liked the idea. Yale bought a house for us within walking distance of my office—a large house on a large lot that cost a good deal more than we could have paid (it later became known in the Yale housing office as "Brewster's Folly").

Meg was going on thirteen when we went to New Haven, and Morellen was ten. I had played with them through the years, mostly on weekends and vacations, and I had counted myself a tolerable father, especially considering my start in the trade. When Meg had been a few days old, just back from the hospital, I had volunteered to change her diaper. Preparatory to attempting this feat, I had held her naked to my naked chest. Suddenly, she let go a stream of urine that hit me just below the sternum. I yelped and dropped her. By fool luck, she landed on a bed rather than the floor.

In New Haven, I discovered I was no father at all—at least, that was what my elder daughter was telling me. Meg had always been strong of mind and wiry of arm. With the teens upon her, and with a radicalizing community to explore, she would greet me each evening with a broadside. We fought about civil rights. We fought about the Panthers. We fought about the miserable way my generation was mucking up the world her generation would have to live in. She knew the jargon: I wasn't even close to being part of the solution, she said, triumphantly. I was part of the problem.

No one else could get in a word, not even at the supper table. She had my full attention, and I hers, to the exclusion of my wife and Morellen. At the end of one particularly rough session, Meg was sitting partway up the back stairs, eyes shining with tears, jaw set. I reached up with both hands and pulled her down to my level. She looked up at me with more than enough scorn to wilt my resolve.

Fields of nodding rumors bloomed with the spring. A hundred thousand people were coming to New Haven for the May Day demonstrations. Explosive materials had been stolen from a Yale chemistry lab. Black Panthers were buying arms in Boston. Few in New Haven went serenely about their lives. The media came to report on our unease, and the alumni began to make nervous noises.

I still retained some connection to alumni affairs. Why not serve as their own May Day correspondent? Kingman approved, and I set up shop in my own home, well away from Woodbridge Hall and other potential takeover targets. It was a calming thing for me, this return to the research and reporting I had been doing before I started up the status ladder. I had an assistant from the alumni office, a phone, a notebook, and good walking shoes.

One week before May Day, I was crossing the Old Campus, reading one of the information sheets generated by student and community groups. Kingman had spoken at a meeting of the Yale College faculty, and when I read his statement I stopped and sagged. "I personally want to say," he had told them, "that I am appalled and ashamed that things should have come to such a pass that I am skeptical of the ability of black revolutionaries to achieve a fair trial anywhere in the United States." He had made it clear that he was speaking as an American citizen and not as the president of Yale. He went on to say that "doing anything to inflame the community would be the worst possible service to the defendants [in the Black Panther matter] . . . The first contribution to the fairness of the trial which anyone can make is to cool rather than heat up the atmosphere in which the trial will be held." This was pure Brewster: forthright, honest, compassionate, and above and beyond the call of prudence. I knew what the media would do with it. And they did. Conservatives across the country lashed out. The Nixon administration thought it had a free kick against the liberal establishment, and it took it. Vice President Spiro Agnew urged the trustees and alumni of Yale to replace Brewster with someone "more mature." The response in New Haven was one ringing endorsement of Kingman after another, from a majority of the faculty, the students—and, as the days went on, the alumni.

I talked to Archie often. I knew that in principle he would back Yale's stance, but I wasn't sure his heart would be in it. If I, in New Haven, was having trouble understanding the radicals in and around Yale, I feared that Archie, on his distant hill, would be deaf to them. Not so. Archie wrote Dean Acheson that Kingman was surely a lucky man, marveling, "Who would have foreseen that the preposterous Spirochete would call for his ouster?" But he gave due credit: "Bill (Peter) says the University has never been as substantially unified as it is this week—something Harvard has yet to achieve."

As the May Day weekend approached, Yale—which is mostly to say the students—settled on a strategy that sounded strange, almost meek, to me. The university would shut down so that it could open up. Most classes would be suspended in order to allow the university community to prepare for what was coming. There would be few gates locked and many opened to handle demonstrators. There would be marshals, volunteers from Yale and New Haven, to help keep order.

Sam Chauncey set up a sort of command center fairly near the New Haven green equipped with lines of communication to college masters, student leaders, the city's mayor and chief of police. In my rounds, I thought I detected a sense of confidence, a sense that all this would work. Then I heard a sound I hadn't heard for sixteen years. Late one night I awoke to the clatter of metal treads. I knew what that meant: armored personnel carriers were bringing military units into the city. By next morning, I heard that the Connecticut National Guard had entered New Haven, while about four thousand federal troops had been flown to various points in New England to stand by.

That afternoon, my assistant from the alumni office, who had been mobilized with his guard unit, phoned to say that some live ammunition was circulating in his staging area outside the city, along with talk about giving the radicals what was coming to them. Sam Chauncey's people checked out the report immediately. I don't know if they turned up anything. But what might have happened if live rounds had indeed found their way into rifle magazines became tragically clear a few days later, when we learned that National Guardsmen had shot and killed four young people on the campus of Kent State University in Ohio.

May Day weekend in the event looked quite different from May Day weekend approaching. The predicted one hundred thousand visitors turned out to be something like thirty-five thousand people, most of them young, many of them sunning themselves on the city green that first day, listening to speakers ranging from Black Panther Hilliard to Abbie Hoffman of Chicago ruckus fame to the writer Jean Genet. There was no violence during daylight. At night, provocateurs were able to sucker a small crowd with the lie that some Black Panthers had been arrested on the green. Marshals locked arms and formed a line between protesters and police. There was no physical contact, but bottles and rocks from one side brought tear gas from the other.

On other campuses, protesters seeing some of their fellows staggering through the streets, streaming tears and gagging, might have reacted with more violence. At Yale, no such incitement was allowed to develop. Sufferers were taken at once to aid stations set up by the students, and those who might have been tempted to raise hell on their own were invited instead to get some rest and relaxation in the colleges.

This system worked overtime, and so did luck. A bomb tucked under some bleachers at Ingalls rink went off in the middle of a dance attended mostly by demonstrators. I have learned recently that the device might have killed a large number of the dancers had it not been for some saving coincidences: there were two bands; the one near the bomb had just taken a break, so when the bomb went off, everyone was stomping at the far end of the rink. I heard the explosion half a mile away in my bedroom and thought for an instant that someone had lost it and called in artillery.

By Saturday night, things were so quiet—and so many demonstrators had already left—that the schedule for Sunday was canceled. Kingman called a press conference to announce his relief and his thanks—to the Panthers and the police, for their self-restraint, and, most of all, to his students. Archie thought Kingman had achieved "something very close to a triumph." More conservative alumni thought otherwise. My classmate and friend William F. Buckley, Jr., devoted a column to Kingman as a "prime example of what a mob can do to the leader." His thesis was that the president of Yale, the grown man, had reversed himself under unrelenting pressure from "the kids."

My own view, when it finally declared itself, was that the triumph at Yale was not so much due to the president as it was to the president having listened to the students. That did not mean he had caved in to them. It meant, to me, that he had heard them, really heard. He had opened himself to them in a way many adults of the sixties were unwilling to do. He saw merit in much of what they said, and to that extent, he encouraged them in their efforts to prepare for May Day. He said what he said about black revolutionaries and fair trials because he believed it. So, looking back, do I.

My efforts at developing the May Day report for the alumni

had given me more room and time to observe than I ever would have had in Woodbridge Hall. I had seen the shifts in generational relations, the growth of respect when young and old had a chance to work together to maintain what they held in common. I was close to believing that I too could learn something from the young.

. . .

Meg, who is now the age I was during the May Day troubles, tells me that she made a practice of disobeying her mother and lighting out for radical territory in New Haven. She hung out with Bill Coffin's children. During the troubles, she performed the preferred coming-of-age ceremony of the times by placing flowers in a rifle barrel or two. Morellen, now thirty-nine, has just sent me one of her short stories, based on the time when she and her sister went AWOL from our house and sold lemonade to a squad of Hell's Angels rumbling by on their bikes. The Angels, Morellen writes, hung out with them a little and were careful to properly dispose of their paper cups when they rumbled off.

After the campus had calmed down, Meg and I continued to fight, but about different things. She had decided she wanted to go to a Quaker school in Rindge, New Hampshire, called the Meeting School. My wife and I were against it. It didn't sound educational enough (for which read preppy enough). Meg was for it because, she said, it sounded to her like a real community. Something about that resonated, something left over from May Day. Why, I said, didn't the two of us go and take a look?

The place was a coeducational farm school with about fifty students and almost as many faculty. I tried to dislike it and failed. Everyone seemed happy, even though it was February.

Adults and teenagers held meetings for worship. They held business meetings in which the affairs of the school were conducted through consensus. They touched and hugged each other more than I thought was either proper or healthy. We went back again. Someone hugged me, and I hugged back. On the way home, I told Meg I thought she should go there.

I kept going up to see her, sitting in the silence of the meetings for worship, listening with half an ear to those few who felt called to speak. I did not believe in the Quaker God; it was the quiet in the room that drew me. If opposites attract, then I, as pygmy shrew, was drawn by a chance to be still. As a child, I had known what it was like to do nothing but breathe and be. At the Meeting School I could swim down to that bliss in the company of other swimmers.

I got to know the clerk, the head of the school, a man renowned in the world of nonviolence for having been at Selma and other freedom marches, and for having sailed his boat, *The Golden Rule,* into restricted Pacific waters in silent protest against the nuclear test due to be set off on an atoll nearby. His name was Bert Bigelow, and as we grew into friendship, he told me about his first wife. She had been seduced by an American in Paris named Harry Crosby. Crosby kept trying to get women close to him to commit suicide with him. His preferred method seemed to be defenestration. But in a New York hotel, Crosby shot and killed Bert's young wife and then himself.

I sat there stunned, knowing what Bert would tell me next. Crosby's widow had asked a friend in New York to sit with her husband's body. The man she called was Archibald MacLeish. Archie had told me many times about the Crosbys, Harry and Caresse, and how their Black Sun Press had published him back in the Paris years. I'm pretty sure Archie never met the master of *The Golden Rule*. I never heard him talk about Bert.

I couldn't stay away for long from the Meeting School. I found myself singing rounds and, one evening, sitting in a room reciting "The Brown Bear of the Green Glen" and telling my listeners how once I had thought I was John, youngest son of Erin's king—John the fool, who saves his father.

Only months before, I had started out with a few perceptions about an elite institution learning to bypass its hierarchies to find new direction. At the Meeting School I had begun to see the personal point: there was nothing to be gained in remaining a square when there were so many more interesting shapes to assume; there was no reason I should continue clinging to what I had been trained and trained myself to cling to for forty years— the assumption that I was, by birth and by gender and by race, someone apart, someone better. I was thinking about all this one spring day while walking past the school's barn when I felt an arm tighten around my waist. I didn't have to look to know whose it was.

Overstaying

AFTER MAY DAY THE QUESTION AT YALE WAS: What's going to happen next fall? Should we stick with what worked in the spring? we asked in the summer. What could we do better? The answer turned out to be nothing. There was nothing to do. There were no confrontations, no demands worthy of the name. The revolution had graduated.

There wasn't much for me to do either. Kingman asked if I'd be interested in acting as executive secretary to an alumni council that brought various kinds of expertise to Yale's affairs, but by then I knew that, secure as it was, the job did not match the man. I had been asked by the Conservation Foundation in Washington to edit a collection of essays for the United Nations Conference on the Human Environment, to be held in Stockholm in June of 1972. It was called *Man's Home* and was well enough received to convince me it was time to find a place where I could do what I did best.

Word came to me that summer that the Woods Hole Oceanographic Institution was looking for someone to run its magazine, *Oceanus*. Woods Hole! My wife and I had driven to Woods Hole on our honeymoon, to catch the Nantucket ferry. As the broad old boat began to move, I had stood at the rail looking across a narrow strip of sea to the brick buildings of the institution, at the glorious lines of one of her blue-water research vessels. "Jesus!" I said to the wind, "Jesus! What I wouldn't give to be a part of that!"

I went up for an interview and got the job. It would be bipartite, the larger part being to add private foundation money to the institution's considerable intake from federal agencies. No matter. I didn't mind development that much, and I had plans for *Oceanus* that might make me a full-time editor. It was water I wanted, like my father before me, but water I could live beside in all seasons.

I was, and remain, almost incapable of expressing my wants to the women I love most. The gender studies so popular in recent years have "shown" that the problem is widespread among American men and that it may have something to do with the myth of male self-sufficiency, the I-don't-need-any-help syndrome. Perhaps so. At any rate, I couldn't tell my wife how much I wanted to go to Woods Hole. Instead, I told her how much fun it would be for the family, how it would help me move further into environmental journalism. My circumspection angered her. It didn't occur to me to ask my wife what she wanted, so she told me. She was just getting to a point in New Haven where she felt secure; she had a growing number of women friends who shared her intellectual interests; she was coming to know Yale and what it could offer her; she did not want to move.

We could neither resolve nor abandon the argument. In desperation, we went out to a favorite picnic spot by the shore. Each of us ended up walking in ovals, a couple of hundred feet apart, looking at anything except each other. Shortly after that, my wife told me she would go with me. We decided she would stay in New Haven for another year so that Morellen could finish up at the middle school she loved, and Meg could have an established home to come to on vacations. My wife also said it would be the last move she would make with me. I was so glad that she would come that I blotted out the condition.

I started driving up to the Oceanographic on Monday mornings and back on Friday evenings. My route took me to Providence, Rhode Island, looped over the head of Buzzards Bay and across the Bourne Bridge onto the flexed arm of Cape Cod—which, by virtue of the canal cutting it from the mainland, is really Cod Island. Then down to Falmouth, past stands of oak cut short and shingled houses silvered by the wind, and on south over ledges and glacial moraines, round a bend to the right, descending, to a village by and for and of the sea: the small harbor on the left with its Coast Guard station, the larger one beyond it with the ferry slips and the big pier for the Oceanographic's vessels; Eel Pond and its confusion of big-money yachts, rotting dinghies, and backyard-built houseboats; the drawbridge over the pond's neck and the graffiti on its bottom for tourists to ponder whenever a skipper wanted it raised. The one I saw that first day was VACATE OUR HOLE.

It quickly became my Hole—and remained mine for ten years, my longest stretch of employment. I still claim it. It is a Brigadoon of a place, so full of what the Buddhists call the ease of well-being, of satisfactions at once mental and sensual, that many, especially the young, can never fully leave. This is one of the great centers of marine science in the world. The Oceanographic and its elder sister, the Marine Biological Laboratory, with its list of more than thirty Nobel laureates, are the stars. The National Marine Fisheries center monitors stocks of cod and haddock and flounder along a line of seaward shallows southwest of the Grand Banks. An office of the United States

Geologic Survey, among other things, scouts this part of the continental shelf for petroleum hydrocarbons. At a more terrestrial level, there are the summer retreats of the National Academy of Sciences, and, a relative newcomer, the Woods Hole Research Center, a small and highly regarded organization specializing in ecological work.

Rigor there should be in these fastnesses of discovery, and rigor there is. At the Oceanographic you can hear—but not necessarily understand—marine biologists or physical oceanographers or chemical oceanographers or marine geologists or marine engineers holding forth at brown-bag lunch lectures almost every noon. Or you can walk toward the end of Water Street and, at MBL ("Mumble" to some), pick up the latest theories on what has come to be known as the id of the squid. A tie usually indicates an outlander or an administrator under duress. Shirts are open and old, and sandals have it over shoes. But if you hang around town some summer evening after a lecture, you will hear what the writer Lewis Thomas heard when he was in Woods Hole—everyone aflame with intensity, everyone interrupting everyone else with "But, Look!" Outside an MBL building stands a bronze statue of three people doing just that. The work is called *The Scientists.*

When I arrived, some of the people who had first put the Oceanographic on the map were still helping to keep it there. One was a former mural painter named Fritz Fuglister, another a failed classics major out of Princeton named Valentine Worthington, a third a would-be minister named Henry Stommel. Not one had a doctorate, yet all three contributed enormously to the knowledge of oceanic circulatory systems, most particularly the Gulf Stream and its gyre. When Worthington learned that the British called those without Ph.D.s "subprofessionals," the three formed So-So, short for the Society of Subprofessional Oceanographers.

By the early seventies the place was awash in exotic degrees. Oceanography enjoyed a boom of new theories and new sensors—moored or drifting or orbiting—to test them. Stommel had enlisted squads of post-docs and graduate students to decorate his ideas with differential equations. He admired their genius with computers, he told me, but this came at a price: many of them had come to believe that if something didn't compute it wasn't true. And, he said, too many of them didn't spend enough time at sea to learn otherwise.

Stommel was of two minds himself about sea duty: "It's a little like going to a wild party. When it's over, you say, 'My God! I'm never going to do *that* again.' And then you see it's just enough fun so you do." My first taste of that party came on a ten-day leg of a research cruise aboard *Atlantis II* in the Caribbean. I can't remember how many experiments were under way on a given day—enough to produce more noise and confusion than I could handle. Standing watch at evil hours raised hell with my biological clock, and the sea did the same with my digestion. Sour and surly, I left the ship with the beginnings of the first of three beards and a determination to repeat the masochist's delight.

My goal was to turn *Oceanus* from the house organ it had been before its founding editor died, into an international magazine of marine science. Several magazine publishers had helped me sharpen the idea, and the director of the Oceanographic was suf-

ficiently impressed to let me give it my full attention. That
meant that my attention to my wife suffered, and her adjustment
to Woods Hole became even more difficult. We had been married twenty years, and, instead of settling down, I seemed enchanted with the idea of sending my life to sea.

I think now that as things changed for us, each became more
unwilling to accept the elements in the other that would never
change. I know that my inability to tell my wife what I felt and
why diminished her trust in me. Her tendency to deny her anger
set me on edge. So did what I took as her sense of moral superi-
ority to me. So there we were, bound and gagged, and seldom
was heard that which needed to be heard. I reacted to my wife
as I had seen Archie so often react to his: I dissembled, I propi-
tiated, as I have done to this day. I tried anything to avoid what
I feared, a loss of control, a fight with the woman I loved. That
only added to the tinder.

. . .

Archie liked to say that he had been "carried in" to Harvard "on
a chair and carried out on a statute." He had turned seventy in
1962, and the university promptly informed him that it was time
to go. He had to keep making some money, and the best way to
do that seemed to be on the lecture rounds. He was by then
master of the rostrum. His public lectures in Cambridge had
often drawn crowds. Struggling through one overflow, a student
asked what the occasion was. "The second coming," was the answer. It was like that all through the sixties, and beyond. It was
almost as if Archie had been taken up as a writer of what
Thoreau called the nation's Scripture. Those who invited him
soon learned to give him room, the biggest they had. I drove to

Providence to hear him talk at Brown University, watched those hands sculpting what he was saying, winced at the crash of applause.

Richard Nixon asked him to write a tribute to the moon landing scheduled for June of 1971. Archie respectfully declined, saying he didn't function well as a command performer. He wrote his own poem, "Voyage to the Moon," and the *Times* published it on its front page next to reports of the landing. This is the version that appeared in his *Collected Poems 1917–1982*:

> Wanderer in our skies,
> dazzle of silver in our leaves and on our
> waters silver, O
> silver evasion in our farthest thought—
> "the visiting moon," "the glimpses of the moon," . . .
>
> and we have found her.
>
>   From the first of time,
> before the first of time, before the
> first men tasted time, we sought for her.
> She was a wonder to us, unattainable,
> a longing past the reach of longing,
> a light beyond our lights, our lives—perhaps
> a meaning to us—O, a meaning!
>
> Now we have found her in her nest of night.
>
> Three days and three nights we journeyed,
> steered by farthest stars, climbed outward,

crossed the invisible tide-rip where the floating dust
falls one way or the other in the void between,
followed that other down, encountered
cold, faced death, unfathomable emptiness . . .

Now, the fourth day evening, we descend,
make fast, set foot at last upon her beaches,
stand in her silence, lift our heads and see
above her, wanderer in her sky,
a wonder to us past the reach of wonder,
a light beyond our lights, our lives, the rising
earth,

       a meaning to us,

             O, a meaning!

Honors generated honors until they overflowed the space reserved for them—the top of an ancient Spanish chest and the
wall above it in the passage leading from the main house down
to the music room. When the MacLeish Collection was established at Greenfield Community College, the curators received
thirty-seven hoods, each representing an honorary degree, plus
a score or more of medals, ribbons and parchment testimonials.
Mail in the post-Harvard years may have dropped off a bit from
the highs after *J.B.,* but secretaries still came in to handle it.
From time to time, Ada pitched in. She told me that she opened
several invitations to marriage. She answered them by thanking
the writer and informing her that Mr. MacLeish was otherwise
engaged.

232 of them mistook him for a hired hand.

People drove the dirt road to Uphill Farm and slowed by the driveway, hoping for a glimpse of him. When they got it, most of them mistook him for a hired hand. One complimented him on his skill with the reel mower and asked if he could come over the following week to do *his* lawn. Another asked if indeed this was the house of poet MacLeish. Archie said it was. Well, was the poet in the house? Archie said he wasn't.

During my early years at Woods Hole, I saw Ken at Conway more frequently than before, and he was a different Ken from the one I had followed around as a boy. For one thing, he no longer killed animals. I too had quit hunting, in my mid-thirties, after my arrow had wounded a doe. I tracked her blood trail until I could no longer see it in the dusk. I lost her and never hunted again. Ken slowed down and stopped some years later, though he kept a collection of handguns for target work.

While we were still hunting together, Ken came over for an afternoon of archery. I had practiced much more than he, and I made a couple of rare shots. He pounded me on the shoulder. But his mood changed as we walked down to the salt-hay butt to collect our arrows. He turned toward me. "Everything I start," he said, "you finish." That was nonsense: he had done, was doing and would do things I would never try or think of trying. But, at that time, that was not important. What was important was my feeling that I had won: Ken, in his way, had at last acknowledged me as someone approaching his equal.

After spending years working for *Life* in New York, Ken had persuaded Time, Inc., to send him to Paris. He had written passionately about Algeria's struggle for independence from France, but a sufficient number of his pieces went unpublished to send him into paranoia and depression. Things got so bad that Archie went over to see him and then, through a friend in Washington, put Ken in touch with the *National Geographic,* where he found a berth.

It was a natural job for him, roaming the world, diving on the Great Barrier Reef, doing the things that had always driven me into crosswinds of admiration and envy. In 1969 he and Archie spent wonderful days together in the Outer Hebrides, courtesy of the *Geographic,* the son taking notes as the father looked on. That also had me spitting nails.

Ken and Carolyn had bought a home on the western shore of the Chesapeake, right on the water. A couple of times a year, I'd go down to Washington on business and spend the night there. I could almost smell the anger in the place, and yet I was surprised when, in 1971, Ken moved out and divorce proceedings started. I think now that the separation saved Carolyn's life, for there was nothing left of the marriage except chaos. It did not save Ken's life. He floundered into another marriage that was disastrous almost from the start and that soon came apart. He began to worry more and more about his health, convinced that his heart was going, but it wasn't his heart. He discovered a lump on his side. He thought at first it was a rib he thought he had broken while hauling himself over a gunnel of a dive boat with his tanks on—not a recommended procedure. The surgeon thought so, too, for a while. But when oncologists analyzed tissue deep within the lump, they told Ken he had bone cancer that had originated as a particularly aggressive cancer in his prostate.

Ken did what he could. He underwent castration to slow

down the inevitable, and found to his joy that he could still function sexually. He established a life for himself in a house not far from the one he and Carolyn had lived in. There he was joined by a woman who had met him in Paris and who had come to love him enough to be with him through the final three years of his life. Ken continued to work, in pain, on legs that had increasing trouble bearing his emaciating body. He mastered lightweight crutches he manipulated with his forearms, and with them he covered ground. One of his last stories had him traveling all over England trying to find the realities in the myth of King Arthur. The Wart would have been proud of him. He sped around Maryland on self-starting motorcycles he couldn't possibly have righted if they had lost their balance; at the end, he had three machines in his garage. And at some point, Kenneth the agnostic hobbled through the doors of the Episcopal Church.

One of the thoughts that deepened Ken's depression when he first accepted his cancer as terminal was that I, until then the spare, would be heir—not only to his parents' money but to Uphill Farm. That would have been impossible. Archie and Ada always wanted Ken to have the place, and went through revision after revision of their wills to ensure that he could. Mimi and I were to be compensated in other ways. Ishbel had told me in my thirties that when she and Alec died, Downdale would pass to me. Well into his decline, Ken called me to ask if I would sell Downdale to him; his executor would return it to me on his death. I had to remind him of what his agony would not let him remember: the Campbells were still alive, Downdale was not mine, I could not help him.

Gradually, the rage left him. Earlier in his disease, he had come close to killing himself with one of his handguns. But when I went down to see him shortly after that, he was calm. We lay on the floor of his living room and listened to Schubert. As I got ready to leave, he limped toward me, and in his arms were his Henderson pipes, silver-chased and gleaming. I hugged him, feeling the fragility. I drove only a short distance before my eyes would not let me see. I pulled over and cried until the bones of my own shoulders ached.

I never saw Archie or Ada cry over Ken. I knew from their close friends that they did, but I also knew they would not let me see them in tears. I could hear the grief only in what they didn't say, what the tenacity of their self-control wouldn't let them say. I was in Conway a few times when Ken visited. Ada tended to him when he needed his morphine, an old woman bending over him, trying to find a blood vessel unscarred enough to take the needle.

Ken wanted very much to die at Conway. That was too much for my parents. I think that they felt it would have been impossible at their age to tolerate the disruptions—the collapse of their treasured routine, the endless alarms, the mess. Beneath that feeling could have been the near panic I sensed at Uphill Farm at the intrusion of illness. I don't know what lay behind it, but I do know that when a friend developed a modest postoperative difficulty, she found herself directed to seek medical attention elsewhere without an instant's delay.

Ken died on the fifth of August 1977. I helped with plans for the funeral. He was cremated, though I later found he had not wanted that, either. There would be no church service in Conway; a more ornate ceremony would be held at the National Cathedral in Washington, where the bell would toll once for each of Ken's sixty years. I wasn't surprised when Archie told me that he had written a tribute for Ken but would have the minister read it at the grave. Increasingly, he had taken to asking me to handle the toasts for Ada's birthday parties. How could he possibly have spoken of his dead son? On the drive to the cemetery, Archie did break down, repeatedly. I am so glad for him that I was not there to bear witness.

The minister began reading what Archie had written.

> Here in this pine grove, this
> hollow in the pines and
> oaks and maples, half a mile as the crow flies
> from the house he knew as a child, the room he
> loved to sleep in as a man, Kenneth has come
> home . . .

It was well crafted, and was later printed in many copies on thick and rich paper and sent to friends in its own envelope. But there was, as there usually was, a poem that went deeper. It was left for us to look at after Archie died. Archie called it "Overstaying." It begins with Ada and Archie walking Uphill Farm years ago and talking about their baby, their Kenny. It reads like a playscript. Ada: "And when we're dead . . . and gone . . ." Archie: "So we go first?" Ada: "It's not in nature to outlive / the life you've borne, the breath you've given." Archie: "But we're entitled, surely, to our day." Ada: "Provided there's no talk of overstaying!" But they did overstay. The poem ends: "Now we walk here in the late last year, / the wood hushed and the daylight almost done. / We do not speak. We keep the silence for our son."

I waited, almost out of earshot, on a knoll above the grave, dressed in the gray plaid of Cluny MacPherson, with the drones of the Hendersons on my left shoulder and the oiled chanter in my hands. When the minister looked up, the drones sounded their octave, held true, and I played "Amazing Grace."

Four months later, I left my wife.

"I Don't Like This Play"

BROILING GUILT, ENOUGH TO BROWN ME. BOLTING
awake with it, four, five, six times a night. How could I have destroyed my family? How could I have walked out on a marriage
that had lasted for twenty-four years? All these excoriations and
then, as a faint continuo, the drone of excitement. My fingers
drumming on my chest—no, not drumming, practicing, working on the multiple grace notes of a piper's march I had been
learning, "The Black Bear." Whatever my shame, some part of
me was up and about again.

I worked with my lawyer, my wife with hers. My lawyer had
a sign on his wall: "Almost anything in life is easier to get into
than out of." I was tempted at times to get back into the marriage, but it was remorse drawing me, not love. I had met a
woman who had been divorced and then widowed years before, and I began to spend too many hours frantically scheming
how to go beyond friendship. A wise friend told me recently
that many men "screw for arms"; they make love not just for
the pleasure of the penetration but the security of the embrace.
At the beginning of my new life, I think that was the case
with me.

My greatest fear in those early days of freedom was an empty
bed. My Quaker friend Bert Bigelow and his wife had a small
winterized cottage off by itself on Buzzards Bay, and they would
rent it to me for next to nothing. Weekday nights there slowed
me down until I could see where I was going. Most weekends, I

spent with my parents. Ada had been all but destroyed by Ken's death. She told friends that she had been a bad mother, and for her sins she sentenced herself to solitary confinement. She would talk to no one. Archie at first viewed her withdrawal as some sort of punishment for him. He tried everything to get to her, even sinking to his knees, but he finally saw that the only thing left on his side was time.

It took Ada months to resume her life, and months more to open herself to Archie. When she did, Archie tried to maintain the connection with his old habits of atonement. "Oh, Ada, how lovely!" he would say as she brought a small bouquet into the room, then, "Darling, can I get you anything?" It reminds me now of a headline in a checkout-counter tabloid: REMORSEFUL HUBBY CRAWLS 870 MILES ON HANDS AND KNEES. But Ada was no longer in a mood to hold in her anger. "She scolds," a friend reported, "he folds." To me, it was a revolution in intimacy. What seldom had been heard at Uphill Farm was finally being said. I could not believe my ears.

While Ada was still keeping her silence, Archie and I spent a lot of time together. We put a day or so into seeing if we could repair an artesian fountain on a rise above Ken's grave. As we sat beside the dry pipe, I asked him how he felt about Ada, and he said the feeling was of a tree growing through his heart. I asked him if he had ever had an affair. Yes, he said, one, "and it damned near killed me." Well, I thought, not quite. Here we were, sitting on warm grass, soaking up sun. We had both survived our failures of love.

Early in the spring of 1978, I left my cottage on Buzzards Bay for a rented house on Eel Pond, in the middle of Woods Hole. I walked to work, waving at friends. I joined a Scottish country-dancing group and began to pipe reels and strathspeys for them—and marches for the annual Woods Hole Black Dog parade. Someone asked me to play Father Christmas in a mummer's show, and I reveled in the role. One evening I came out of a folk music concert at the community hall and walked under the stars the long way around the pond to my house, tingling with a sense of comfort I had never felt before. I—not as son or husband or father but as myself—for the first time had a place of my own. And when her mother returned to her home city, Morellen came down to stay with me. She was nineteen and filled with a love for language and music and handsome young men, and found a sufficiency of all three in the village.

A physical oceanographer and fellow country dancer invited me to come aboard *Atlantis II* for a month of bobbing and rolling in one of the world's more active oceanic regions, Rockall Trough, way west of the Hebrides. We would be part of an international effort to further knowledge of how energy is passed back and forth between sea and air. The exercise was called JASIN, for Joint Air-Sea Interaction Experiment—a pretty good acronym, but not up to the level of Fritz Fuglister's DREAM, thought up for a Gulf Stream cruise years before and standing for Damnedest Results Ever Achieved by Man.

Ken was dead, Archie was declining, and so the writing path seemed open to me. I contacted the *Atlantic Monthly* about Rockall Trough. They expressed interest, and off I went for a second go at self-torture. We mustered at a Glasgow dock, boarded an *Atlantis II* low in the water under the weight of huge buoys, miles of hydrowire, tons of equipment designed to measure wind velocities, temperatures, conductivities, air pressures, and the behaviors of waves both external and internal (the troughs and crests of subsurface water layers). We settled in but not down, for the passage out was rough enough to unhinge digestions. Someone had tacked a helpful suggestion on a bulletin board: cover your belly button with duct tape and stand facing into the wind. I skipped the tape, but the bite of the wind staved off the heaves for a couple of days.

I could deal with the nausea, but not the distance separating me from home. I tried to call every week, but patching through is never easy at sea, and we were close to Soviet radar—so close that I could hear nothing on my receiver but a chorus of hammerings and peckings. I knew all about what could happen if you lost hope on an oceanographic cruise. Many years earlier, a scientist had become so overwrought that he suddenly dove overboard. When they were drying him out, he explained that he had seen his sweetheart paddling by in a blue canoe.

I did my best to describe the endless confusion of JASIN. There were fourteen research vessels assigned to the program from the United States, Britain, West Germany, and the Soviet Union. Three aircraft overflew the area. Sensor arrays rose hundreds and thousands of feet from the bottom to their subsurface buoys. Floats followed the undulations of internal waves, chirping their whereabouts to the labs aboardship. From the sea to the wind to the instruments, nothing was ever quiet.

The *Atlantic Monthly* said thanks but no thanks: lots of action, but nothing happens. Nothing does happen in this kind of science, I said, not right away. It takes months of analysis to figure out what you found and then see what it tells you about how energy moves through this maelstrom of wind and water. I sent the piece down to *Smithsonian* magazine and waited. And waited. I called to ask about the manuscript. What manuscript? I sent another copy and, in a few days, I got a letter from Don Moser, soon to be the magazine's editor. He liked it; they would run it. They ran a dozen or so others. Moser's first assignment for me was to spend time on a Danish semisubmersible drilling rig anchored a hundred miles east of Atlantic City, New Jersey, in over four hundred feet of water. From the two-hundred-foot derrick jutting up from its one-acre deck, a string of metal tubes tipped with a fistlike tungsten bit was drilling a test hole inches wide and miles deep in the ocean floor. Offshore drilling for oil and gas was nothing new in the Gulf of Mexico or off California, but it was new on the East Coast. I went out to the rig on the service boat and threw my back out on a particularly nasty roll. From the boat's fantail, I flew up to the rig's deck in a rope basket and spent days getting to know the roughnecks and roustabouts and drill pushers and squads of specialists. I listened to Australians and Scots and Norwegians and Cajuns and Texans. The hole produced some gas and a little oil, not enough to be profitable. But the story, coupled with my month out on Rockall Trough, convinced me that I wanted the sea as my beat.

From Conway came letters I had not expected. "We have always been proud of you," Ada wrote, "but it is piling up. . . . We have done everything but read it aloud in the P.O." Archie wrote, "Well, my lad, it is a piece of *work*. And it works. You keep yourself easy and it reads like talk. An expository triumph. (That word is TRIUMPH). Even I can understand it. It's as vivid as any exposition Pappy [Hemingway] ever wrote and that's so in spite of the fact that your subject is so much more difficult than any he 'addressed' (Jesus! That bloody word!). I'm proud of you."

They were by then reaching the end of their ability to live their lives on their own. "Your eyes change. Your handwriting changes," Archie wrote in his "Definitions of Old Age." "You can't read what you once wrote. / Even your own thoughts sound wrong to you, / something some old idiot has misquoted." The poem talks about getting up "at seven every morning, / right on time for nothing left to do but / sit and age / and look up 'dying' in the yellow pages." And then this ending:

> old age
> level light
> evening in the afternoon
> love without the bitterness and so
> good-night

Archie never asked me for help, but Ada did. Not long after Ken died, she broke down when I was leaving after a weekend's visit. "You're about the only one we have left," she said. That wasn't true. She had Mimi. But Ada would not accept that. Mimi had proved too strong for her, had become the woman Mimi, not her mother, had in mind. A little later, again as I was leaving Uphill Farm, Ada said, "Don't let us lean too much on you." I said, "You can't," and left her to figure out what that meant. My memory tells me that I didn't know myself.

As she had all my life, Ada still confused money with love. I had always taken the checks she sent me with gratitude, for I think she had passed her confusion to me at birth. This financial dependence on my mother had troubled my marriage, and my wife had tried to get me to see what was wrong with it. I suppose I did, in a way. And so, occasionally, did Ada. Once, when I had driven her somewhere and taken her to lunch, she thanked me with a delighted smile and said, "I'd like to put some money in your account"—and then caught herself. "It's not for what you *did,*" she said, and then blushed. We both laughed.

Toward the end of his eighties, Archie told Bill Moyers in a filmed interview that the sorrows of his life were becoming part of the delight, that he was "remarkably unafraid of death." He was still vigorous, looking if not young then permanent. His marriage was once more his support. He and Ada were the "Old Gray Couple" of his poem "They know that love, like light, / Grows dearer toward the dark."

The death of friends troubled him. Each one left him closer to isolation in old age, alone, as he put it, to face the oncoming generation. Ernest was the first from the Paris years. I think the last time Ada and Archie saw him was in the mid-fifties, when they sailed over from Antigua to Cuba and went to his *finca*. He was in bad shape, with a body that had been broken—by air crashes, by his way of living—and a mind that was sinking further into depressions. Ernest had stayed his course, while Archie was beginning to understand the price he had paid for straying so often from his. Ernest had won the Nobel in 1954, and Archie honored Ernest's triumph with "Poet":

> There must be
> Moments when we see right through
> Although we say we can't. I knew
> A fisher who could lean and look

Blind into dazzle on the sea
And strike into that fire his hook,
Far under, and lean back and laugh
And let the line run out, and reel
What rod could weigh nor line could feel—
The heavy silver of his wish,
And when the reel-spool faltered, kneel
And with a fumbling hand that shook
Boat, all bloody from the gaff,
A shivering fish.

When Ernest shot himself in July of 1961, his widow thought it an accident, "in some inexplicable way." Archie thought of Ernest's father, a suicide by gunshot, and wrote in "Hemingway," "Oh, not inexplicable. Death explains, / that kind of death: rewinds remembrance / backward like a film track till the laughing man / among the lilacs, peeling the green stem, / waits for the gunshot where the play began, . . ." Three years later, Gerald Murphy died of intestinal cancer. He and Archie had repeatedly closed and opened the distance between them in the years since that spring morning in 1945 when he had given Hopkins' "The Windhover" to Archie. There was time in his dying for letters back and forth. When Gerald was close to death, Archie wrote to him, "When one expects to go on 'forever' as one does in one's youth or even in middle age, horizons are merely limits, not yet ends. It is when one first sees the horizon as an end that one first begins to see." The letter went on, "Death is the perspective of every great picture ever painted and the underbeat of every measurable poem and the enviable men are the ripe men who can sit as you do and look at a featureless sky above an endless sea that does, nevertheless, and at that point, *end.* I like to think of you there, looking."

There was time for Archie to tell Dow that the Museum of Modern Art had accepted and would hang Gerald's painting *The Wasp and the Pear,* a work that had hung in the music room at Conway during most of my life. And time for Gerald to hear and say, "How wonderful!" before he sank into senselessness. Archie and I went down to Long Island for the funeral. As Gerald's godson, I was asked to carry his ashes. There was to have been a cortege of cars, but the distance was short and the autumn day warm. I asked Archie if he thought Gerald would enjoy the walk. Yes, he said, and so the three of us led the mourners to Dow's grave beside his dead sons.

Felix Frankfurter and Adlai Stevenson died the next year, and Carl Sandburg two years later. Dos died in 1970—he had wanted to see Ada and Archie before, as he put it, "the men in white" got them all, and then "the men in black," but I don't know whether he did. Dean Acheson died in 1971, and Archie and I flew to Washington to see Alice in the beautiful house on P Street. Ezra Pound went the next year, not exactly a friend, not after years of scolding Archie about his work, not after turning against his country during the war. Pound had been committed to a mental institution in Washington, and Archie had played a large hand, along with Robert Frost, in getting him out—primarily because Archie had remembered what Pound had been at his best: "Maybe you ranted in the Grove— / Maybe!—but you found the mark / That measures altitude above / Sea-level for a poet's work."

Mark Van Doren died the same year. Although theirs had

been a strange, late-blooming friendship, Mark was the one man I heard Archie say, and say often, that he loved. When he died, Archie remembered his voice and the sound of the brook that ran below Mark's workplace, the two in discourse. "Year after year they talked there; now / the brook is mute, is winter-bound, / and Mark . . . / no winter knows, can sound, / the silence where his voice is drowned."

Archie was never one to build friendships quickly, and there was only a decade remaining to him. That may be one reason why he and I began to settle into the closest relationship I have ever had with a man. My close woman friend told me that Archie and I were like lovers together. She told Morellen that she thought my father was my only comfort, and that, at the time, may have been true.

• • •

At the beginning of his ninetieth year, Archie began to retain body fluids. The men in white fixed that with pills. But then he began to lose weight alarmingly. In the early spring of 1982, X-rays showed a polyp that was constricting his colon. He had had a similar one back in 1956 that had been benign, and the radiologist was fairly sure this one was too. The question was whether or not to operate. Two of Archie's doctors were against it, saying that, given his age, the costs in stress would outweigh the benefit. But the surgeon argued for it and, as surgeons tend to do, he won. I thought the operation a poor idea, but I was only barely aware of the politics of medicine and deferred, as was my tendency, to what I considered superior male authority.

Archie called me at Woods Hole to tell me the operation was scheduled at Massachusetts General in Boston. The problem was, there was no one to drive him down from Conway. Ada had given up driving years before, after he had become so obsessed with her safety that he would sometimes follow her car in his own. Age and Ken's death had weakened her mental equilibrium to the point where she could not be left alone long. By the greatest of good luck, Ada had hired a couple named Cummings to cook and look after the place. But by then, Roger Cummings was himself too ill to drive Archie to Boston. His wife, Phyllis, had to stay with Ada.

I told Archie I'd come and drive him down. There was a pause, then Archie said, in a breaking voice, "Of course you will." We said little to each other on the way to Boston. I believe we were both thinking different thoughts about the same thing: would he make it through and, if so, what then? I don't believe Archie had any faith in an afterlife, so he must have been faced with simply ending, stopping, and then nothing. I twitched in the driver's seat, thinking of that. I looked over at Archie. He was dozing.

I felt the beginnings of a long tension, anxiety about settling his affairs, about tending to his wife and their place. How would we arrange things for him at Uphill Farm if he survived? Visiting nurses? And if the operation killed him, who in the press needed notification? Who at Harvard, who in New York, Washington, Boston; where else? How to handle all that for a man still famous? Who would handle the body of the famous man?

I left Archie in his room at the hospital. The elevator was close by, but I headed for the stairs; they were healthier, I thought. As I went down the corridor, his nurse had started her paperwork. I couldn't hear her voice, just his. "Archibald MacLeish"; "Pine Hill Road, Conway, Massachusetts, oh-one-three-four-one"; "May seventh, eighteen ninety-two." With that came my first tears.

I drove Ada to the Ritz Carlton on the day of Archie's operation. We waited for an hour past the time the surgeon said he'd call us, then two. Ada said she was sure Archie was gone. When the call finally came, we were told that Archie was fine. It had just taken a lot longer than expected to put him safely under. Later, we would hear that Archie's tumor was benign (Archie called it "beneficent"), and that a number of nodes elsewhere in his intestines were cancerous but inoperable. They had taken the innocent and left the ominous.

The recovery room was full of light and tubes and steel and people in pastels padding about. Archie was lying near the desk, on his side. Ada bent over him, and I could hear his voice, so soft and high. He saw me and began moving his hand under the covers. I reached for it, and he grabbed a finger and pinched hard, either as a reflex or a way of telling me that he still had the conn of his life.

It took Archie days to swim up to the surface. Ada came back to see him early in his recovery. The surgeon was with him, and he called Archie "Professor." "Professor, your wife is here," he said. "Professor, turn your head to the right to see her." Archie did and whispered, "Hello." She didn't hear him. Thinking he hadn't recognized her, she broke into tears. It took several efforts in the car going home to Conway to convince her she had not been rejected.

My daughters went to see Archie, as did Ken's children, Martha, Bruce, and Ellen. A couple of times I accompanied Ada and sat and watched him in his dreaming. The bones of his head showed through the skin. The only features left unchanged were his eyebrows. I sat and watched him, my head inches from a bank of bouquets, and smelled the smallest smell of rot. I was pretty sure it was from the flowers. Once, when Archie seemed to rally, I tried again what I had muffed a few months earlier. I leaned over him and said, "I love you." He opened his eyes, raised his hand to my cheek, and said, "Yes." Then he waved his arm and told me the feeling was mutual.

One of the nurses said, with admiration, that Archie was a survivor, that he was stubborn, doing just what he wanted to do. As days passed, it seemed that Archie wanted to do nothing. The surgeon looked worried. He came, he called to the professor; the professor lay doggo. "He may be giving up," said the surgeon.

They got Archie into a chair, where he held a kind of court. Family and friends came and went in varying degrees of solicitude. Archie was there. He recognized them; he made introductions when necessary. And he would drift off, come back, and let us know where he had been. Once when I was alone with him, he motioned me over and asked, "Do you think we should contact those people over there who are whistling and shooting?" Morellen arrived as I was leaving and, for the first time in our lives, held me to comfort me.

Archie talked a good deal with my daughters. They thought it wonderful that an old man would tell two young women what he could not tell his wife: that he wanted the curtain down. He said to them, "I don't like this play." He was trying to pull out the tubes running into his arteries, his penis. (Ha-body noises, Mr. Stanley! Ha-body noises.) I wanted him to wake up and say, "Hello, Bill, I'm dying." And I would say, "I know." And we would wait it through. I would say to the man who always had felt so much in debt to his life, "You are owed this passage. You don't owe anyone anything anymore. I am watching you go for freedom. Go gentle."

Archie died on April 20, 1982, just two weeks shy of his ninetieth birthday. In his last days, letters of congratulations arrived, one from the White House: "You have given the American people many wonderful gifts—your poetry, your plays, and outstanding service to this nation in the time of great need. . . . Thank you for a lifetime of contributions to America." Ronald Reagan signed the letter. I thought it was a pity, considering Archie's observation in the book room those few months before, that he never saw it.

I worried, yet I knew I needn't, that Ada would collapse—or collapse and die. She stood her ground. I was more fragile. A messenger carrying Archie's personal effects had been mugged on his way to the post office and Archie's wallet had been stolen. When I heard that, I stood beside my father's big desk in the music room and screamed and pounded the leather top, over and over. That was the start of my mourning.

We planned the funeral and carried it off. Archie was cremated. A couple of years before, he had selected yellow quartzite boulders from old stone walls around the farm and had them laid in a line on the MacLeish plot in the Pine Grove cemetery. His stone was on the left. Ada's came next, then Ken's, then Brewster's. The baby bones had been moved from Uncle Billy's plot in Farmington in 1981.

I stood during the short ceremony, not thinking of it. I thought about being the only man-child of Archie's left in air, about how I was standing over men who had stood over me most of my life, about how fine it would have been if Archie had followed through on his fantasy and been buried behind the wheel of his Mercedes.

Afterward, family and surviving friends sat in the spring sun on the east terrace at Uphill Farm and ate and drank and remembered, laughing. Ada laughed, too, to cheer up the guests.

The Bald Orphan

ON ARCHIE'S NINETIETH BIRTHDAY, GREENFIELD
Community College went through with its plans to hold an
Archibald MacLeish symposium. What took place was half en-
comium, half wake. Ada and I attended most of the two-day affair. She sat in the front row, listening to poets and academics
analyze Archie's poems and prose and plays, his private art and
public persona. I spoke last. I talked about Archie's death, his
wanting to die. I said I hoped that he had put all his passion, all
his curiosity, into going. Then I read the beginning of an early
poem of his, one that, to me, could stand as a log of his last voyage. It was "Epistle to Be Left in the Earth."

> . . . It is colder now,
> > there are many stars,
> > > we are drifting
> North by the Great Bear,
> > the leaves are falling,
> The water is stone in the scooped rocks,
> > > to southward
> Red sun grey air:
> > the crows are
> Slow on their crooked wings,
> > > the jays have left us:
> Long since we passed the flares of Orion.
> Each man believes in his heart he will die.

Many have written last thoughts and last letters.
None know if our deaths are now or forever:
None know if this wandering earth will be found. . . .

I looked over at Ada as I finished the poem segment. Her mouth was open in a silent keen. She was rocking back and forth in her seat, alone in the crowded auditorium. All I could think of was that my voice, reading Archie's words, had been too close to his for her to bear. "I should have known," I kept saying to myself as I went to her. I held her, apologizing, reassuring. In a few days, she began calling me Archie, first as an occasional slip, which she caught, and then as a habit.

I shuttled back and forth between Woods Hole and Conway, too busy with phone calls and mail to feel much, grateful for the adrenaline that kept me moving and not thinking. I drove Ada to Harvard for a memorial ceremony, and she was as poised as ever I saw her. Archie's old colleagues, faced with that awful urge to say something soothing, were instead soothed by her wit and affection.

Phyllis Cummings made it possible for Ada to continue living at Uphill Farm, even as her own husband's life was passing slowly into mental vacuity and death. Her ability to run the house was fully equal to Ada's, and her compassion for the old woman and new widow went beyond my comprehension. There seemed to be no financial problems on any horizon. In matters of physical comfort, my mother was unthreatened.

What worried me was that after sixty-six years of almost impossibly close union, loneliness would become Ada's mortal enemy. But no. Ada asked Phyllis to spend the evenings with her, and by a year after Archie's death, the two women had formed a kind of family. Ken's younger daughter, Ellen, completed the support system. She had moved to Conway in 1978, and she and her husband regularly came up the hill with their children.

With Archie gone, who was left to worry? I was. I sat in his chair in the book room, at Ada's behest, and fretted that I was going to be asked to assume his mantle. Taking heart from his fame was one thing, taking his place quite another. No older male in the family now walked point for me. I was at long last out on my own—only to find that duty might soon call me back to the home hearth. As it turned out, Uphill and Ada had no need of my guiding hand. Neither did my children or Ken's. Everyone seemed to like having me around, but none looked to me for guidance. My ego took on the look of an old balloon, and I retreated to my own life.

• • •

Well before Archie's operation, my close woman friend had become my lover. She was the most stirring woman I had ever met, but I didn't meet her enough. For some months we saw each other a few days each week, and then she'd go off to a second home at another end of the country. She had great interest in love but none in marriage. I seemed in need of constant companionship. The result resembled a rubber band. I would pull and haul until I thought I had what I needed, then she would snap back to what suited her. We did that four times in four years. The last snap—our final rupture—occurred early in the winter before Archie's death.

Friends in Boston had asked me to their house for New Year's Eve. They wanted me to pipe in the New Year. I noticed a young woman standing close to me. She had Viking eyes, broad shoulders, lovely breasts, and dress buttons held on by safety pins.

She was teaching at the University of Kentucky, and she was a poet. Her name was Elizabeth Libbey. Close to midnight, I put on my kilt, warmed up the pipes, and at the appointed time began to play "Auld Lang Syne." I kept my eyes on Elizabeth's eyes. She told me later that she kept hers on my knees. When the drones died away, I walked across the room and kissed Elizabeth Libbey. She felt very good to me.

My hosts asked me to return the next day for brunch. I did and so did Elizabeth. We stood talking, then sat talking, and then lay on the floor talking. I learned that she had been married twice, that she was nineteen years younger than I. I had only begun to turn my life around in the sixties. She had taken the decade head-on, going to jail for a Vietnam War protest, dropping acid, living as she liked. I decided to ask her, as a poet, how she rated my father as a poet. Good, she said, but not great. Seeing me off balance, she took my hand and smiled at me. And that, I like to think, is when love began.

After a while, we noticed that everyone else had left the room—to watch pro football, they said. A few nights later Elizabeth asked me to spend the night with her. We both loved the love we made. I overslept and had to rush down to the coastal town of New Bedford. A big stern trawler was going out that morning for five days fishing on Georges Bank, a rich ground about a day's run out to sea on the continental shelf. The trip was one of many I had planned for a book called *Oil and Water,* about Georges Bank and the struggles that control of its resources had set off among offshore oil drillers, fishermen, government regulators, and environmentalists. But the harbor was iced in, and I drove home to Woods Hole.

A couple of months later, I went to see Elizabeth in Lexington, flying straight from Miami, where I had landed after a week or so of drug patrols in the Caribbean for a *Smithsonian* story about the Coast Guard. The cutter that carried me had stopped several suspects, one at night, and had put a boarding party on a cabin cruiser loaded with marijuana—and a few illegal parrots. I was feeling quite the adventurer. But the minute I saw her at the airport, I knew I could never keep my swash buckled when she was around. She and I went to see her parents outside Washington. Not long after Archie died, she moved in with me on the shore of Eel Pond.

I had just left the Oceanographic to turn to full-time writing. I don't remember being particularly scared about the decision, just sad about ending such a fine time. The institution had helped me find a grant for *Oil and Water,* so I had the lucky combination of a woman to try to keep up with, and a pursuit to pursue. Elizabeth and I were both worried about how Ada would react to us. Her divorce was not yet final, and we were living together. At the very least, I expected that Ada would put us in separate bedrooms, but she was delighted with us. Perhaps her own loss made her look more kindly on our affair, or perhaps we gave off so much warmth that she simply pushed aside her mores to take in as much of it as she could.

The Campbells let us use Downdale. Ishbel was by then almost completely blind, and Alec had taken to thinking too many beautiful thoughts to be trusted to drive the five hours from their home to their summer home. I used Archie's stone house for my work, looking out the open door at Ada's gardens and the house beyond, listening to wild turkey hens and their poults muttering in the hay outside and giving me an occasional goggle-eyed ogle from the threshold.

Ada would take herself off to bed early in the evening. The stairs were too much for her by then, but she had found a solution. She would hobble over to the stairway, bend over, and cry "Uppadee!" —something she used on me when I was a toddler frightened of the ascent—and scramble up on all fours. Late in the summer of 1982, I asked Elizabeth to marry me. She had told me in the beginning that she had no intention of going that route again, and at the time I didn't think I did either. I was no longer frightened of being alone, I told her, I was finally my own man and . . . and . . . I wanted her to be my wife. After a while, she said it would be all right if I were her husband. When we told Ada, she whooped. She asked us to get married in her house, down in the music room, and we did. We said our vows before the fireplace. A close friend, Jill Conway, then head of Smith College, gave us a reception at the president's house in Northampton, and then Elizabeth Libbey/MacLeish and I drove down to Woods Hole. It was New Year's Eve, a full orbit of earth since we had examined each other's eyes and knees.

I was by then fairly comfortable with the freedom of freelance life, of writing pieces for *Smithsonian* and having the time and financing to go pretty much where the story took me—to barrier islands along our eastern coasts, to sea, to pilot boats in New York harbor. *Oil and Water* meant years of that freedom, years of roaming and writing, years of the joy of finding out and the fear of missing out. I was ideally positioned to do the book. People who could give me my basic education in fisheries management, oil geology, pollution problems worked right in Woods Hole. The drillers' base camp was less than two hours away, as were the offices of the environmental lawyers who were preparing to challenge the federal government and the oil companies in court.

Elizabeth worked on her poems; I went to sea, aboard trawlers and scallopers, research vessels and a research-submarine tender. Helicopters and service boats ferried me to a semisubmersible rig drilling on Georges Bank. Coast Guard aircraft carried me over the bank to count whales and sea turtles and fishermen fishing where they shouldn't. Meanwhile, the oil companies kept on until they hit what they were after. The trouble was there wasn't enough of it, for them or for me. Without the draw of a commercially viable find on Georges to heighten reader interest, *Oil and Water* drifted and sank.

In the fall of 1983, Elizabeth went down to the University of Alabama at Tuscaloosa for a year's teaching. I went with her, heading back to Georges when I needed to. Preoccupied with earning her living, she had practically no time to write. I had more than I needed, and that satisfaction kept me from seeing the considerable difference between us. She was the established writer, with two books of poems published. I was the newcomer.

Visiting Ada was a problem; I couldn't afford the trips, but Ada's lawyers used her trusts to finance enough travel to put me, and often Elizabeth, in Conway almost every other weekend. Ada's mind was slowly fogging. She forgot the calendar, even forgot that her house was hers. She told me that some kind gentlemen, presumably her lawyers, had told her she could stay where she was until she died. Elizabeth and I invited Ada's friends to come for pond picnics and, sitting at the head of the table, looking out over the water, she reconnected: "Mom, here are your glasses." "Good. Now where are my eyes?" We recited

old limericks, most of them naughty, including one she was particularly fond of: "In the Garden of Eden, as Adam / Was con-
tentedly stroking his madam, / He chuckled with mirth / To
know that on earth / There were only two balls and he had
'em." We sang close harmony on songs like "Don't Beat Your
Mother, Boys, It's Mean." We took her out to lunch in Archie's
Mercedes and annoyed nearby diners with our fun.

In April of 1984, Phyllis called to say that Ada was in the hospital with a stroke. She seemed to rally when they got her into
bed, but now she was failing. Elizabeth and I headed north.
When we walked into Ada's room, she was already well into
what medicine calls the Cheyne-Stokes respiration—heavy, labored breathing trailing off to nothing and then repeating itself.
She was lying on her side, facing away from me. I spoke to her
when I was rounding the foot of the bed, and when I got close to
her, I could see that her eyes were shut tight—and that a big grin
was spreading across her face. She never spoke. She died a few
days later, four months short of her ninety-second birthday.

She died in the night, alone, as Archie had been. I could have
been at either bedside; perhaps I felt I wasn't needed. Archie as
much as told me I wasn't. A day or so before he went, he had
said to me, "You get along." I asked him if he meant back to
Conway, to Ada, and he said yes. Perhaps Ada had welcomed
me to her deathbed and, with that same grin, released me. And
perhaps the thought of actually watching the two most powerful
people in my life lose all power was more than I could bear. I
went back to the hospital early the next morning, thinking I
might find something of her there. The room was empty, of her,
of everything about her. I drove home to Uphill Farm, walked
into the book room and fell on my knees before the faded yel-

low, butt-sprung armchair that had been her command post. I saw her sitting there in one of her long velvet robes—the maroon one, I think. It was at the end of my last visit. As I was leaving her then, I had turned at the door. She had given me a look, long and calm, and said, "You've been a wonderful son."

I don't know what I said. I spoke too quickly—probably something about her being a marvelous mother. What I wish I had said was that she was a remarkable woman, a fascinating person, and that I loved her. But I had botched it. Standing a yard from where I had tried to tell Archie much the same thing two years previously, I had botched it again.

• • •

Elizabeth and I went back to Tuscaloosa to pick up our things, turned around and drove north through frantic thunderstorms to empty Uphill Farm. None of us surviving heirs felt up to taking on the place. Its upkeep would require more money than any of us could afford. We had thought about turning it into a writer's colony, but there was a sufficiency of those around the region, and we had little chance of raising an endowment big enough to keep it going. The practical thing was to sell it.

During his interviews with teachers from Greenfield Community College, Archie had spoken about how he would like to dispose of his poetry collection. "I know that my only surviving son is going to think that he wants them very, very much, but they would never stir from the shelf. . . . He is a very good writer, but he's one of those charming active people who always, given a choice, wants action and not sitting in a chair." I was angry about what he had said and furious that he hadn't said it to me before going public. He was right on some points: I had seldom looked at the books while they sat on his shelves. What upset me was that he had forgotten that he had given me some poetry volumes he loved. One was Yeats. He had inscribed it, "For Peter, this cherished book, with my love, Dad." It is in the shelf behind me now. I use it—hold it, smell it, cherish it, read it. I am forgetting enough now to forgive him.

I had known for years what Archie and Ada wanted to leave to us. They changed their wills early and often with the shifts of circumstance, and each time they sent us all copies of the changes. I had never paid much attention to the paperwork, taking the lofty view that their assets were theirs to do with as they willed. What they had willed, finally, was to leave the same amount of stocks and bonds to Mimi, to me, and to Ken's estate. Ken's four children received their shares free and clear. Mimi's portion and mine were to be held in trust, managed by estate lawyers in Archie's old firm.

The strategy had been popular for generations among those well enough heeled to employ it. Uncle Billy had done so with Ada. There had once been some tax advantage to it, but that had disappeared by the time Ada and Archie had finished their fiddling. It is now looked upon by many who study such things as a good way to infantilize one's children. I certainly saw it that way. When I had absorbed the gist of my situation, I went out into the woods, sat down under a big white pine, opened my mouth, and let fly. Goddamnitohell! By what right were they telling me from the grave how to lead my life? I could have answered, by right of my silence on the matter when they were alive, but that would have derailed my rant. Where did they get off putting their dead hands on my tiller? Fucking trusts! If they were for anything, it was to show parental distrust of me. So it went, until I could no longer create satisfactory sonic booms.

I had no idea how we were going to divide the contents of the house among the heirs. A half-century of collecting had filled every room and most of the huge attic. There were books everywhere. There were the two pianos, a magnificent highboy—the one Uncle Billy had stolen for a set of false teeth. In fact, there were antiques out of mind, many of them the fruits of Ada's auctioning. There was silverware, glassware, glorious linen and china. By then we had an inventory from an appraiser. But what to do with it?

Ken's children knew. After he died, they had taken turns picking items from the list of his things. Then each paid or received enough cash to balance the process. It worked beautifully. We all knew from the beginning what items each of us treasured, and in most instances, honored those preferences. We sat in the music room for four or five hours and then left with cools intact.

In their last years, Ada and Archie had talked to us about choosing parcels of Uphill land for ourselves. Mimi had chosen a field across the road near where I had shot the kit fox. Ken's elder son, Bruce, picked a field farther on, a big one, with the best hay on the place. Ellen, who had been living downstreet, took some lovely property toward the village and built on it. I went for what meant most to me—water: the upper pond, the lower, and the brook that fed them and flowed down into the Campbells' ravine. By then, though, I knew that it would be impossible for us to live year-round at Downdale. It stood at the bottom of a long, steep, unplowable driveway. It had no heat or insulation. Winterizing it would have cost a great deal. It had no cellar, and contractors told me there were enough big glacial boulders beneath the soil to make a nightmare of digging one. What normally went into a cellar probably would have to be put into an extension, and that would ruin the perfect simplicity of the place.

Elizabeth and I had to find a home. We talked about moving out to her country, Montana or Wyoming. That appealed to me, but I was afraid it was too far from New York publishers for a very late-blooming writer. Woods Hole was closer, and dear to me, but its cost of living was dearer still, and rising. We started looking north of the Deerfield River, around high hill towns like Heath and Shelburne. Ada had put us on to them. She said nothing about living in the town of Conway; the land to look at, she said, was across the river.

We did a lot of exploring before we drove up a steep slope in Charlemont and stopped by a house in the middle of a long sloping hayfield. Down below us was the river valley and above us Bald Mountain. It was the most supersaturated land for miles around, just a foot or so of soil above an impenetrable lens of clay. Long and lean as a ship, the house had columns at one end and, at the other, a stretch of shed made from old barns and so sagged in on itself it probably would outlive the living quarters. It just seemed natural to call it Weird Hall.

The sale of Uphill Farm went a lot faster than anyone thought it would. I had brought in a local realtor, who brought in Sotheby's. The sales pitch was different this time around: no talk about sweet pine groves and nonmalarial climate. "Uphill Farm, Conway, Massachusetts," went the listing. "Situated on fifty plus-or-minus acres of pasture, pond and woodland, a beautifully restored late 18th Century Federal residence, formerly the home of Archibald MacLeish." A buyer appeared within weeks. He was fairly young. He was involved in investment banking and very active in the Republican Party. (I imagined a turbine's whine rising from our lot down in Pine Grove Cemetery as Archie spun in his urn.) The price paid for the house and 175 acres in 1927 had been $5,000. The price paid for the house and a third of the original land in 1984 was about $340,000. I believe at the time this was something of a record in Franklin County.

The new buyer gave us the time we needed to clear out. Elizabeth and Phyllis Cummings and neighborly neighbors and I hauled clothes and canned food to the Salvation Army, a surprisingly small amount of junk to the Conway dump, and our share of household goods to Charlemont, where Weird Hall was still undergoing extensive shoring up. Guests invited to our third anniversary party arrived just hours after our new refrigerator started making ice for their drinks. Within a few months, Elizabeth's parents, the Boggses, had moved up from suburban Washington to the hill town of Rowe, just eleven miles northwest of us, and I had family again.

Ida Boggs and I got along from the beginning, talking music and laughing at each other's word play. Her husband, Marion, and I probably would never have understood each other well on our own. He had an analytical mind that had brought him success at the State Department and later at Eisenhower's National Security Council. His politics had started with FDR and moved right to Reagan. My mind had always followed my imagination, and what passed for my politics had started with Roosevelt and staggered to the left. It was our love for Elizabeth that broke our ice and, in time, brought us close.

The pressure of emptying Archie and Ada's house had kept me from thinking about how it would be to leave it—to leave most of what for so long had led me back into childhood: the winey smell of the cellar; the attic where we had played Murder on rainy days; the fireplaces, especially the one I got dressed before on winter visits during my early years. But when we did leave, when I turned the key in the lock, there seemed to be little to weep about. I had known since boyhood that Uphill Farm was a place to have fine times in, not to dream of having; the dream had been Ken's, and Archie's for Ken. I had wanted it, of course. But for some reason the hankering disappeared in the rituals of hauling and dusting and locking up. I have never stepped inside the house again, although the new owner has asked me to. I hear it has been substantially remodeled, that it has a sauna now. Certainly it has more light than it used to. And so do I.

. . .

During my days on Georges Bank, I had heard marine scientists talk about how the Gulf Stream sent eddies of warmer water up onto the shallows. Late one fall, I passed through one on a Woods Hole research vessel and thought I was in the middle of spring. Why not a book about this magic? T. S. Eliot called the river of his native Mississippi a "strong brown god—sullen, untamed and intractable." He wrote, "The river is within us." The Gulf Stream became the blue god within me. I resolved to trace it, to travel on, over and under it, right around the North Atlantic gyre, the great oval that runs from the Gulf Stream's northern courses toward Europe, rounds south to Africa and then heads home through the Caribbean to the stream's natal jet off Florida.

Robie Macauley of Houghton Mifflin, the very man who had introduced me to Elizabeth, bought my proposal. For the next five years—each of my books, as if responding to some hidden metronome, has taken roughly five years—I filled a box of notebooks with excerpts of interviews, scientific papers and books, and my own attempts to turn sight and sound and sea into language. A huge chemical carrier, bound for New York, carried me from Baton Rouge down the Mississippi and out into the Gulf of Mexico, round the tip of Florida and straight up into the stream, where it caught a ride that saved its owners several thousand dollars in fuel costs. Another giant, a containership, took me along the northern arc of the gyre to London.

The trip of my heart was along the southern arc, on a craft scarcely one-twentieth as long, a tops'l schooner owned by Arthur Snyder, a Quaker banker from Boston. She carried the name *Welcome* to honor the ship that had carried another Quaker, William Penn, to his grants in the New World. Snyder and his daughter had taken her across the North Atlantic to Scotland and from there down to a port in southeastern Portugal, near the river where Columbus had first hoisted sail for his western adventure. I went aboard there, with a two-person crew making a film for *Nova* based on my book. Snyder went into shock when he saw how much gear we had with us, but somehow we got it stowed. The next morning, we headed south for Madeira. We were not sailing *to* the island, Art said. That would be tempting fate. Instead we were sailing *toward* the island. Look, he said, at our situation. We were a tiny thing on a great ocean, three hundred and fifty miles west of the Sahara desert. I remembered that two of Captain Moses Hillard's brothers had lost their lives fairly close to where we were, one at sea, one on Madeira itself. The man who drowned had been only nineteen. Yes, toward.

Christopher Columbus had topped off his supplies in the Canaries, and so did we. He and we had the sight of volcanoes rising more than two miles above the sea, and to the west, nothing but long and lonesome water. I advanced slowly, from movable ballast to apprentice helmsman. I handled my first squalls satisfactorily, checking the schooner as she tried to break free of the course. But a few nights later, the wind suddenly gusted past thirty knots, and before I knew what I was doing or what to do, the ship lay down on her side like a tired hound. Those off watch came boiling up from below, dropped the mains'l, and *Welcome* came to.

We saw what Columbus had seen—long rollers under the trades, flying fish fluttering in the scuppers (and delicious in the mouth), the birds. "Nothing was wanting," he wrote, "but the singing of nightingales." The admiral's lookouts had twice mistaken clouds on the horizon for land, and even with Snyder's smooth navigating, we were often tempted to do the same. Once, the wind brought me the smell of what I thought was bacon cooking. It's the smell of the Sahara, my watch mate told me. He said that winds regularly brought not only the scent but the dust of the desert to the Antilles, even to Florida. Perhaps the admiral too had caught the smell, crushed the grit between his teeth. How would he have felt, with no explanation but deviltry? Dolphins were as familiar to him as chickens to a farmer, but how would he have explained a dolphin's head breaking the surface and burning with the green fire of bioluminescence?

Our landfalls were far apart, his in the Bahamas, ours in the Leewards. He is said to have seen a light moving in the night shortly after he raised the island, perhaps a native jacking fish. We would encounter a light we knew was there before we started, the light at the entrance to the dogleg passage into English harbor at Antigua. The trouble was, it wasn't there. It had failed weeks before, and nobody had fixed it. We scooted right past the entrance and, when we determined that we had, turned and beat back for hours against the heavy wind. The next morning, I went on deck and looked out at the arid hills of southern Antigua and the British battlements where Ken and I had dug up bottles and buckles dating from the time Lord Nelson was having it out with the French. I hugged Snyder and anyone else I could find and departed. Within the hour, I lay sprawled and snoring across my first bed in a month. Late in the afternoon, a fine alto voice awakened me singing, "O come let us adore him," and I reentered the seasons.

· · ·

Where do you come from? This is the question that most often brings stutters and sighs in our increasingly migratory culture. It has taken years for me to be able to answer it straight. I, the bald orphan, the son of no one alive, now say I come from a hayfield above the Deerfield River, and I believe it is my last and true home. Elizabeth, herself a wanderer, belonged to Weird Hall from the day we arrived. She prodded me to take time from cutting grass and brush and other distractions ("Willy, Stop-p-p!") to see what was really here. She taught me to pay close attention to home birds, from wintering chickadees to the wild turkeys that pace our meadows like Quakers on the way to meeting.

My daughters have liked it here. Meg's first child, Lucia, old enough to remember how strict Ada could be at Uphill Farm, did what she wanted here, knowing we'd keep an eye but not a leash on her. She and her younger brother, Jacob, helped me plant fruit trees, walked the dirt roads that wind up into the hills, and, as the years changed their vocabularies, gave me to understand that what we had was way cool.

Both my children had divorced within a decade of my divorce, Morellen in 1984 and Meg in 1990. I floundered around, at once trying to help and not knowing how to help. My old guilts came alive. Was mine the example they followed? What exactly had driven me to separation? Did I follow Ken? Had we both taken a hopelessly idealized image of marriage from the matchless match of my parents? Neither of us was ever actor enough to approach their performance. When we found we had neither the craft nor the stage to keep our show running as long as they had, each of us may have opted for his own reality and walked away.

Morellen left Woods Hole and her marriage for Boston. She had little trouble finding work. She has had more trouble with choosing her paths and in that she is quite similar to Archie and to me. She has a natural gift for composing songs and singing them, for writing short stories—and for helping people work out their problems. She was only twenty when my first wife and I divorced. She hated what we were doing, hated being caught between us, yet she did what she could for us.

I didn't pay much attention then to how much the divorce bruised my daughters. Because they rarely complained, I felt free to concentrate on my own bruises. A decade or so later, I sold Downdale. We had Weird Hall to keep up, and I was worried about the additional time and money involved in maintaining a second property, especially since we no longer used it. Only after it was gone did I come to understand how much Morellen had loved it.

What a daughter! I said to my friends. I told them about traveling to Scotland with her, how much she helped me in researching the history of the Highland clans for what turned out to be a stillborn piece for *Smithsonian,* how she fit in: on one lunch break, as I was making my way against a press of students, a good many of them from abroad, I saw a young woman with fair skin and red in her hair coming toward me. Now, I said, *there's* someone who belongs here. Then Morellen waved and made me a liar.

I began to fancy that what Morellen and I had was what Archie and I had had in our relationship. Only recently did I realize that I was right—and that I had better do something about it. My father and I had suppressed tension between us because we were afraid of losing our ease and delight with each other. As a result, we came to treat each other with an affection that was at once deep and curiously lacking in curiosity, and that was the way I had been treating my daughter. In recent months, Morellen has been telling me as much. She says she doesn't like acting Glenda the Good in my play. She says it hurts that I know her so slightly. I react with tension. I am ashamed that I have been so blind, angry that she has waited so long to tell me (or is it that I have waited so long to hear her?), and fearful of what will become of us. Perhaps my jam has broken.

I see my intensity and drive in Meg. It spooks me sometimes to see those traits looking back at me through the eyes of my firstborn. Meg moved from New Hampshire to Vermont after her divorce and began devouring college courses with a bright and feisty mind that eventually would put her in a doctoral program. Not long after she had started her surge, she told me that she was a lesbian. She introduced me to her partner, Alison, a skilled dancer and choreographer. I was surprisingly unsurprised. I was pretty sure that homosexuality had occurred earlier in the family, and it didn't shock me that it should have reappeared. What did unsettle me was how swiftly I became a villain in the lens of Meg's newly discovered orientation. She said I had tried to raise her to be little more than a flunky to men, that I had derided homosexuals, over and over. "Now that I am a homosexual," she wrote, "that doesn't make you a very safe person."

I wrote her a nasty letter and then tore it up. I thought about my own first exposures to the idea of homosexuality, how Archie had almost shuddered over what he called the "perversion" of the thing. I thought about my own worries in early adulthood that my attraction to one or two males made me a "pervert." The best defense I could find then against what I now see as wonderfully close friendships was a shield of homophobic blather.

In the fall of 1992, I listened to the religious right at the Republican Convention announce in so many words that it talked to God and that God said, "Get the gays!" My imagination started in on the old and barren scenarios of how I would get the reactionaries. But this time, when I climbed back to reality, I had a promising plan. I would honor what Meg had found in herself by writing about it. When *The New York Times Sunday Magazine* showed interest, I talked to Meg. She and Elizabeth and Alison and Morellen were helping me clean out Downdale for the new owners. Meg and I walked out by the ravine, and I told her what I had in mind. Her eyes glistened, and I thought of her, back in New Haven, facing me down from the middle of the back stairs. Then, I had reached out to discipline her. Now, she reached out to draw me in close, close enough to see the love.

The *Times* took the piece, and it attracted more positive and passionate comment than anything I have written. I read it now and feel lofty and, for a while, at one with my daughters. We are all travelers then. I see Morellen walking by the Spey, a muscle of a river in eastern Scotland that courses by farms where our people once lived. I see Meg and Alison and the children walking hundreds of miles through Spanish hills to Santiago de Compostela, pilgrims in a country I have always yearned to live in. It is wonderful for them to be on their roads: Meg, with a heart of a face, a Castilian face; Morellen, the true Gael. They are a continuance, what comes after.

Across the River

NOT TOO LONG AFTER HE DIED, SOME OF ARCHIE'S friends decided on a way to mark his passing. They wrote to the Postmaster General, urging a commemorative stamp. Silence, then, the decision: Archie was out; Elvis was in. In America, no poet is going to displace the king of rock. I knew that. But it reminded me of what Heywood Hale Broun had said in his memoir, *Whose Little Boy Are You?* "The children of the famous may resent the shadow in which they dwell, but when it disappears, they know sadly that parent has died for the second time." I had dwelt under Archie's sun, not his shadow, but otherwise Broun reflected my condition: the twilight that followed has unsettled me. In fact, I may be writing this memoir to mention the name in Sheboygan—in hopes of another sunrise.

At first, I liked to say that Archie made one of his perfect dives into oblivion. That isn't true. What really happened was that his fame began to flake and fall like old house paint. Some of his books are still in print. *J.B.* is still around. "Ars Poetica" is apt to appear in the anthologies for some time to come. Archie's Internet citations are plentiful, but his royalties have gone down substantially. Not many teachers teach him, and not many scholars refer to him. One sympathetic academic searched an international bibliography recently and found only one entry for MacLeish—as against about a hundred for Robert Frost and over two hundred for Emily Dickinson. The new American Library collection of twentieth century American poetry carries mostly his earlier poems.

Some people have told me Archie pined for the Nobel. If he did, I never heard a word of it. He lived far enough into this frantic century to know that it was just a matter of time before the bitch goddess took up with someone else, and he seemed to accept that in the same way he accepted old age. The laurels that came late to him were, he said, "like the touch of hands." "Any poet wants to be admired, to be a great poet," he said to a writer from *The Paris Review*. "But who is a great poet? Maybe a handful in the world's history. So that's irrelevant. What's really going to come out of your work is something else. If you have succeeded at all, you have become part—however small a part—of the consciousness of your time, which is enough. No?"

Family friends say he might come back, that like Hemingway, MacLeish is down but not out. When they do, I nod a little and think of a decade ago when I was diving with scientists from Woods Hole. We were on a wall that dropped a couple of thousand feet from the western edge of a Bahamian bank just east of the Gulf Stream. I hung even with the lip of the wall, level with schools of fish shining on the golden shallows beyond, not seeing but sensing the abyss beneath me. I felt the hug of deep water, and I thought of Archie, how this was just the sea for him. I knew Ernest had dived in Gulf Stream water not far from this wall. He had said that it was awfully nice down there, that he was tempted to stay. It *was* awfully nice. I tricked myself into seeing the glint of Archie's back as he turned to look at something beyond the branches of a staghorn coral—Ernest, perhaps. I too wanted to stay, but I left. The vision stayed.

I don't know if Archie will come back any time soon. We like our culture "lite" these days, and works of weight and passion can have difficulty staying afloat. But since change is our basic constant, we'll probably be taking ourselves seriously once more. We will pay more attention then to the language we now relegate to captions. When we do, people may read Archie again, or some of him.

One of Archie's grander utterances is the epigraph to *The Hamlet of A. MacLeish:* "No man living but has seen the king his father's ghost. None alive that have had words with it." I have never seen Archie's ghost, not even in my dreams, only sensed it among the throngs of strangers in the huge rooms my dreams take me through. I have never had words with it. But I hear it, or him, every time I speak one of his best poems. To that extent, I am haunted by my father.

This is neither pleasant nor easy to reconcile with the conceit that one is entirely one's own man. I am not even close to being so. A psychologist friend of mine recently told me, "You are putting your life on hold for your father." Fury shook me, when what I should have said was: I am living my life more fully than I ever have. It's just that there's this ghost in here with me, and I don't feel like getting rid of him.

• • •

Some years after Ada died, I began to lose interest in playing music. I'd reseason the pipes from time to time and buy new reeds—and new strings for the guitar—and then leave the instruments in their cases. Ada herself slipped away for a long while—in fact, until I began shaping this book. I think what happened was that I found such fresh delight in writing that words overwhelmed notes. It may have been that I allocated more of my consciousness to the writing parent than the singing one.

During a night watch aboard *Welcome,* I found myself thinking about the continent a thousand miles beyond the bow, the country Columbus approached but never saw. What if I could evoke what it had looked like the instant Columbus had seen the light moving near his landfall? I played with the notion until it had grown into a story of how human beings have altered the nature of North America from the time, at least twelve millennia ago, when we first entered it, up until the present. The title went from *The Day Before Columbus* to *The Day Before America.*

I thought at first that I would be spending most of my research time in libraries and museums. I spent some, but a lot more in the open watching archaeologists and paleontologists and palynologists and a bevy of ecologists working at their trade. A Makah elder on a hill at the mouth of Juan de Fuca Strait in the state of Washington showed me how his people had lived for hundreds of generations before the whites came, and a Mohawk elder did the same for me in his office at Cornell University.

I finished *The Day Before America* with the realization that before we are anything we are meddlers. When I look at urban sprawl, I'm liable to think that there is little hope we can keep from ruining most of what we touch. But we are also adaptive—who knows that better than I? Perhaps, perhaps . . .

· · ·

Although my books have attracted reviews that pleased me, none came close to paying royalties. The fact that I wrote each one because the subject matter—rather than the market potential—drew me to it probably helps explain the best-cellar result.

Many writers start out with low or nonexistent earnings from their first efforts. But it is one thing to do so at thirty and another in one's fifties. Hope is a help but hard to maintain when you consider the demographics of publishing. The most promising market for books, as for films and television programs, appears to be among adolescents of one form or another. And though we live in the Age of Information, the demand for printed information seems to be dwindling. More than two hundred years ago, Dr. Samuel Johnson wondered why so much writing was being done when there was so little reading to go along with it. He should see things now.

Under normal circumstances, I would have been forced to curtail or give up full-time writing, possibly after the first and probably after the second book. But my circumstances aren't normal. My share of Ada's and Archie's estate, carried aloft by what I regard, in my dark Gaelic soul, as an insanely optimistic market, now makes me an affluent man. I have on my wall a notice from the *Reader's Digest* announcing: "You Could Be Millionaire Number 5,271,881." I don't know what my number is, but it's smaller than that. Yet despite my luck in coming into some money at just the right time to quintuple it, I kept on sticking stamps on the *Digest*'s sweepstakes offerings for years, telling them that, if I won big, I: (1) wouldn't show up in Pleasantville, New York, to collect; (2) didn't want a weekend at the Waldorf; (3) didn't want a Cadillac to labor up our dirt road with its trunk stuffed with cash (or was that a pitch from Publishers Clearing House?). What I wanted was a substantial annual payment for as long as I lived, and to hell with the taxes.

To stay in the race, I was willing to buy an occasional book telling me how to boil an egg or unfreeze a pipe—even if the

Reader's Digest assured me that no purchases were necessary. I was willing, even though the minuscule print on the reverse side of the entries told me that the chances of my winning were on the order of one out of 207 million. When I finally admitted that the odds were roughly similar to those involved in my being knocked out of my shoes three times by lightning during the same storm, I quit sticking stamps.

Something tells me that Ada used to play around with sweepstakes or something like them. I believe she did it because the Depression had taught her just how chancy security can be. She may have also played out of self-assertion. Her wealth came from Uncle Billy's luck and skill, Archie's from Andrew's. Perhaps she—and later I—shared a yen to stir up some luck on our own rather than merely accepting someone else's.

That acceptance came hard. My parents' posthumous gifts put me in the steerage compartment of a class I had resented and feared and refused to understand—while openly admiring a number of its members. When I learned that among the truly monied of, say, New York, I would be lumped with the "little rich," I breathed a small sigh of relief. I know these are not exactly mainstream attitudes, not in a society that has moved from "greed is good" in the eighties to an advanced case of Midasitis in the nineties. It is now almost blasphemous for those who are thus shot with luck to wince at our wounds. Only recently, with the onset of wisdom or simply that old desire to move on, have I come into some balance with what is in the bank. It is not that I think I deserve it; it is that I have stopped wanting to give it back.

Heirs, at least new ones, are also apt to worry more about the future than those who make their own money. Only in the last year or two have I refused to become airborne when the market dives. I know from my youth that what goes down eventually comes back up. Of course, I also know, from what Ada and Archie told me of the twenties, that what goes up eventually comes down. If it comes down hard next time, experience tells me I could survive, but in a somewhat altered state. What would surely crash with the crash would be much of my hard-won self-respect. I would still have my name and what fame adheres to it. But I could not continue living in the special way that first made me feel apart. Although we might be able to keep Weird Hall, my ability to do for the most part what I want to do would be gone, and with it my cover. And that, I have to admit, is what scares me most about losing my shirt. It's not so much the shirt, it's face.

· · ·

Memoir writing, I find, is better left to the accomplished masochist, which must be one reason I have kept with it; the pains encountered are wasted on a more balanced soul. First comes the unnerving passage into the heart's core for a look around. Next, the jolts of discovering what others think of you and those who produced you, and what those who produced you think of you. I have read what dozens of people have had to say about Ada and Archie. Some were friends, some strangers, some enemies, some friends acting like enemies. I have read that Archie was passionate, that he was cold, that he was gregarious, that he was a loner, that he was a great lyric poet, that he was a depressingly mediocre poet. I have read that Ada and Archie created a trophy life for themselves at Uphill Farm, turning an imperfect reality into a perfect fake.

I have read that Ada would have been much more at ease if she had not committed herself to the full-time job of looking after Archie. I have read that Archie was much too worried about offending and perhaps losing Ada to even think of having lovers, that he had lovers; that Lillian Hellman pulled his pants down and they then proceeded from there. I have read that Archie and Ada brought their children up cruelly, playing favorites, that they took no pleasure in us. I recorded most of these readings, and I can hear myself on the tapes, laughing, snorting, cursing, and sobbing.

Innards do not like this kind of tweaking, particularly if it is prolonged by doubts about accuracy and guilt over telling this or not telling that. Mine have gone on strike several times over the past five years. I look forward to the time, after revisions are complete, when I can restore balance to my digestive system—before the book comes out and I look at it and cry, "My God! What have I done!" and the cycle repeats. But I now know these innards immeasurably better than I did before the process began. Elizabeth says she writes to find out what she means, and I suspect that is mainly why I have done what I have done here.

Elizabeth and I have fought, and fought hard, ever since the beginning. Fighting her still scares me, leaves me depressed. Sometimes it leaves her feeling sick. She fights to preserve her most sacred boundaries, and I find I fight to preserve old customs that have lost their relevance. Yet in spite of our battles—or perhaps because of them—we appear to have found a way of staying together that feels most days as if it will last. We are both stubborn, and we both admit, with considerable justification, that we are hard to live with—but then, most people worth marrying *are* hard to live with.

When I'm in the middle of my writing, I can walk right past Elizabeth and not see her. This riles her, as does my penchant for letting my attention sag in mid-conversation while the writing mind nibbles, like the mice in our walls, on bits of sentences. She is not amused by my insistence on acting the dominant male, even when I insist I'm not one. In this role, I am strong and competent; in command, yet loving; involved with my life yet ready to rescue hers, without asking, whenever I think it is in disarray. Elizabeth can describe her feelings to me with what seems to me to be consummate ease. True to my maleness, I haul and twitch at mine and usually come up dumb. After such moments, I feel as if the floors of Weird Hall are inches deep in eggshells.

What we do find occasionally on our pine floorboards are the droppings of field mice, house mice, and now and again of squirrels, red and flying. We once had a family of rats, but I think the multitude of mice suffocated them. The bears come by regularly, and it takes a lot of banging on a pot with a big spoon to get them to go away. They munch on our bird feeders. The deer munch on our young apples. There is always a doe hanging around in the fall. One already dark for winter runs the lower field. She sees us, advances two paces, holds, then climbs the air. Her flag is up, and she gives us the sight of white dancing among dark trunks of the pines.

We have always had dogs here—the present pair are young German shepherds, sisters, one with a sleek, Egyptian look and the other with a sable coat and the hot eyes of a wolf. Their predecessors were also shepherds—one German, the other Aus-

tralian. When the nights froze, the four of us piled into our bed
together. Elizabeth made a poem out of the two-dog sleeps. She
calls it "Lair":

> The four of us abed, blizzard
> full-on, toying with this
> historic wreck, carpenter's architect's
> phantasmagoria we call
> Weird Hall, devoid of one single
> right angle.
>   We make up for
> that tonight. Me, my husband, our
> two dogs, here in the king-size
> Hollywood bed, snuggled
> spine against spine, paw slung
> across chest muzzle in armpit hand on flank
> until we establish geometric
> perfection a moment, then someone
> snores awake, turns, settles
> back, and we all turn-settle
> new into this nest of quilt and fellow
> body, most efficient of turbines
> powering our group furnace through
> whiteout, zero seeping
> wall into headboard into pillow into.
> Let me tell you:
>   separate, any
> one of us might just be burrowing
> ourselves a burying hole. But we're no
> bunch of random animals tossed together.

We're the pack! Come!
It's beautiful, it's art, it's fun watching
us get the job done.

When he was well along in years, the mythologist Joseph
Campbell said he didn't feel old, he felt like a young man who
had something wrong with him. I feel a little that way now that
I'm stepping off from seventy. I still fill out a turtleneck in what
seems to me an acceptable way, but when I look in the mirror
closely, I see a turtle's neck coming out of that turtleneck. I still
run in the hills, two miles every other day instead of my customary four, but my knees are often not in favor of it. My ears have
given up on the high notes, and I will soon need longer arms to
accommodate my eyes' surrender to presbyopia. I think about
death more each month.

In the spring of 1988, Elizabeth's mother was diagnosed with
lung cancer. Elizabeth and I spent the last night of Ida's life with
her in the hospital, and we brought her home the next day to
die. Elizabeth and her father, Marion, and I were with her,
around her bed. We each kissed her. Then she gave a shrug and
was gone. Ten years later, Marion broke a hip and never recovered. He spent most of the next seven months in a nursing
home, and we saw him every day. Elizabeth had promised that
she would bring him home to Rowe to die, and we did, at the
end of February 1999. He came alive for a couple of days, delighted with being where he belonged. Then he sank, slowly at
first, but then so fast that he was dead before we could get to
him. Elizabeth and I were with him for hours, watching the skin
of his face turn the color of old ivory. I sat very still, sensing my
breath, touching a body that had stopped breathing. And sud-

denly I was looking at Archie, the corpse of Archie I never had seen. With the sight, I was able to weep for two old men who had gone ahead.

In the days since, I have found myself able to look longer than before at my own ending. I still dodge it, saying I'm going to miss me when I'm gone, or laughing at the perfect title someone invented for a *Reader's Digest* article: "New Hope for the Dead." But at least I can now see me dead. My corpse is now so familiar that I can watch it rejoin the soil without too much horror. I can accept the obvious fact that mine will be but one of 100 billion or so human bodies that have supplied sustenance to new life since the species started.

Marion feared dying more than death, and so do I. He had his living wills and medical proxies, but he was also in the hands of a medical establishment that often seems nowhere near as accepting of death as its patients are. I think of the old ways of dying—of the elder, sure that she can no longer keep up with her clan, rising from her sleeping robe, lifting the flap of the lodge, and slipping out into the blizzard. I doubt I would have that kind of courage. If the actuaries are to be believed, I still have another couple of decades to go, though how long I will want to continue going is another matter. I don't think I would end my life while I was still strong enough to walk. I would wait instead, cozened by hope, by the latest drugs, so that when the urge to end finally did come, I would, like the proverbial frog in the pot, be too weak to act or too muddled in the mind to remember what it was the urge would have me do.

I seem more interested in people than ever before, more willing to desert the old securities of solitude. I have joined a group of men who help each other to be honest about being males. We

call ourselves the Mankind Project, but no name really fits what
we do. What moves me is the trust we can build. Men, in my experience, have trouble trusting men. Yet now I can hold and be
held by men, some of them young enough to be my sons or my
grandsons. That is a form of safety I find I am starved for.

I still go out on an occasional clear night to drain the dogs and
myself. I roll my head back and look up at the lights. The full
moon rides over Hawk Mountain, and I think of Archie and his
unanswerable question: what are we to make of ourselves in the
presence of this incomprehensible cosmos? Lately, I have been
taking comfort in what the sky scientists say. The sun, in its
time—several billion years—will die. It will swell into a great
red star that incinerates the earth and then collapses into a small,
impossibly dense white dwarf. A billion years later, our galaxy
will crash into another. This may be chaos, but it is as common
to the universe as the dirt in our garden is to me. We die. Stars
die. Assemblages of stars die. If this were not so, if there were no
death to release old substance into new existence, nothing could
ever be.

Archie believed that life had purpose of some sort, that it
"tended toward." I think he was right. I sense no God, as the few
gods I know about are defined, but I sense Design, and that
seems enough for now. It may not be later. I have not forgotten
how Sara Murphy turned to *le bon Dieu* at the end, how Ken did
the same.

For all my digging and discovering, I am probably no closer
to constancy than I ever was. I can spend hours thinking about
how nothing fails like success—or contemplating what Buddhists call the extraordinary qualities of being ordinary. Then, in
an instant, I can be recording a commentary for public radio,

thundering at the far right from a patently exalted position. I can say I am pulling in my horizons: writing about whole oceans and continents and millennia passing like so many sunsets no longer interests me. And then I read Henry James, exhorting himself in his aging to "go on, my boy, and strike hard: have a rich and long St. Martin's summer. Try everything, do everything, render everything." And my heart leaps.

I can read Shelley's "Ozymandias," telling of a ruined monument in the desert, the torso and head toppled. The ending seems to speak to my condition as a son of fame.

> And on the pedestal these words appear:
> "My name is Ozymandias, king of kings:
> Look on my works, ye Mighty, and despair!"
> Nothing beside remains. Round the decay
> Of that colossal wreck, boundless and bare,
> The lone and level sands stretch far away.

Instantly my imagination creates a local chapter of Ozymandians Anonymous where I stand and say: "I'm Bill . . . No, I'm Peter. Yes, I'm Peter, and I'm a recovering MacLeish."

But then another voice speaks in me, for me. That would be Mr. Stanley. "But wait a minute!" he says. "Why stop now?"